D1643497

THE ENGLISH
COUNTRYMAN

Books by H. J. Massingham

ENGLISH DOWNLAND, 2nd Ed.
COTSWOLD COUNTRY. 2nd Ed.
CHILTERN COUNTRY
REMEMBRANCE: AN AUTOBIOGRAPHY
Etc., Etc.

Edited by H. J. Massingham

THE ENGLISH COUNTRYSIDE
ENGLAND AND THE FARMER, 2nd Ed.

All fully illustrated, and published
by BATSFORD

1 " Rest from Labour " (1808) : from an engraving after George Morland

THE ENGLISH COUNTRYMAN

A Study of the English Tradition

BY

H. J. MASSINGHAM

"This Isle, this England"

LONDON

B. T. BATSFORD, LTD.

15 NORTH AUDLEY STREET, W.1

Dedicated to
My Fellow-Members of the Kinship of Husbandry

First published, Autumn, 1942

MADE AND PRINTED IN GREAT BRITAIN BY WILLIAM CLOWES AND SONS, LIMITED
LONDON AND BECCLES

CONTENTS

ACKNOWLEDGMENT

A small portion of the material of this book was printed in a different form in *The Field, Time and Tide* and *The Fortnightly Review*. The author is grateful to their editors for allowing him to reprint it.

FIG. 71 is reproduced from a painting in the Royal Collection, by gracious permission of His Majesty The King. The publishers must also acknowledge their gratitude to the Tate Gallery, for permission to reproduce fig. 47; the Victoria and Albert Museum, for figs. 22, 45 and 84; the Guildhall Gallery, for fig. 66; the Harris Museum and Art Gallery, Preston, for fig. 14; the Rothampsted Experimental Station, for fig. 59; and Major Guy Paget, for fig. 68. As in other books, they must express their sincere obligation to Messrs. Walter T. Spencer, of New Oxford Street, for the loan of so many subjects from prints and drawings in their unrivalled collection.

Of the photographs, fig. 32 is by Mr. G. P. Abrahams; figs. 9, 49 and 52 by the late Brian C. Clayton; fig. 53 by *Country Life* Ltd.; figs. 7, 8, 48, 51, 56 and 77 by Mr. J. Dixon-Scott; figs. 3, 5, 18 and 39 by Dorien Leigh Ltd.; figs. 6 and 78 by Mr. Herbert Felton; fig. 76 by Mr. W. H. A. Fincham; figs. 43, 44 and 83 by Fox Photos; figs. 19 and 38 by Mr. G. G. Garland; fig. 10 by Mr. A. W. Haggis; fig. 36 by Mr. H. D. Keilor; figs. 30 and 35 by the Keystone View Co.; fig. 50 by Mr. Sydney Pitcher; figs. 40 and 42 by Mr. C. F. F. Snow; fig. 81 by Sport and General; fig. 34 by Mr. John H. Stone; figs. 25, 33 and 37 by Mr. Will F. Taylor; fig. 20 by Mr. W. J. Watkins; fig. 41 by Miss M. Wight; fig. 64 by Mr. C. H. Wood; and fig. 24 by Major Richard Wyndham. Most of the remaining subjects are from the publishers' collection.

PREFACE

THIS BOOK should have been the study of a lifetime and in a sense it is, since a great deal of my own experience and thought about its subject over more than a decade has gone into it. But even if I had devoted my whole life to this one book, readers would still find that the enclosure of so wide an acreage had as much hiatus as hedge. My object has been to trace back to their sources in the country scene the more durable elements of the English character through the representation of half a dozen of the basic types whose functions and characteristics have largely contributed to its building up.

These types are the Peasant, the Yeoman, the Craftsman, the Labourer, the Squire and the Parson, with the Tenant Farmer more incidentally observed. They are all rural types and we are not accustomed nowadays to think that we owe anything as a nation to the country—except, for the moment, our daily bread. Also, it would be easy, too easy, for a protestant (with a small p) to point out that not only have various urban types (not to mention the Sailor who is neither rural nor urban) contributed to the generalized character of the Englishman, but that I have not included all the country types (the Doctor, the Innkeeper, etc.). Granted, but I have chosen what I consider are the organic, the fundamental figures and in our depths we are a country, not an urban, people. Such forgetfulness has sadly mislaid us in the guidance and control of our destinies. It is high time that we sought out the springs of what Matthew Arnold called our "buried life." This book is an attempt, however fragmentary, to reveal them.

Such a study is necessarily historical, economic (and economics are a part of history, not, as Marx made out, the whole of it), and environmental, but it also includes literature and personalia. I have tried to do justice to all four quarters of the whole, but I should have liked to have given a separate chapter to a seventh participant in this workshop of character—the Country Artist by pen, brush or melody. The more so as one day the Brains Trust was asked a question as to what were the proper educational subjects for boys between sixteen and eighteen and not one, not a single one of the cerebrating directors of the Trust, made the arts one of these subjects. But I had not the space and the Country Artist does play a very considerable part in the life-histories of the others. All six have been artists in one way or another for the simple reason that, though we have done our utmost in our latest manifestations of energy to root out this quality, we are really an artistic nation. Of course, I recognize no distinction in kind between the arts and the crafts.

I have set aside the last chapter to outlining the dubious prospects and stressing the imperative need for the survival of the English tradition as represented by the types discussed and proliferating into one of the richest and greatest cultures the world has ever known. In this development, of course, the town has played its part. But we have to remember that before the advent of the Industrial Revolution nearly all towns were country towns. The type-figures of a country town would make a grand book of itself, but it is clear that the ambit of this book is already wide enough.

I have to thank my friends, Arthur Bryant and Adrian Bell, for valuable suggestions in reading the MSS.

January 1942   H. J. M.

"Ill fares the land, to hastening ills a prey,
When wealth accumulates and men decay."

OLIVER GOLDSMITH

"Whatever the future may contain, the past has shown no more excellent social order than that in which the mass of the people were the masters of the holdings which they ploughed, and of the tools with which they worked and could boast, with the English freeholder, that 'it is a quietness to a man's mind to live upon his own and to know his heir certain.' With this conception of property and its practical expressions in social institutions those who urge that society should be organized on the basis of function have no quarrel. It is in agreement with their own doctrine, since it justifies property by reference to the services which it enables its owner to perform. All that they need ask is that it should be carried to its logical conclusion."

R. H. TAWNEY, *The Acquisitive Society*

"The abdication of the Christian Churches of one whole department of life, that of social and political conduct, as the sphere of the powers of this world and of them alone, is one of the capital revolutions through which the human spirit has passed. The mediaeval church, with all its extravagances and abuses, had asserted the whole compass of human interests to be the province of religion. . . . It had even sought, with a self-confidence which was noble, to bring the contracts of business and economic life within the scope of a body of Christian casuistry. . . . The Churches of the 19th century . . . acquiesced in the popular assumption that the acquisition of riches was the main end of man, and confined themselves to preaching such personal virtues as did not conflict with its achievement."

IBID

"The true past departs not. No truth or goodness realized by man ever dies, or can die; but all is still here, and, recognized or not, lives and works through endless changes."

T. CARLYLE

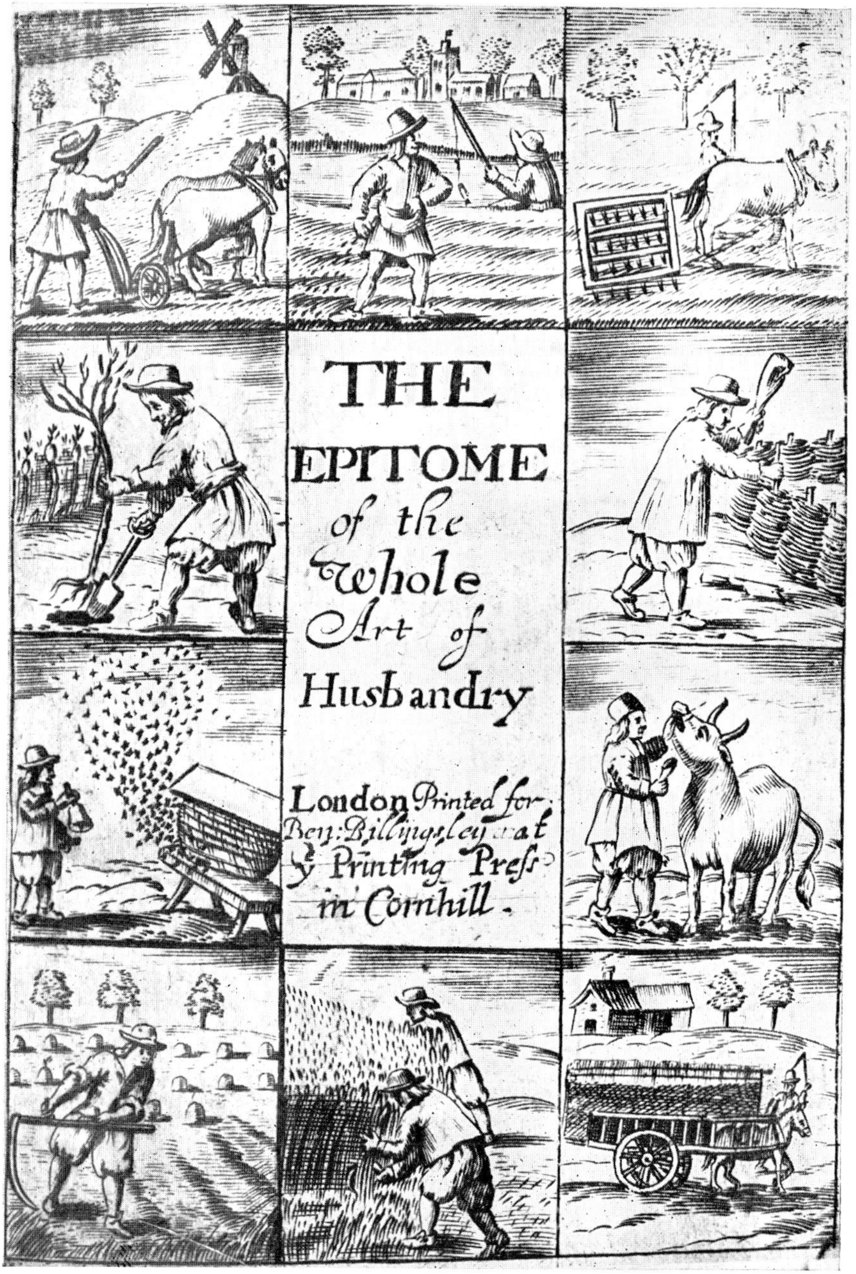
THE
EPITOME
of the
Whole
Art of
Husbandry
London Printed for
Ben: Billingsley at
ye Printing Press
in Cornhill.

2 English Husbandry in the 17th Century: from a contemporary title-page

3   A Sussex Shepherd

Chapter I

THE PEASANT

I THE PEASANT COMMUNITY

The most important fact about the English peasantry is that it no longer exists, while my reason for heading these chapters with its all but extinct society is that the base of the pyramid which we call civilization is the peasant cultivator. I know of no exception to this general rule: it is a despised historical truism. In England, a peasantry, ruled, so far as we can gather by inference, by a theocracy whose earthly sovereign was the divine king and Almighty was Nature represented both as the source of life and the queen of heaven, colonized our virgin territory about two thousand years before, as a soldier who was excavating a tumulus once said, " the birth of God." " Coeval they with Adam's race " is a true description of the peasant ancestry of all civilization.

With varying fortunes, ours remained in actual possession of the land until the middle of the last century, A.D., when the General Enclosure Act of 1845 finally put an end to it. Its aristocracy, the yeoman class (also recruited from the lesser or impoverished gentry), still maintains a depressed and precarious foothold upon the land as the " owner-occupier." But, except at two pinpricks on the map, the " commons of England " is no more. They were slain by what is curiously worded the " Commons." The contemporary smallholder has too mixed an origin to be described as of peasant pedigree as the copyholder certainly was, though he may one day be the founder of a new peasantry fathered by the towns. The agricultural labourer is indeed a lineal descendant from the peasant community, but a landless proletariat working on the land is an anomaly having no organic relation with a people rooted in it and the rich humus of its own traditions. The land was anciently regarded as the measure of all human rights, and to turn its uses from permanent livelihood to incidental employment is to cut the heart out of the peasant economy. The wage-earning labourer is essentially an urban idea.

The average definition of peasant as small landowner is misleading. When his society flourished, every secular acre was king's land and every sacred one God's. In prehistoric days, it is probable that this dual ownership was combined into one. Even the freeholder or yeoman only possessed his land by proxy, and the land of the pre-manorial free vill or the patriarchal Celtic " trev " or hamlet, grouped into " tyddyns " or households,* " belonged " to the village or sectional tribal unit as a whole rather than to the individual farmer. Up to the 14th century, land was not purchased or even bequeathed by legacy but bestowed in trust and in return for certain services. It was not even held by law, much less by a money transaction, but by custom alone and so upon a traditional basis. Only when these services—week-work and boon-work on the lord's home-farm—were " commuted " into rental during the 14th century did money play any but an insignificant part in the village economy. Thus, the foundations for the peasant's immemorial disregard for

* 9 Tyddyns—1 Trev, with smithy, bakehouse and song-maker.

cash valuations in respect either of holding property or disposing of his produce were laid during the many centuries when communal ownership was the condition of private possession. What is called " the open-field system " of peasant cultivation, whereby each village or (later) parish held two or three large fields of unfenced arable in conjunction with meadow-land by the stream, common and waste, was an arrangement by which private property in portions of land was inseparable from co-partnership in the whole. In other words, each village was a single farm or self-sufficient complex of production in which every member of the hierarchy was at once servant and master, owner and shareholder.

The meanest bondman, villein or cottar, had more security of tenure than the most secure of modern landowners, great or small, but he could not crop his land at his own times nor sow it with his own choice of grain. Such matters and their methods were the arbitrament of the village. But he *was* the village as well as himself, and he chose the council or moot or jury or court-leet which adjudicated upon them and appointed the officers (the reeve, the hayward, the pinder and the others) who herded his cattle, drove his swine to the woods, kept his beasts off his own and his fellows' corn and unfenced the meadows for common grazing. One for all and all for one— the principle of collective responsibility within a complete regional unit— was thus the mark of the village community from prehistoric times to the Enclosures. Whatever its faults, there is no doubt whatever that the peasantry of our open-field system did actually achieve and live an extremely durable and tenacious peace between Socialism and Individualism. The community gave its adhesion to neither because it represented a fusion of them both. In it ownership and co-operation made a match of it.

If our village community be impartially analysed without the prejudice of modern urbanism and the abstracted thinking of modern ideology, it will be seen how closely it approximates with " A.E's " passionate plea for a Co-operative Commonwealth based on region and on land as an alternative to " State Socialism, the Servile State and the industrial anarchy of *laissez faire*." The self-governing village community is a fact of history; to George Russell it was an ideal, a way of salvation out of the chaos of industrialism and the dark autocracy of the State. He does not mention it, but in a hundred passages he describes it :

> " One man," he wrote, " in every hundred is a freak, a person lit up by a lamp from within. He may be a poet, an artist, a saint, a social reformer, a musician, a person who has found the law of his own being and acts and wills from his own centre. As for the other ninety-nine, they are just what the social order makes them." And again, " The parish is the cradle of the nation." And again, " What is a nation ? It is a single yet multitudinous being, giving evidence of unity and individual character by the power of growth from within which it manifests." And again, " A country must first of all safeguard its producers. It depends absolutely on them to create wealth, and they must be allowed to create it under the best possible conditions they can devise."

That " one man in every hundred (or a million) " was himself, but the social order he outlined for the ninety and nine is simply a rendering into modern terms of the village community's as it once actually existed, " a little damaged " (as Lamb once said of Coleridge) by the frailty of human nature and our mortal state, but essentially what he pictured as a vision of regeneration. And I challenge any sociologist to disprove me. Only the modern incapacity to understand what social life really is has separated ownership from co-operation.

Ownership there certainly was, not so much of the land but of its tillage—namely by the ox and the plough. A " hide " was not only 120 acres but the eight parts of a team of oxen that could plough it comfortably in a year. The man who owned an ox, therefore, was entitled to a " bovate " (15 acres) of land, two oxen a virgate or 30 acres. Thus, in Anglo-Saxon times, a total team represented more often than not a joint ownership. But the oxen by themselves could not be separated from what they drew—the plough—and this too was privately owned either in its several parts or as a whole. Thus, " coaration " or communal ploughing was linked with individual ownership of the plough itself. This explains at once the striking difference between

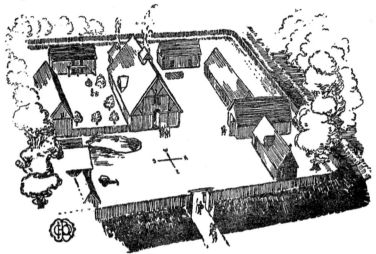

An Anglo-Saxon Homestead, reconstructed by Marjorie and C. H. B. Quennell

the little rectangular fields of the Iron Age Celts and the long strips or " lands " or selions (Lincs) or rigs (the north) or lawns (Dorset) or loons (Wales) or baulks (the Fens) or stitches (the south) or raps (Somerset) or pauls (Sussex) or dales of the Lakeland dalesmen or " statesmen," whose standard length (modified according to land surface) was 220 yards and breadth 22 yards, with a water-furrow (not a baulk, as has been mis-stated) between them. This furlong (furrow-long) was a day's ploughable land so that the strip was what Adrian Bell has called the " ploughable unit."

In their book on *The Open Fields of Laxton in Nottinghamshire*, with the Isle of Axholme in Lincolnshire (much more broken up) the only surviving examples of the old peasant community, the Orwins contend with sagacity that what led to the ploughing of the long furrow was the evolution of the mould-board. The scratch-plough that preceded it was itself evolved from fitting what survives as the Hebridean " caschrom " or mattock into a plough-beam. It could never have determined the " lands " of Saxon and mediaeval

England as did the heavy plough with coulter and mould-board by " opening up a top " in the middle of each " land " and ploughing two furrows on either side of it to close the top and form the ridge.

The whole system of ownership and commonalty was thus based upon the needs of the village community as a whole, needs in organic relation with the land itself and the means of cultivating it. Social organization was indivisible from agriculture, both from Nature. A man's relations with his neighbours were as interlocked as oxen with plough and plough with earth. This co-ordinated peasant life has been regarded by Arthur Young and Sir John Sinclair, his colleague at the Board of Agriculture, as " barbarous "; by modern agrarian economists as " primitive " and by most people as simple. But the interdependence between private and public, owning and sharing, individual and communal, free and obligatory, is seen on a closer view to be a highly complex one and not to be fitted into the more unbalanced modern notions of Socialism, Communism, Liberalism or Individualism, all of which show a tipping of the scales too far in one direction or the other. The theory of Hobbes's *Leviathan* that naturally predaceous man could only be held in leash by the absolute State, and the theory of Rousseau's *Social Contract* that tradition was an impediment to man's full enjoyment of his own true nature (the one a precursor of Fascism, the other of Communism) are both denied by the traditional self-government of the old village community. Rightly so, since both are false. Our conception of the English peasant must be partial and unbalanced itself unless this factor is given its due.

II   THE FREE PEASANT

Nor can it be doubted that the peasant community was democratic in a sense more integral than that covered by the counting of heads. This democratic element suffused every facet of the peasant life—his sport, his festivals, his labour, his economy, his administration and his institutions. Dr Orwin's analysis of the Laxton villagers puts this neglected truth beyond controversy. Tillage and husbandry were the joint concern of the village and were conducted by common consent, while the system made differential treatment between tenant and tenant impossible. A shared responsibility, a common law governed each for the sake of all but without sacrificing the individual to the community. If each man ploughed, sowed and harvested at the same time and submitted to all the seasonal punctuations dictated by the Field Jury, rotations and Nature alike, he was allotted his fair share both of the best and the worst land, and he could crop as he pleased and do what he liked with his own " closes." The right to graze the common was reserved for the poorest, and if the number of animals was restricted and there were fines for over-stocking, neglecting to cut thistles, to repair gates, to ditch and to drain, for trespass, unfenced fields, selling hay off the " toun " (tun), turning the stock on the stubble before the church-bell rang and others, these regulations were enforced by an elective body in the interests of good husbandry.

There was (and is) a network of them—bye-laws as it were for tethering stock on the " sikes " or unploughed roughage of the arable fields, for the limited use of bulls and rams among the stock, for opening the aftermath of the Lammas meadows. Yet these rules were not formulae nor forms to fill up nor impositions applied from the top downwards, but adaptable, informal, flexible, spontaneous and annually born of the common need. When the Duke of Portland's keepers were fined for taking anthills off the common as pheasant food, it is clear that they were operated without fear or favour, and that if they were voluntary at source, they were also firm in execution.

The co-operative system at Laxton, thus locally developed out of the needs of the soil and the villagers who live on it, is an utterly different concept from that of the modern Board of Control which is imposed on farmers from the top downwards. This speck of a land democracy surviving in an age of industrialized masses, a living museum piece, has been the only one in the countryside which the village lads do not leave for the town. Why should they? As individuals they enjoy personal responsibility; as social beings a community life; as ambitious to get on the chance of moving up from the part-time allotment or smallholding to a proper farm, and as villagers the privilege of managing their own affairs in their own way. For Laxton, a pure democracy, is still healthy and vigorous, still productive and stable, and is supported even by the large farmers on enclosed land in the neighbourhood.

Yet we know from the records that this village community of peasants whence Laxton is the uniquely lineal and authentic descendant, was a hierarchy. It was ruled by a feudal and manorial lord. Its services to him were onerous and exacting, while, previously to enfranchisement by payments in money or kind in lieu of service, many of its members were bondmen. Outside the freeholder or yeoman class, every mediaeval peasant before the 14th century was obliged to labour on the home farm or demesne at his lord's own time. He had to have his corn ground at the lord's mill and, yet bitterer grievance, fold his sheep as fertilizers of his lord's ground. The peaks of the domestic round, " a wedding or a funeral," were the occasions of a fine. Even as late as 1794—so vast is the period of time covered by the term " peasant community " and so regional were its fluctuations—the peasants of Cumberland were

> " getting and stacking the lord's peats, plowing and harrowing his land, reaping his corn, haymaking, carrying letters, etc., etc., whenever summoned by the lord."

Since feudal tenures were originally on a military basis and the free vills appear to have preceded the manorial village, it looks as though these dues of obligatory labour on the lord's demesne were the effects of political conquest. Certainly the Norman occupation bore more heavily upon the villagers than did the Anglo-Saxon: the taxes were more stringent; the acreages of many of the freemen shrank; the hundred courts held in the manor hall tended to supersede the entirely democratic assemblies gathered under a tree or in some traditional place of sanctity; forced services were increased; the markets for surplus produce were more strictly controlled and the persistent trouble about the peasant's corn being ground at the lord's mill—the " mill-soke "—first came into notice. Montague Fordham points out that the Saxon squire, he who gave his name to *tun* or *ham,* was himself of peasant stock, replaced by a foreign aristocrat less restrained by the custom of the village. The term *adscriptus glebae* is Norman and, so far as I know, there is no Saxon equivalent. The game-laws were tightened up, if they were not a novelty, and peasant backs became more difficult to straighten. In short, king's land was on the way to becoming lord's land and a baronage, coming between the

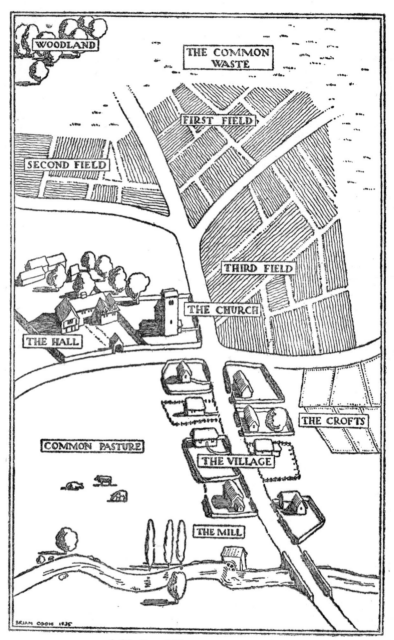

A Mediaeval Manor reconstructed

king and his people, tends to exercise a more despotic power than the mediaeval royalty ever did.

To understand the meaning and character of our English peasantry, it has been necessary to underline this shadowing of the village destinies. For this significant conclusion emerges from it. The personal liberty won by the 14th-century peasant was not an evolution from servile conditions, as most modern historians, partly responsible for the modern theory of progress, choose to represent it. In Domesday Book, there are distinct traces of the earlier system of the free vill, while another sign of the pre-manorial village community is that hidage was paid not by the lord but the tenants, once free men paying their taxes to the king. Scrutt's *Commons and Common Fields*, again, points out that the Salic Law " De Migrantibus " indicates the consent not of the lord but of those " qui in villa consistunt " when a man moved from one vill to another. If the system of customary rights was not developed independently of manorial overlordship, how could the lord have been fined for trespassing, as he was many centuries before the example given by Dr Orwin from Laxton? Vinogradoff insisted that the communal organization of the peasantry was " more ancient and deeply laid than the manorial order " and it was this which gave its members the control over their own lives which Tawney truly called " the essence of freedom." The reflection of that freedom even in the most burdensome days of serfdom is seen in such free institutions as the frank pledge, in the popular courts of the tithing and the hundred, in the inviolability of land and stock-in-trade and other rights. (See Garnier: *Annals of the British Peasantry*.)

Slaves do not free themselves; they have freedom thrust upon them. In other words, the peasant was originally a free man in free association with his fellows who recovered his freedom from a temporary depression superimposed upon it. And the cork screwed into the bottle itself became part of it. The new Norman lord whose motte and bailey dominated the village street shared his arable strips and his meadow doles with the common cultivators. It was as much his interest to preserve the village economy as it was that of his customary tenants. He interfered with the peasant custom to prune but not to uproot it and the peasant rising of 1381, the revolt of the " great society," was not a revolution on behalf of abstract rights and Utopian conceptions but a battle for the restoration of the ancient custom. It was a *conservative* revolution. How far back does that customary freedom extend? Who knows? Perhaps to the palaeolithic communism of primitive society.

Be that as it may, the term " serf " is a very misleading one. Not even the manorial serf had the ground cut from under his feet. The bottom class in the community had his one acre as a bondman and his five acres as a cottar, and this land was his in usufruct and possession as inalienably as was the hide of the freeholder who paid rent in kind to the lord. Apart from the squatter who marked out for himself a plot or " assart " on the waste, no villager was without rights of commonage on arable, meadow and common and the custom of the manor was virtually ownership without a written agreement. And since the village was an organic inheritance, it may be said that the meanest bond-servant owned it. The day of the landless labourer, that is to say of the ex-peasant, was not yet. Even after the villeins had emancipated themselves and the lord was hiring his labour for a money-wage, he was a rare bird indeed who had no land at all. Though the bondman's services were forced, still they were a kind of payment for his holding.

THE ENGLISH COUNTRYMAN

There are other indications beside these that the mediaeval serfdom could not have originated (as Seebohm claimed) from the Roman servitude, and so that the village community could never have been in the line of evolution from the Roman villa. At the time of their military occupation of Britain, the Romans had become capitalist farmers and the fact that 800 wheat ships were despatched thence to the garrisons in Gaul during the Imperium of Julian the Apostate is clear evidence that the export of corn was one of the main incentives for the Roman invasion of Ultima Thule. Rome's relation to Britain was in fact similar to our own towards India and the new colonies before the establishment of Dominion status. She desired British wheat for the same reason that we desired the best part of the colonial harvests—to feed an urban proletariat. Nor were the methods of satisfying that need very different—exploitation by means of slaves in the one instance and of machinery in the other. At the beginning of the Empire, the Roman *latifundia* or large-scale farms run by slave-labour had completely supplanted the yeomen farms of the old-time virile peasant stock during the Republic,* and the soil-erosion or exhaustion which are the anxiety of nearly all nations in our own period certainly occurred in the Sahara and elsewhere when the Roman magnates were organizing their villa-system in Britain. No wonder that Egypt mattered as it did to Rome when the unfailing regularity of the Nile flood was an insurance against loss of fertility by large-scale farming among the wheat lands of the fellaheen.

It has even been contended that one of the principal causes for the fall of the Roman Empire was the soil-exhaustion consequent upon the excess development of the *latifundia*. Though I have never seen it pointed out, it is evident from the reconstruction of many Roman Villas in England that they *were latifundia*, cultivated by slave-labourers housed in *ergastula* or underground slave quarters and controlled in gangs by overseers. How then could the Saxon and mediaeval peasantry of the Open Fields have drawn its system from that of the Roman Villa? And what relationship could there have been between the Celtic household or " tyddyn " and the separate holdings of the Coloni or ex-servicemen? Up to the withdrawal of the Roman legions in the fourth century, the two systems, the patriarchal and democratic Celtic and the servile or small-holding Roman must have co-existed side by side with no more inward association between them than there was between a Palladian house and park in the 18th century and any small mixed farm in the next parish. Indeed, it is probable that there were only differences in degree, between the Celtic and the Bronze Age and Neolithic peasants. In the Neolithic and Bronze Ages, the villages appear to have been more commonly sited within the earthwork or fortified market town; in the Hallstatt and La Tène Iron Age, the villages were grouped about the market hill-town, just as the Saxon *tuns* and *hams* were about the little valley-towns.

Whether the rather sophisticated Romano-Celtic villages of Cranborne Chase were occupied by a degraded peasantry supervised by the Romans for the mass-production of corn or were more or less genuine settlements of the village community under the Roman eye is a debatable point. It hardly is that the Roman Villa by its capitalistic purpose and methods embodied an idea totally alien from that of the self-subsistent manorial farm-village.

* See Toynbee's *Study of History*, Vol. IV, pp. 58 *et seq.*

8

4 Ploughing in the 14th Century: from the Luttrell Psalter

5 Ploughing To-day

6 The Mediaeval Moot Hall at Elstow, Bedfordshire

7 The Mediaeval Tithe Barn at Bradford-on-Avon, Wiltshire

ROMAN VILLA AND BRITISH VILLAGE

When the Barbarians overcame the Roman Empire, they planted out new communities of peasants in the Roman provinces (at Lille, for instance); when the barbarous Saxons invaded Britain, they left the Romanized townships and country estates to fall to pieces and established a new civilization in their place which modified the Celtic and ignored the Roman. Here was a mutation, not an evolution.*

I make no apology for stressing at some length this differentiation, so rarely made, between the Roman capitalist and the Celtic and Saxon peasant farms. It is not merely vital to the theme of this book, which is an attempted rediscovery of the English tradition from its rural sources, but is of primary importance in any proper estimation of the national character and its free and democratic origins, now overlaid. The *latifundia* and the village community are separate and opposite entities, like oil and water. It is against the nature of things that the one could have been derived from the other. The English peasant was a free man by virtue of his possession of land and stock; if he went into eclipse, he regained what he had lost in a new form, and when he lost his beasts and his holdings from the Enclosures, he disappeared altogether. His history came to an end. The serf was a free peasant in the toils; he became the commons of England. The *servus* might become a freedman but never a freeman. We owe the English sense of liberty to the peasant, not to the slave. At a time when the Roman idea of the *latifundia* is being revived in high places and our countryside is in danger of a new slavery, this historical verisimilitude cannot be overstressed.

III   THE PEASANTS' REVOLT

We gather then that the English peasant was a social being and that peasant society was in essence a cluster of free and localized democracies, just as were the Guilds in the towns. The social content and the democratic ethos were functional in that they were based upon the cultivation of the soil, and traditional in that they relied for the preservation of their liberties and the maintenance of their identity upon the " custom of the manor." This is what Tawney calls " the sanction of immemorial antiquity." The interlocked working of the village community both as an organism and in its economy was, however, conditioned by military conquest, Saxon, Danish, Roman, Norman, from external sources and this resulted not in the breakdown of its institutions but in various restrictions upon individual freedom. By the time of the Black Death, this freedom had been largely restored through the commutation of forced services into rent, which was a novelty almost unknown to the experience of past generations. But this by no means explains how the process of emancipation was effected. Nobody knows how it was done, but it surely must have been by the exercise of a stubborn and continuous self-determination which might be interpreted to-day as a kind of passive resistance. It called for qualities of patience and endurance and inflexible resolve quite inexplicable upon the theory of an evolution from a state of previous servitude with no knowledge of what freedom was. Such doggedness of temper perfectly illustrates the saying of Chesterton that " whatever has roots must have rights." These roots were in the land.

But these little democracies of property holders were to exhibit the home-

---

* How could the peasant village have originated from the Roman *latifundia* when the latter postdated the former?

spun stuff they were made of in a more instant and dramatic manner than by nursing generation after generation the sacred flame of independence, gathering the fuel for it stick by stick, fanning it by the breath of their devotion, fatting it with the sweat of their bodies. The immediate cause of the Peasants' Revolt was, of course, the Poll Tax, as Ship Money was of the Civil War. The underlying one was the Statute of Labourers, a desperate expedient of the Government to prevent the demesne lands from falling out of tillage in a depopulated countryside. It reintroduced the principle of forced labour by manorial tenants bound to the soil and lowered the wages bill to the pre-Plague level. In other words, it attempted to " put the clock back," and the peasants retaliated by a rising aimed at swinging it back a good deal further. The exactions of tithes and fines both showed the corruption of ancient principles, while the first stirrings of enclosure by force for sheepwalks and the harsh extension of aristocratic hunting and fishing rights were equally undemocratic and anti-traditional. So were the power-encroachments of the higher clergy against which the poor clerks and the lower clergy like John Ball and William Grindecobbe, the peasant leaders, expressed their protest. It was against these violations of what mediaeval society regarded as *natural law* (how different from the later predatory and then mechanical concepts of it!) that " John Nameless and John the Miller and John the Carter and John Trueman and all his fellows " rose like Shelley's wild west wind.

Apart from its drama, the most interesting thing about the great Revolt is the light it throws both upon the past and the future. The peasants found a widely distributed leadership that went far beyond the household names of Wat the Tyler and John Ball, and they were in London before the Government had time to stretch out a hand for the sword. The conventional idea of the peasant either as a submissive beast of burden or as an archaic straw-chewing Hodge or as a reactionary as tied to his tradition as the circling horse to a cider-mill collapses before such swift action and so high a degree of organization.

He pounced but with discipline and on the whole with a capacity for restraint and forbearance very different from the despairing flare-up of the Jacquerie in France. The looters before the murder of Wat were the London mob, not the peasant army. The peasants hanged a few lawyers but their violence was principally directed to burning the manorial documents which has displaced the hereditary witnesses to their liberties of the custom of the manor. Miss Levett's *Sketches in Mediaeval History* shows clearly that the reason for this paper-war was the written imposition of baronial councils, forerunners of the J.P., upon the democratic manorial courts. Centuries of orderly co-operation surely underlay a spontaneous movement distinguished by so much tolerance and a giant's strength singularly free from a tyrannous use of it. As for the future, the reknitting of the ancient handhold of the king and his people over the heads of the baronage was broken by the Parliament who forced young Richard to forswear his pledge. It was the Commons which betrayed the commons of England, as it was the Commons who, four centuries later, destroyed them. This is a queer reflection upon the free use of the term " democracy " in modern parlance and the still freer manipulation of the facts of history by later historians.

The conduct of the peasants in all their upheavals—1381, the Pilgrimage

8   The Village Common, Goathland, Yorkshire

10 The Mass: carving on a 15th-century font at Gresham, Norfolk

9 The Geddington Cross

of Grace in 1549, 1550 (Kent), 1552 (Bucks), 1554 (Sir Thomas Wyatt's rebellion), 1569 (Derbyshire), 1575 (Oxon) and 1607 (the Midlands)—was in marked contrast with that of their masters who made no scruple in moving on from perfidy to bloody reprisals and twice after Kett's rising and the Pilgrimage of Grace called upon barbarous German mercenaries to redress their own incompetence. If the peasants had won, or, I would rather say, if *only* they had won, England would never have rooted out her peasantry, England would never have mislaid her soul in that avid pursuit of wealth which is the history of the 19th century. In spite of their betrayal they did win—but only for a time. The attempt to force the peasants back into servitude failed in England, whereas it succeeded in Germany after the Thirty Years' War.

And so a likeness of our old peasantry begins to take shape and lineaments. They rose because their property was in danger and so the very existence of their communities was at stake. Yet these peasants were no theoretic doctrinaires : on the contrary, they were conservatives striking for the restoration of old usages based on experience. The kind of spirit actuating them is manifest by the contemporary doggerel :

> " Mr Pratt, your sheep are very fat,
> And we thank *you* for that;
> We have left you the skins to pay your wife's pins,
> And you must thank *us* for that."

Not very edifying, no doubt, but there is a kind of free-heartedness and good fellowship behind it which tells us more about the English peasant in his prime than volumes of moralizing. The specifically English note is there, the ribaldry " i' the imminent deadly breach," the hazard taken with a jest. This is something quite different from the Teuton solemnities, justifying racial abstractions by the methods of hell and the *jusqu' au boutiste* logic of the Frenchman, mowing off heads in the name of liberty, equality and fraternity.

IV PEASANT RELIGION

Yet the 14th-century peasant was also a religious man, though not at all in the Covenanting sense. The integral relation between the peasant and his religion is pictorially presented by the siting of every parish church to every village. The fields, the cottages and farms and the church—God, Man, Earth—these ultimates of life are represented by the subordination of the fields to the houses and of the houses to the church. They form an indissoluble trinity of individual and separate entities in an hierarchical order and as such are permanent truths. To the church as the pivot of the village came both the people *and* their fields. Only the Harvest Festival now remains to manifest this universal trinity. But this particular aspect is more properly the concern of a later chapter. Here I am trying to find my way into the peasant's religious mind.

In his march upon London, the name of Christ was freely upon his lips, and there can be no doubt that he conceived his Saviour, as John Langland did more mystically and John Ball more in terms of the social contract, as the friend of the poor. The Christ " of the Trades," of the farmyard and the carpenter's workshop, was a living being to a countryman who knew all about sowing and reaping and the ox at the manger—who better could appreciate the Parables of Husbandry? If the peasants rose against oppressors who would push them back into serfdom rather in the spirit of a down-tools May-Day festivity, Christ still sat at the head of the feast, the village Christ of the Gospel stories, painted on the walls of the church. Their religious imagination was concrete, pictorial, realistic, not revolutionary in the abstract sense but from the example of one who rode upon an ass, picked the ears of corn on a Sunday, threw the money-changers out of the Temple and turned the water into wine. This, of course, was largely due to the maternal influence of the Old Church, and there is no manner of doubt that, in spite of such examples as Gloucester Abbey, where week- and boon-work was particularly exacting, the monastic landlords were more indulgent to their tenants than the secular. Otherwise, the Pilgrimage of Grace, partly agrarian but also a protest in arms against the suppression of the monasteries, would scarcely have been so formidable at it was. The Church really did stand in the same relation to the peasant community as the church in any average village stands in geographical relation to the cottages and farms grouped or aligned about it—namely the shepherd's to his sheep.

Nor did the Church, having absorbed not a little paganism into its own ritual and ceremonies, offer any very strenuous resistance to the same phenomenon in the peasant rites of seasonal observance. The survivals of pagan nature-worship in the festivals of our mediaeval peasants is due to something more than the inherent conservatism of peasant life. The intimate contact with nature that governed every phase of the old village life was partly responsible for it. The recognition of the unity of creation lies at the back of B.C. and can be read by any sensitive observer of the works of megalithic and Iron Age man upon our downs and wolds. They translate the designs of nature into their own and are themselves drawn into the larger circumference of nature's order. The very buildings of the mediaeval peasantry, whether sacred or secular, express the same concept, though that strange feeling for the high places and for far horizons is lost. The transcendental sense of the archaic peoples of Albion was transmuted into a new universal; it was reinterpreted in the light of a new and definitely historical religion, but not destroyed. That was the work of modern civilization. Owing to the fact that the Romans never drove a wedge into the continuity of the old Irish culture, the transition between the pagan and the Christian can be more closely marked—for instance, in the Irish sculptured high crosses. That did not mean that the early civilization of Christian Ireland was the less deeply and passionately Christian.

So with the rural population of Christian England. Pasteur said that the older he grew, the more his faith became that of a Breton peasant and he hoped it would become that of a Breton peasant's wife. What the faith of the English peasant was John Langland is witness. In *Piers Plowman*, the peasant Christ takes on a definitely Anglicized form: Piers Plowman is conceived as the peasant Messiah. It has been well pointed out that Langland's provincialism and conservatism are far more representative of the English mediaeval countryside than are even the most rustic of the Canterbury Pilgrims. Langland spoke from its depths and his traditional right to do so is stressed by the very place where he was born, the very Malvern hills of his dream, Wulfstan of Worcester being the only Saxon bishop to survive the Conquest. Langland shot bitter shafts against both the Church and the peasantry but as a revolutionary no more than did Sir Thomas More against the former.

For Wordsworth the leech-gatherer was a symbol of patient toil redeemed and dignified by the service of the earth; for Langland the ploughman was the symbol of a divine humanity whom he actually identified with Christ, the divine Craftsman. There is nothing Wycliffite about him and he was not in the least a precursor of Puritanism, severe moralist as he often was. The ploughman with his vocation was the guardian of the Christian Faith and the pillar of all true civilization—" Piers Plowman tilleth for all "—and he supported the Canon Law because it explicitly recognized the moral superiority of the ploughman as the creative worker to the merchant, still more so to " Lady Mead," the personified Dalila of the power of wealth, and even to the scholar :—

> " None sooner are ravished from the right creed
> Commonly than clerks that know and read most,
> And none sooner saved and surer of faith
> Than plowman and shepherds and poor common people,
> Unlettered labourers and land-tilling folk."

The sweat of the plowman quenched hell-fire.

As S. B. James puts it in *Back to Langland,* the ideal peasant was the Son of Man. So Christ and Piers were mystically identified and " God speed the plough" acquires a spiritual profundity in his pages that goes beyond Bunyan's idea of the New Faith as embodied in the valiant person of Christian. Christian was the true Christian but Piers Plowman the " Christ of the Trades."

To understand the essence of the peasant culture in its relation to Christianity, a man should make a pilgrimage to the Northamptonshire village of Geddington. At the cross roads, not far from the banks of the Welland where the shires come down to drink, and spanned by a powerful mediaeval bridge with massive cutwaters built of the local oolite limestone, stands an Eleanor Cross, built of this same stone and surrounded by a group of cottages walled and roofed of this same stone. The names of the craftsmen who built this monument commemorating a king's grief in the village through which the funeral procession passed, have not come down to us, though sculptures of equality in beauty with it but wrought some sixteen centuries before it, are known to be by Pheidias and Praxiteles. The supernatural loveliness of the Geddington Cross, had it stood in the nave or chancel of Chartres Cathedral, would have drawn the eyes and heart away from them. It was chiselled and set up in a village of peasant quarrymen and peasant tillers of the open fields, just as Christ was born in a farmyard. It is only to us that the setting of this matchless work of art appears incongruous with it. It would not have seemed so to the peasants who gathered round it when it was blest or consecrated perhaps by the parish priest himself. They were accustomed to think of the King of Heaven being woken from sleep in the straw by the stamp of a cow. Their appreciation would not have been exclusively aesthetic, and doubtless their minds and feelings were filled with three reverences of different degrees in one, for a work of master-craftsmanship in memory of their own king's queen now at home with the Queen Mother of the King of Heaven. The idea of collecting masterpieces into a gallery or museum would to them have been entirely unintelligible. That

13

the Geddington Cross has actually not been removed to the Victoria and Albert Museum, but still remains in the little square of Geddington, shows that, in the hinterland of our minds and in spite of all appearances, we do understand a little about our lost peasant rural-Christian culture.

V FOLK MEMORY

A character that could so mingle pagan and Christian beliefs is no simple nor merely primitive one, and this complexity is both enriched and confused by his tenacious hold upon the past. Whole millenia were poured into the peasant mould and his folk memory stood in the extremest contrast with the urban theory of Progress to which forgetfulness is tantamount to virtue. His dependence upon the earth, his concrete imagination, his hopes and his fears were fed from many convergent waters whose sources were derived from the very springs of the human sense of the supernatural. If the custom of the village was the watchword of his liberties and the custom of the seasons the guide to his daily work, the custom of his ancestors was the granary of his mental life.

Nowhere was the stamp of the past more sharply impressed upon him than in his recreations, sports, pastimes and festivals, or in what we should call his leisure from the fields. But this too was a complex activity since it is impossible to separate it from his work. Therein it differed fundamentally from the leisure of the modern proletarian, whose significance is that it has nothing whatever to do with his work. But in the life-cycle of the true peasant, work and play were organically intertwined. In a sense he had no leisure at all. Not that he lacked abundance of holidays, which again were holy days, so that his Bank holiday was really Sunday, though by no means a Nonconformist Sunday. Walter de Henley, writing in the 12th century, numbers the peasant holidays as eight weeks in the year, a sum of more than 50 Bank holidays for which the modern wage-labourer may well envy him. But they were not what we mean by leisure and still less leisure *from* the fields. They were self-acting patterns, set to music, so to speak, by tradition, to theme by the Church and to punctual celebration both by the Church and the seasons. Thus the peasant world was in very truth a cosmos, the cohesion and integration of many parts into a whole.

Just as in a country scene pieces of wild nature will compose with others of domestic husbandry to make a harmonious whole, so the pagan and Christian traditions met and mingled in the peasant mind. Few were the commemorations and observances which could or can be called pagan alone or Christian alone. In certain of them, it is possible to view the two traditions juxtaposed without being fused—as, for instance, the Hodering Horse (see Miss Christina Hole's *English Custom and Usage*), a memorial of the Celtic horse-cult, pictured on Iron Age buckets and visualized in the Berkshire White Horse, introduced into the Soul-Caking Play at Comberbach in Cheshire, which survived up to 1914. In the Mummers' Play, the pagan predominate over the Christian elements, while in other ceremonies it is the other way round. But in every festival or ritual, the peasant's drag-net was sunk deep.

How immeasurable a landscape unfolds by the bare mention of such memorial terms as Christmas, Twelfth Night, Plough Monday, May Day, Hock-Tide, Shrove Tuesday, Ash Wednesday, Midsummer, All Hallowe'en,

14

11　A Cottage Scene in Essex (*ca.* 1820): from an engraving after Bigg

12　An 18th-Century Alehouse: from a print by Collet

13   The Thresher (*ca.* 1800): from an engraving after Westall

14   A Cottage Interior (*ca.* 1850): from a painting by Thomas Webster, by
permission of the Corporation of Preston

the sun's farewell of the Celtic Samhain as the festival May Queen was linked with Beltane and Lammas Day (Aug. 12), when the hay-meadows were opened to the stock, with the Feast of Lugh! Rush-bearings and the summerings of St John's Eve were then something more than names to conjure with. Church Ales and Whitsun Ales now only stir the brain-cells of the antiquary, but the ghosts of the villagers who kept them are "thick as the leaves of Vallambrosa." Who remembers Dunstable Down or Cooper's Hill or White Horse Hill for the cheeses that were rolled down their turfy flanks; or Silbury for the wheaten cakes that were eaten on its summit; or Abbot's Bromley for the dance of the horned men; or Ashbourne for its Shrove Tuesday street struggle for the football that in the beginning of beginnings was perhaps the mummified head of Osiris; or Tissington for its well-dressing; or Charlbury for the Beating of the Bounds; or Dover's Hill for the Cotswold Games; or Stroud for its Maypole; or Randwick for its Wap of the Feast of Fools and the Lord of Misrule; or a Devon orchard for the wassailing (*was heile*—hail to you!) of the appletrees; or every farm-house in the land for the Feast of Proserpine? "I ha'un, I ha'un," the man in the centre of the circle of scythemen chanted, as he held up the "Neck"—wailing as older reapers mourned the death of Osiris.

In former days, I used to entertain myself with wild goose chases after the origins of these and other carnivals and rituals; there was hardly a legendary haunt in England I did not know; hardly a Sphinx-like monolith I did not question nor a storied hill I did not tread nor a Mummers' Play I did not puzzle over. A world of monsters, fairies, giants, hobby horses, corn-spirits, dragons, kings and queens, shepherds, mythical smiths and historical personages all jostled and jumbled together with a seasoning of the Devil in the peasant's memory.

Oak Apple Day appears to commemorate only the restoration of Charles II, though I misdoubt me whether, when the villagers of Great Wishford fetched green boughs from Grovely Wood on Oak Apple Day and paraded the village street in forester's dress and the women with faggots on their heads, they were not thinking of a queen rather than of a king, and her ageless as the deep dark wood of Grovely. Or their forefathers were, which amounts to much the same thing. Also, Oak Apple Day was the signal for the annual sheep-shearing and that was appointed by an eternal queen not a transitory king. On June 29th, the Feast of St Peter and St Paul, the procession still streams down to the quay at Mevagissey, though no longer headed by the image of St Peter, to bless the waters. So at Chipping Campden I have seen the parson issue from the church-door at Rogation Tide to bless the fields. Padstow still has its Hobby Horse Day and Helston its Furry Dance. On Henry Best's Yorkshire farm, the 17th-century household dragged "the fond plough" round the parish on Plough Monday with a bladder tied to the driver's whip and "Captain Caufstail" prancing alongside in motley. Near Shaftesbury, on the Springhead Estate, Plough Monday is still celebrated. These and like ceremonies go right through the top-soil of Christianity into the subsoil of the pagan recognition of the earth's bounty. Now there is no longer any soil at their roots.

The folk memory of the Mummers' Play, versions of which I have from time to time collected from villages of the South Midlands, is quite literally unfathomable. Before the Industrial Revolution, there must have been as many variations of the original as there were villages, and the plumbless depth of its oral antiquity is partly suggested by the sheer gibberish of some of the lines spoken in many of the surviving versions and partly by the extraordinary hotchpotch of stock figures—" King George," " The Turkey Knight," " Bold Slasher or Soldier," " Father Christmas," " Beelzebub," the " King of Egypt," the " Man-Woman," " Fiddler Wit," " Jack Vinney " or " Finney " and other fantastics. I have seen the Play performed at a village pub (years and years ago), and the actors might have been Bottom the Weaver and his hempen homespuns.

But the consistency of one of the *dramatis personae* and the invariability of one of his actions are even more revealing. This character is the Doctor and his deed is the magical restoration to life of the foeman slain in the combat. The Mummers' Play, in short, is not a secular drama at all but a sacred ritual, ragged and windowed with the attrition of centuries, even of millenia, in which is recreated the hoar story of the divine king, put to death for the welfare of the agricultural community and reanimated. If this be so, the Mummers' Play (" Mummers " because the peasants played the parts of the deified ancestors in order to exert a direct influence upon the courses of nature) is not merely pre-Crusades and pre-Christian but pre-Iron Age, when the personified myth of Light overcoming Darkness at the turn of the winter solstice was ritually represented. The marvel is that the accretions, desuetudes and interpolations of this knock-about village pantomime, daubed on or scraped off by the long Ice Age of human forgetfulness, have not utterly blotted out the medicine man's magic formula and elixir of life. What is Beelzebub (" don't you think I'm a jolly old man? ") up to prancing on the scene with a club over his shoulder like the Naked Giant of Cerne Abbas? The blue-blooded old clown does not know that he is moving about in worlds not realized either by him or his tap-room audience. It is probable that the Mummers' Play was rewritten in the 17th century, but assuredly certain of its stock figures date back, as the rustic says when he wishes to express a sense of vast antiquity, to the times " when Adam were a little bwoy," or, as Sir Toby Belch said, " since before Noah was a sailor."

Time's impact upon the peasant, then, was like the weather's on the rock. He changed but it is difficult to catch him at it. He was not by nature progressive and so the legend has grown up among those who have only seen his modern shade and him only from a distance, that he was dull of wit, the finite clod untroubled by a spark, or the quaint boor who chews a straw. Progress is a worse historian even than Little Arthur. This is the finite view that fails to look out upon a limitless horizon. We no longer sing the ballads that came from his spontaneous lips, ballads like the wild flowers he was the first to name, Ladies Smocks and Gilliflowers, Whitsun Bosses and Love Lies Bleeding. The highly expressive, matter-of-fact field names marked in old tithe-maps or to be drawn from some veteran of the village, no longer delight us with that intimacy and poetic suggestion which is a by-product of their once functional utility. Only the older rustics now tell his tales and pronounce his proverbs. His weather lore and prognostications of change by the movements of animals, the behaviour of plants and the subtleties of the very air he breathed, are now at their last extremity from the siege of the Research Institute and the wireless weather report, as often wrong as he. Under the tides of modernism his cargo is sunk, food for the fishes of Lethe.

THE GOTHIC SHAKESPEARE

VI THE PEASANT AND SHAKESPEARE

None the less, a source there is whither we prisoners in the present may grope our way back to the peasant's communal mind as reflected in his speech, leisure, entertainments and observances. No less than Shakespeare. It must be done with caution since between Shakespeare and the English peasant were the three barriers of his town-life, the bugbear of Popery and the Renaissance learning. The Tudor " Inclosiers " made war on the peasants' work by turning husbandmen into beggars ; the Puritans upon his leisure partly by direct persecution and partly by raising prejudice against his music, dancing, poetry, sports, festivals and customs as " the dregs of Antichrist " —" Dost thou think because thou art virtuous there shall be no more cakes and ale ? " Yet successive Tudor governments set their faces against enclosure for sheepwalks and the development of unrestricted business enterprise, while the Puritans, completely breaking with mediaeval ethics no less than with mediaeval religion, lent their weight to the encouragement of both. When James I made a progress through Lancashire in 1617, he found that the Puritan magistrates were punishing the people for their " lawful recreations and decent exercises," and in the next year he restored the May-poles and Whitsun Ales. In 1648, all ballad-singers were arrested and vast numbers of organs, lutes, viols, " harpsicons," flutes and theorbos were destroyed. All, as Stiggins used to say, "vanity." The Puritan was the first figure in our history to tip the national scales from self-subsistence in the country to business in the town, and his zeal was directed towards making a solitude of that crowded ground between the peasant's work and his religion which was filled by his communal recreations.

Richard Carew's *Survey of Cornwall* has an imaginary dialogue :—

" Of latentimes, many ministers have by their earnest invectives con-demned these Saints' feasts as superstitious and suppressed the church-ales as licentious." But they had a purpose, " raising a store, which might be converted partly to good and godly uses, as relieving all sorts of poor people, repairing of churches, building up bridges, amending of highways."

Antichrist had indulged, even organized these feasts and ales and so they were tainted, heathenish, a foe to godliness. By this action, Stubbes, Prynne and their far from merry men split the peasant integration between work and play and religion as their descendants split the nation and, philo-sophically speaking, the very soul of man.

Thus (apart from his need to make a living far from Stratford), Shakes-peare had the Reformation and the Renaissance between him and his Gothic inheritance. Nevertheless, the Whig historians have laid far too much stress upon the sundering flood between the Renaissance and the Middle Ages, the golden age of the peasant. Mediaeval man was baulked of the full development of his powers, so Berdyaev has argued, by the severity of his spiritual discipline. The Renaissance opened the locks and the flood poured into the new age of splendour and spaciousness. To my mind this is a much more satisfying explanation of the Renaissance genius than the conventional one, and it certainly explains much of Shakespeare as indeed it does the whole of St Thomas More. The Gothic Shakespeare is a promising theme ; we could spare much Shakespeariana for its exposition.

To what extent, then, does Shakespeare hold the mirror up to the mediaeval peasant?

In his very speech for one thing—the examples are far too numerous to dwell on, and years ago I gathered a glossary of Shakespearean words and phrases from the *extant* talk of the North Cotswold hillmen, a hundred or so and I but a stranger among them. Not only is much of Shakespeare's colloquial idiom of peasant derivation but there are many examples of his lifting the proverbial folk-speech into the plays. *The Merry Wives* (see *Shakespeare's England*), for instance, has " on a line " for " in a rage," while Iago's " speake within doore " for " speak softly " is the Warwickshire " speak within the house," still current.

Shakespeare's connections with the Warwickshire folk bob up in several odd corners of his dramatic landscape. Barton-on-the-Heath was the home of Christopher Sly the tinker, while Justice Shallow ran his greyhound in Captain Dover's Games on Dover's Hill (see Chapter V). Again, Justice Silence's " By our Lady, I think 'a be but goodman Puff of Barson," is a reference to the fat man of Barcheston, the village of Richard Hyckes's tapestries (see Chapter V). Nothing, again, is more characteristic of Shakespeare than plain Saxon lines of one syllable and an extreme simplicity. " In sooth, I know not why I am so sad," " It will have blood, they say blood will have blood," " That struts and frets his hour upon the stage, And then is heard no more," " It is the cause, it is the cause, my soul," " The long day's task is done And we must sleep," " Soft now, a word or two before you go," and scores of other examples, often when the dramatic situation is at its tensest. This is not so much peasant speech as the peasant's love of words that are like physical presences, " things that you may touch and see " and, but for his yeoman blood matched with a daemon unparalleled in literature, these lines could never have reached so consummate a pitch of intensity. The songs, too, that run like a sunbeam through the whole forest of the plays from first to last, these are peasant songs, however rarefied. " And greasy Joan doth keel the pot " reveals a Shakespeare of the farm and at the farm, just as the scene of the two carriers in the inn-yard at Rochester (King Henry IV, Pt. I) must have been his report of what actually happened.

In her masterly *Shakespeare's Imagery*, Dr Caroline Spurgeon demonstrates that Bacon draws simile and analogy from husbandry more than Shakespeare. But though the dramatist Webster shows some interest in bird-life, Shakespeare easily excels all his fellow playwrights in the wealth of metaphor and imagery he drew from country life, the face of Nature, the movements of birds, the weather, rustic manners and customs, and his own provincial landscape, especially River Avon.* A small anthology might be compiled of his gardening terms and orchard predilections. Dr Spurgeon makes a vivid contrast of his country-mindedness with Marlowe's temperamental choice for lunar, solar, astral, firmamental imagery, cold and majestic beside Shakespeare's concrete rural warmth. I have quoted elsewhere his electric simile of Cleopatra's flying fleet with the cattle stampeded by the gadfly (the " breeze "). Lace-making is a country craft allusion among many.

In the " heathen devilry of dancing," the references to formal dances

* Viz: the double and contrary current under Old Clopton Bridge, Stratford, is minutely described in *Lucrece*, Ls. 1667-73

imported from Spanish, French or Italian sources, such as the pavane and the galliard, have to be distinguished from those to the peasant or popular ones, such as the Morris, danced with treble, mean, tenor and double bells behind the team of forty oxen drawing the Maypole to the village green. When Hentzner in 1598 described the English as " excelling in dancing and in the art of music," he meant no doubt that music and dancing were to the whole community what cricket was before the War. Indeed English country dances became very fashionable abroad. Did not Pepys record how King Charles called for the country dance of " Cuckolds all awy? " And how greatly old Pepys with his succession of melody-making servants loved singing and instrumental music! He records how at the Fire of London nearly every escaping boat had a pair of virginals in it. Shakespeare's " The Nine Men's Morris is filled up with mud " (from the floods of the Avon Valley) refers to a peasant game not a dance, but some indication of the urban fashion in folk-dances may be gathered from a few lines in Heywood's honey-titled, *A Woman killed with Kindness*—

Jack Slime " Come, what shall it be? Rogero? (a foreign dance)." *Jenkin* " No, we'll dance ' The Beginning of the World '." *Cicely* " I love no dance so well as ' John, come kiss me now '." *Nick* " I that have ere now deserv'd a cushion, call for the Cushion Dance." *Jenkin* " No, we'll have the ' Hunting of the Fox '." *R. Brick* " For my part, I like nothing so well as ' Tom Tyler '." *Jack Slime* " ' The Hay, the Hay! ' There's nothing like The Hay." *Jenkin* " Let me speak for all, and we'll have Sellinger's Round (the ancestor of Sir Roger de Coverley)."

Shakespeare himself probably danced many a Morris dance with its traditional figures of the Hobby-Horse, the Moor, Robin Hood, Maid Marian, Little John and Friar Tuck, and with them the Dump and the Roundel, dances which he knew and wove into his imagery. Many of the old figure-dances (Dargason, for instance, described by Baring Gould in *Old Country Life*—

> " It was a maid of my country
> As she came by a hawthorn tree,
> As full of flowers as might be seen,
> She marvelled to see the tree so green, etc. "

were sung at the same time, and one of these song-cum-dances, Kiss-in-the-Ring, survived up to the nineties of last century.

The same differentiation between the imported and the home-made must be kept in his familiarity with games. Bowls and tennis were originally king's games, while quintain (described by Trollope in *Barchester Towers*) was knightly before it went rustic. But foot-racing, football, wrestling (still surviving in Cornwall and Lakeland), loggats, quoits, shovel-board, prisoners' base, barley-break or last-in-hell (the Puritans called it " the ready way to hell ") push-pin, cherry-pit, hobman's blind and handy-dandy, all peasant field-sports, were the guests of Shakespeare's poetry as cricket has been of Edmund Blunden's and Francis Thompson's—" Oh, my Hornby and my Barlow long ago ! " Ballads, again (and here, too, the line must be drawn between the contemporary and usually scurrilous ballad and the traditional), are scattered in spadefuls over the Plays like rich earth round flowers of speech and character—Ophelia's, Desdemona's, the Fool's in *Lear* —" When that I was a little tiny boy," the echo of the Gothic voice on Bankside. " In a trice Like to the Old Vice "—here in *Twelfth Night* he speaks it.

So it is with folklore, not the scholastic drawn from Scot, Roger Bacon, Harsnet, Ovid, Pliny and others but the folklore harvested from the unrecorded tales his mother told him and his country neighbours knew by heart:—

> " In winter's tedious nights sit by this fire
> With good old folks, and let them tell their tales
> Of woeful ages, long ago betid,
> And send the hearers weeping to their beds."

These were not the " tales told at the Mermaid," but tales of the far away and long ago, stored from who knows what sources into the timeless memory of the peasant. Tales of Giant Colbrand slain by Sir Guy of Warwick, of the Man-in-the-Moon and the Wiltshire Moonrakers, tales tougher than old oak, of the were-wolf that Dr Marett went to seek in Jersey and of the Mandrake, Justice Shallow's nickname at Clement's Inn, of which Jimmy Teapot, still living near Chipping Campden, disclosed one night at the Baker's Arms that it " shrieked like a babby when it was draw'd up by the roots."

Actually the story of the moonrakers is only Wiltshire by accident, though it may have originated thence. Like others of its kind, it became a stock *fabliau*, distinctly Chaucerian, and bandied from county to county as village ammunition in the wit-combat. The humour of the peasantry was almost invariably social (from its communal structure), concrete and pictorial (from its intimacy with the earth) and narrative in form (from traditional inheritance).

All these examples (and there are many others) appear in Shakespeare, and he frequently takes over the magical associations and beliefs connected with animals and plants and derived from heathendom. The " cursed hebenon " for the yew; the plant " Love-in-Idleness " used as a charm; the toadstone which was the " precious jewel " in the toad's head are peasant borrowings and to be distinguished from Setebos which was picked up from the Brazilian voyagers and the scraps purloined from the classical erudition of the times. Troilus's " As true as steel, as plantage to the moon " is simply an old wives' tale which modern science begins to recognize as a biological verity, as the medicos do the peasant respect for black currants as a specific against disturbances of the belly—even administering the syrup for duodenal ulcers. I have known many of the older countrymen who to this day plant at the waxing of the moon and geld their lambs at the waning. Tusser has :—

> " Set garlic and beans at St Edmund [Nov. 20] the King
> The moon on the wane, thereon hangeth a thing "
>   and
> " Sow pease (good trull)
> The moon past full,
> Fine seeds then sow
> Whilst moon doth grow."

The reference to the wicked stepmother in *Cymbeline* is as pure a folk-tale as Perdita's milking of the ewes was contemporary peasant practise. Such proverbs, again, as " time must friend or end " and " a little pot and soon hot " are Shakespeare's debt to the peasantry. The following proverbial sayings are not actually Shakespearean but coined from the peasant mint and in currency during this century:—" As okkard as a cat in pattens," " as bug (vain) as a pump with two spouts," " as fine as a new-scraped carrot," " as greedy as a fox in a hen-roost," " as pleased as a dog with two tails," " as welcome as flowers in May," with its opposite, " as welcome as snow at harvest." This earthly rural idiom might easily have been uttered by Bottom, Feste, Juliet's Nurse, Dogberry, Stephano, Touchstone, and even the immortals of more social consequence. On the other side of time, my old friend, Samuel Rockall's proverbial saying:—" Blacksmiths' horses and shoemakers' wives go the worst shod " is probably very old.

Many grand old corduroy words that Shakespeare might have used with profit survived into the beginning of the 20th century, " quimple " of running water, a portmanteau word from quiver and dimple; " blowth " (blossom); " shut of day " (Saxon); " underminded " (mean); " bofflement " (worry); Milton's " rathe " for early; " flutterby "; " woontitump " (mole-hill); Ben Jonson's " flittermouse " for bat; " Candlemas bells " (snow-drops); " giglet " (a flighty girl) and many others. " Shiny as silver and black as a raven's wing "—I once heard a labourer say that of a dark pool.

Not less peasant-born were the characters Shakespeare gave to animals, the nine lives of the cat, the melancholy of the hare, the occult significations of bat, ape, hedgehog, owl and serpent. The witches in *Macbeth* are Shakespeare's own, but his " beldam trot " and the " wise woman " in *Twelfth Night* are the peasant's " old wife." She is legitimately descended from the Mother Goddess or corn-spirit of the ancients into a multitude of hag-shapes and christened the archaic green trackways, whether Ridgeways or Drove Roads, as " Old Wife Trods," the green carpets of Proserpine who likewise crowned the cornricks as the dolly or the mell or the kern. The Rollright Stones which once were kings' men changed by the " Elder Mother " stand right on the ancient greenway that links the Edgehills with the North-Eastern Cotswolds. The devilry of witch-hunting celebrated its excesses in post-mediaeval times and King James's demonology is not to be confused with traditional peasant superstitions. The Puritan temper which broke with tradition (did not a Puritan cut down the Holy Thorn of Glaston-bury?) was certainly more witch-possessed than the mediaeval whose witch might be placed as a kind of stepmother to the mischief-making Puck. In the matter of witch-hunting, peasant beliefs should not only be sharply distinguished from the perverted and pornographic erudition of the 16th century and from the literature of certain circles in the 17th century which treated witchcraft as a kind of reactionary Gothic horror and profanity, but from the theorizing of the mediaeval church itself. Mediaeval demonology was largely derived from neoplatonic and rabbinical conceptions of occult and Satanic powers, many of which were pagan ex-deities, at war with Christendom. Peasant thought about witches was at once simpler and deeper, in the sense that pagan supernaturalism was not so remote from it as to be demonized. To the peasant the witch was no intellectual abstraction but simply " the wise woman " whom it was as well not to offend but whose good will was as useful as moderns find the chemist's shop. Shakespeare's volatile and childlike fays are certainly emigrants from the peasant's Elfland, whose horns were the signal of mystery rather than evil. Fairy lore and the charms, spells, omens, cures and conjurations associated with it are relics of the ancient nature-worship rather than a diabolist chimaera, while, if savage sports like bull-baiting have stained the name of our yeasty Renaissance countryman, the fashion of that lusty time rather than the ageless peasant culture may be held responsible. Both Walter de Henley and Tusser three centuries after him are so insistent upon the good feeding, treatment and care of farm-beasts that " Thou shalt not muzzle the ox that treadeth out the corn " may be considered an injunction generally obeyed by our peasantry and true to the reputation of the English.*

Looking at the past as a landscape " broad as ten thousand beaves of pasture," of this we may be certain. When John Stow wrote of the Londoners going maying into Epping Forest " They went into the sweet meadows and green woods, there to rejoice their spirits with the beauty and savour of sweet flowers, and with the harmony of birds, praising God after their kind ; when, again, Fynes Moryson wrote of the popular passion for dancing :—

> " What shall I say of daunsing with Curious and rurall musicke . . . upon all hollydayes by country people daunsing about the Maypooles with bagpipes and other Fidlers, besydes the jollityes of other seasons of the yeare, of setting up may-pooles daunsing the morris with hobby horses, bringing home the lady of the harvest, and like Plebean sportes in all which varietyes no nation commeth any thinge neare the English "

—they were describing, not a national ebullience confined to a cross-section of time, as the Whig historians have misled us to believe, but the common disposition and continuous practise, especially in the 14th and 15th centuries, of the immemorial English peasant. The creator of " Merry England " (which the progressive moderns regard as a myth) was the peasant, not Queen Elizabeth. It long preceded her reign and bits of it even survived Oliver Cromwell and the Whigs—as Goldsmith testifies —

> " How oft have I blest the coming day
> When toil remitting lent its turn to play,
> And all the village train from labour free
> Led up their sports beneath the spreading tree.
>
> .   .   .   .
>
> These were thy charms, sweet village, sports like these,
> With sweet succession, taught even toil to please;
> These round thy bowers their cheerful influence spread;
> These were thy charms—but all these charms are fled."

Or as another country poet has sung of a yet later age :—

> " An' there we play'd away at quaïts,
> An' weigh'd ourzelves wi' sceäles an' waïghts,
> An' jump'd to zee who jump'd the spryest,
> An' sprung the vurdest an' the highest,
> An' rung the bells nor vull an' hour,
> An' play'd at vives ageän the tower.

* Dr Caroline Spurgeon's review of Shakespeare's imagery from field-sports reveals that his sympathies were invariably with the hunted (hare, deer, bear, bird), not the hunter, baiter or snarer.

PEASANT TENACITY

An' then we went an' had a taït (see-saw)
An' cousin Sammy, wi' his waïght,
Broke off the bar, he wer so fat!
An' toppled off, an' vell doun flat
Upon his head, an' squot his hat,
　　　Because 'twer Easter Monday."

Even in the 20th century, when only the ghost of the peasant walks, a gelded communal rejoicing survives in the village fête, outing, club-walk, mop, wake, ploughing match, whist drive, old folks' dinner and annual flower show—and, a little before them, the annual supper of the village choir and the ringers. But his tuneful voice is now silent and surely we know from Cecil Sharp the bitterness of that loss.

VII PEASANT CONSERVATISM

The conservatism of the peasant, in work and in play, in mind and in the work of his hand, is thus gigantically manifest. In these revolutionary days, of course, the very word " peasant " is associated with ignorance and crudity, or " uneconomic units," so false have become our values. For our education is knowing words not things, but the peasant's traditional contact with things drawn from Nature, custom or his own labours was an education in itself.

This obstinacy of his, together with the close-woven mesh of his social organization, can alone account for his survival through a series of post-mediaeval catastrophes. Owing to the new profits to be won out of the sheepwalks, the dealer made his appearance in the late 15th and the 16th centuries. As early as 1514, there was legislation against the engrossing of farms (throwing them together), and by 1530, the Field Juries had lost much of their unofficial legal powers to the J.P. The Dissolution threw 80,000 peasants out of the Abbey estates into beggary. The " covetous and insatiable cormorants " of the Tudor despotism devoured villages by the score, and over one-fifth of the land two shepherds took the place of forty husband-men. Sheep, in More's phrase, were eating men, while farming for profit drove a great wedge into farming for subsistence, which was the peasant livelihood. In Elizabethan times, contemporary literature is full of the paupers and vagabonds swarming into the towns from their village farms turned down to pasture. The rise of Puritanism under the Stuarts was fatal to the social life of the village by starving much of its aesthetic play-activity and snapping its link with the Church. The Puritan movement, being urban and commercial, was also favourable to enclosure and suits in Chancery for it deprived the villager of his right to defend his own property. By the Game Laws of 1670, game became the property of the squires, while the strengthening alliance between squire and parson still further detached the governing from the labouring classes. In the next century, the peasant community was to be metamorphosed into the " labouring poor."

Yet it survived these successive batterings upon its independence and integrity of being. In 1798, 20,000 out of the 23,000 arable acres of Middle-sex were still open fields. When Latimer was preaching against enclosure, a copyholder died whose live and dead stock was valued at £55 and in bed-furniture alone his effects were 3 bedsteads, 4 mattresses, a flock bed, pillows, coverings, hangings and 10 pairs of sheets. Yet he was but a peasant. What the peasantry did not and could not survive was the hundred years' war upon it between the middle of the 18th and the middle of the 19th centuries, when the forces of government, law, parliament, wealth, religion and commerce were arrayed in one solid phalanx against it. A new destitution and a new serfdom became inevitable and the ground was cut from under the co-operative peasant's feet. He vanished and only at Laxton and to some extent the Isle of Axholme did a speck of him remain. He lived by and grew from his own land and he was plucked out of it. With fluctuating fortunes, the peasant proprietary of Albion, Britain and England had lasted for nearly four millenia. From 1845 onwards, when the General Enclosure Act was passed, only the diminished yeoman (and a few of the squires) stood between the town and the total commercialization of the land. The tenant farmer abetted it or was Laodicean in his attitude; the landlord paid for his victory by being nearly snuffed out in his turn, while the smallholder has been victimized partly by finance and partly by dumping him on the land without adequate training. The peasant has not been there; only the ex-peasant in the person of the landless labourer. He had turned into an agricultural proletariat, and the social individual ended as an economic unit. This process was called progress.

It is generally held that the peasant was destroyed by very reason of his conservatism, it being presumed that conservatism implies lack of elasticity. How far is this true? The example of Laxton, a still-thriving self-supporting peasant community, a mere dot in the middle of an industrialized England and a capitalized agriculture, is not a happy one for this theory. It hardly appears likely, again, that his society could have weathered so many storms, military, dynastic, political, economic and natural, unless, like a tree on the Downs, he knew how to give and to sway to their pressure. When it is observed how frequently the peasantry rose against both economic and religious oppression from without, how persistent was its passive resistance to achieve copyhold from villeinage, how mobile and plastic rural society must have been even in the 13th century, the deficiency which the landed aristocracy put forward as the pretext for dispossessing it of its lands would appear to have been not so much lack of enterprise as of the competitive spirit and profit-hungry motive.

In the flood of pamphleteering let loose during the last period of enclosure by force, little enough can be read of enclosure by mutual consent among the peasants themselves for the sake of convenience and the improvement of farming. Yet the process of exchanging and re-allotting the strips to form enclosed blocks of them made strong headway from the 15th century onwards and reveals a sensibility to change in farming methods which acquits the open field system of rigidity. Had this gradual approach to a more individualistic type of husbandry been allowed to develop organically from within, not only would the English peasantry have survived as a check to excessive urbanization and the financial control of the land, not only would agriculture have been spared a half-derelict England during the 20th century, but the horrors of the last stages of enclosure in the 19th century, when the commons were being hanged or transported for stealing the mutton to save their families from starvation, would have been averted. The village Hampden might have been spared the slavery of Botany Bay.

Because the prayer that was prayed from the pulpits in the reign of Edward

VI was not granted, the prayer that the landlords would not add field to field and house to house so that they might have mansions in heaven, the process of enclosure as it was actually carried out in the 18th and 19th centuries was regarded as inevitable, as progress has been regarded. That it was not thus inevitable is clearly shown by the numerous bargains struck (see p. 24) at the close of the Middle Ages between landlord and peasant holder (enclosure by consent) for the latter jointly to take over the demesne lands. This indicated a smooth transition from " champion " to " severalty " tenure, and would have rid the original strip system (itself the only practicable one for ploughing small units) of such disadvantages as trespass from cattle, the absence of root-crops from the three-field rotation and the difficulty of cross-ploughing and cross-harrowing the " lands." It was maintained by Young, Arbuthnot, Eden, Davies and others of the early 19th-century propagandists (not to mention Tusser, Fitzherbert and " W. S. Gentleman " in earlier days and practically all the moderns) that open-field cultivation was a false economy. The scab decimated the common fold and the rot was rampant in the ill-drained fields. Pedigree stock was a Utopian dream for the mixed herds and flocks of the commons. Much land was wasted by headlands, baulks and the like, and dung too, by spreading over an area too wide, not to mention the labour in cartage to the scattered strips. The routine of the body of partners was too stringent, so that no single innovator could depart from it. The thistle-heads of the sloven's land blew into the clean furlongs of the devotee. Bickerings were frequent between the two and time as well as words were wasted by a farmer moving his implements from one parcel of land to another. Straw and cow-dung were too often burnt as fuel.

Many of these complaints were certainly not the fault of the commoners but arose from the disappearance of the reeve who had directed the proper rotation of the crops, the hoeing-up of weeds and the throwing of the grain for the heaviest seed-corn, while the looting of the monasteries, the great husbandmen of the earlier Middle Ages, coincided with a steep decline in agricultural practice. Nor were scab and rot by any means a malady incident only to the village community, as the history of 19th century tenant-farming amply demonstrates. Again, the commoners were often blamed for a stubbornness towards what was politely called economic change which threatened the dislocation of the peasant's attachment to his land. Others of these charges are flatly contradicted by the example of Laxton which can hardly have been exceptional. The inference that one man's neglect would recoil on all his neighbours was so well understood there that the Manor Court or Field Jury, the executive of a joint responsibility, was (and presumably still is) very much alive to all individual shortcomings in good husbandry. It visited with prompt fines such offences as the overstocking of the common, trespass, failure to cut thistles, clean ditches, fence and the like, disregard of the regulations for grazing, sowing, weeding, etc. And it was, by Orwin's testimony, an extremely efficient administration. It is no exaggeration to say that the peasant farmers of the 14th century were leasing the whole of the demesne land available to divide among themselves, quite apart from intakes (" assarts ") from the waste. Thus took place what Tawney has called a balance between communal custom and individualism. The tragedy of the Enclosures (that is to say, the destruction of the peasantry)

4   25

was not merely the rapacity that was at the back of them and the consequent suffering they entailed, but that their social effects were unnecessary. If the peasantry of Denmark were saved by the enclosures there being accompanied by the compensation of from 4 to 6 acres per cottage (an allotment almost identical with the Elizabethan law), so could ours have been.

The vitality of the peasant community, that would have saved agriculture from being bound to the wheel of commerce, is proved by facts that have been kept out of our histories by the dominance of the Whig aristocracy and of the urban capitalism that succeeded it. And unless those facts are given the prominence they deserve, it is impossible for us, living to-day in an age which has completely lost touch with the peasant values, to have so much as a glimmering of what they were. The peasant's sense of freedom was inseparable from his conservatism, and the custom of the village was the generator of both. Our conception of freedom being purely individualistic, it is very difficult for us to appreciate how it was combined in the peasant mentality with co-operation. The earth itself is the real secret. Its possession as an inherited and customary right was the foundation of individual responsibility; a self-subsistent fellowship in work was the condition of its tillage. A democratic system depending on votes but not land may secure political but never economic freedom. The profound symbolism of the Son of Man, the liberator, being born in a manger can never be understood without realizing the place of the peasant in human society and human history.

VIII   THE SHEPHERD

As a last sight of him, I should devote a little space to the shepherd. For these reasons. He was a figure closely interwoven into the tapestry of peasant life—in fact, as Eileen Power pointed out, the typical sheep-farmers of the 15th century were the peasantry with a sprinkling of squireens and new men from the towns. This indeed was the age of the small man. At the same time, he stands a little apart from his fellows and appears to have enjoyed special privileges throughout the centuries. He was rather more of an individual than the rest and with his remote sheep-fold and wheeled cabin containing his medicine chest, tackle and thatching tools, he might even be called a small yeoman, except that he played a more intimate part than the freeholder in the peasant economy. An illuminated MS. of about 1350 (Egerton MS, 1894) depicts the movable shepherd's hut on wheels and of a design almost entirely " modern." For centuries he was buried (especially in Sussex) with a lock of wool, to wave on the last day as quittance from church on Sunday. His customary rights included a bowl of whey and buttermilk all through the summer, ewes' milk on Sunday, a lamb at weaning time and a fleece at the shearing. Unlike the rest of the peasants, he kept his own sheep with the lord's flock on the best pastures, and for a fortnight at Christmas folded his lord's sheep on his own bit of land. His status was almost equal to the reeve's and superior to that of the village officers like the pinder, the hayward and the swineherd, particularly in the 15th century when there was a great variety of copyhold, ranging from 15 to 200 acres. The class of prosperous peasants in that golden age of the small man, when co-operative marketing was organized and credit cheap, small corn-growing flourished and sheep were closely interlocked with it, made the shepherd a power in the community.

26

15 A 15th-Century Sheep-farm in the Yorkshire Hills

16 A Shepherd in his Portable
Hut (14th century)

17 A Piping Shepherd (14th century)

18 Sheep on the Hampshire Downs

19 The Sheep Fair at Findon on the Sussex Downs

Then again he has been immortalized in literature and, though he lost his land after the Enclosures like the rest of the folk, he may be called the sole survivor of the true peasantry into our own period. He is the supreme Biblical representative of the peasants in the Gospel narrative—" And there were shepherds in the fields, keeping watch over their flocks by night." As carols innumerable have sung the glory shed upon him from the Eastern Star, so his fraternity was specially honoured in the Wakefield and Chester Cycles of Miracle Plays. In the pastoral convention, he is celebrated as a joyous and melodious figure, piping to his sheep * *sub tegmine fagi*, the long-term ambassador of Arcady from Anacreon to the Shepherd's Calendar. His reputation for trustiness and wisdom has in a sense been more illustrious than that of any other human type except the saint on earth, so that, though Langland chose Piers Plowman for his English Christ, the world's preference was for the Good Shepherd. His crook, the " shepherd's long arm," as a shepherd called his once in my presence, was symbolized in the crozier and has become more famous than Excaliber, the sceptre of royalty or the rod of Aaron. It was as a shepherdess that Joan of Arc saw her visions. So universal has been the tribute of his praise that mankind may be said to have instinctively recognized in him the debt it owes for its virtue and its stability to the peasant.

The *Rectitudines Singularum Personarum* of the 13th century said of him, " It profited the land to have discreet shepherds, watchful and kindly, so that the sheep be not tormented by their wrath but crop their pasture in peace and joyfulness." So Mascal in 1596, " A Shepherd ought to be of a good nature, wise, skilful, countable and right in all his doings." When Queen Elizabeth visited Sudeley Castle, she was addressed by a shepherd who said :

" This lock of wool, Cotswold's best fruits and my poor gift, I offer to your Highness : in which nothing is to be esteemed but the whiteness, Virginity's colour : nor to be expected but duty, shepherd's religion."

John Stephen's shepherd of 1615 spoke very much like Corin in *As You Like It* :—

" Sir, I am true labourer ; I earn that I eat, I get what I wear, owe no man hate, envy no man's happiness, glad of other men's good, content with my calling; and the greatest of my pride is to see my ewes graze and my lambs suck."

King Henry VI longed to be a shepherd :

" So many hours must I tend my flock;
So many hours must I take my rest;
So many hours must I contemplate;
So many hours must I sport myself.

.   .   .   .

So minutes, hours, days, months and years
Past over to the end they were created
Would bring white hairs unto a quiet grave."

From Mopsus to Gabriel Oak and Caleb Bawcombe the verdict of the ages is repeated.

It is true, so at least I have gathered from what experience of shepherds I have. The piping shepherd is no figment of poetic fancy because he was a virtuoso in the tunefulness of his sheep-bells and a traditional singer at the sheep-shearing. Nor was his attribute of wisdom—a sense of values and right discrimination gathered from solitude and intimacy with the earth—

* The Arundel MS represents a shepherd piping.

a fictitious one. Nor his learning in the ways of Nature. Nor his profound sense of family and of home, of vocation and inheritance—all facts of the peasant's conservatism. I know a shepherd who gave me the sheep-bells that had belonged to his grandfather and of another whose daughter gave me the smock she had made for him and that he wore for forty years until he died past ninety. " Sweet Stay-at-Home, Sweet Love-one-Place " might be the peasant's epitaph, because he was *wedded* to the land, the husbandman. Yet the shepherd, wandering with his flock over the unhusbanded Downs, also drew in a sense of the wider world from their spaces and of eternity from the skies. Thus, he was more often graver than the average peasant. Shepherd's gear, again, could never be mechanized on the lonely Downs. The shearing gangs gave him social respite from his solitude, as did the tales of which Drayton wrote in the Polyolbion :

> " The Cotswold shepherds, as their flocks they keep
> To put off lazy drowsiness and sleep,
> Shall sit to tell and hear these stories told,
> That night shall come ere they their flocks can fold."

No shepherd that I have known was an ambitious man. He never confounded making a living with making money, and that is the peasant. He thinks in terms of fruits, not counters. All shepherds were lovers of animals and knowledgeable. Said one :

> " Ther' bent no two ship the same, neither in temper nor yit in face. Ther' be just as much diff'rence, bless 'ee, atween they as ther' be atween you an' me."

Were there ever such dominies of dogs from Caleb Bawcombe to many a shepherd I have known?—one instructing his among the flock without ever so much as opening his mouth. All too I have known taught by gentle ways :— " they be like 'oomans an' must be spoke soft to an' humoured."

Shepherds were men of thoughtfulness and a pondering nature. They had reverence for the " works of creation." Their speech was often an unconscious poetry like the earth's unconscious beauty, so that they were not so remote from Colin Clout and Thyrsis. But great men too for citing the Bible. And their years were patriarchal. It is authentically told of one questioned as to whether he ever needed a doctor :— " We dwunt ha' no doctor: we just dies a nat'ral death." And they were customary men, though I never met one who counted his sheep by the Celtic numerals—Yan, Tan, Tethera, Pethera. . . . But I knew one who remembered the great sheep-fairs at Weyhill and the " tenantry " sheep-farming on the Berkshire Downs. I have seen a pair of them roll up the fleeces after the shearing with motions and rhythm as on a Greek vase. Men " of quietness and slow time "—no men more. In Abraham's time, the shepherd walked in front of his flock; now he (all that is left of him) mostly walks behind it, but still not always. They no longer make his crook at Pyecombe, Kingston and Falmer and he no longer wears the smock. But these things are the measure of his changes. Neither do the Downs change. Who wants them to? Who wants the shepherd to ? Pepys's *Diaries* record how he met a shepherd on the Downs with his little boy reading the Bible to him, " the most like one of the old patriarchs that ever I saw in my life, and it brought those thoughts of the old age of the world in my mind for two or three days after."

EVESHAM VALE PEASANTRY

Equally dateless was Mitchell of Newark, who died in my lifetime. He used to doctor not only sheep but cattle and all sick animals, so that no vet. was ever seen on his master's farm. Day and night he watched the sheep, year after year rearing a record number of lambs and never sleeping at shearing-time except at the week-ends. He lived for his farm and his garden and had never been inside a town. Every year he took first prize at the local flower-show; he knew the name of every wild flower and grass in his neighbourhood and every year he was the discoverer of the first bird's nest. His master said that he had never been known to be troubled, to lose his temper or speak without thought. He educated his master's children both in husbandry and natural history and sat at his right hand at the harvest home. In 1889, when he was sixty, he had worked for three generations of the same family. Pepys's, Hudson's, Adrian Bell's, Mascal's, John Stephen's shepherds seem to live as much in fiction as in fact, in Handel's *Faithful Shepherd* as in time. He, the flower of the peasantry, helps us to see the peasant as he was—one in true and timeless relation to the ageless earth.

IX THE MODERN PEASANT

In distinguishing the peasant from other types of English countrymen, he is to be regarded as the co-operative villager, living by the land which he owns not by deed nor purchase but by custom. The trace of him to-day is that of a footprint after snow. The last sign manual of England's true peasantry was the cottager's pig. Since the local bureaucracy ordered the pigsty to be removed 60 yards from the cottage, the ex-peasant's patriotism can hardly be what Arthur Young said it might be from the possesion of a pig. The dalesmen or " statesmen " of Lakeland are rather small yeomen than peasants. Colonies like the Bruderhof and others are not a peasantry, though they may be co-operative. They lack " soil-wisdom "; they are not villagers; they have no customary inheritance and their education in the values of husbandry has been largely theoretic. These lacks and financial tribulation added to them have caused most of them to fail.

But the smallholders of the Vale of Evesham, of whom I gave an account in my *Shepherd's Country*, are half-way to a peasantry, partly because the most powerful section—the asparagus growers—are co-operative, and partly because their tenancies are held under the beneficent " Evesham Custom " (giving the tenant a property in his improvements and a right to nominate his successor) which survives from the open field system. Thus, they compete on the whole very successfully with the big fruit combines and companies. But their farming is more specialized than mixed; it depends on mass-production for the urban market and the tenants no longer possess rights of commonage. It is significant that the Vale villages still speak many different dialects and that the cottagers make or made quantities of jam and cider from their own crops. Here are definite traces of a regional peasantry, and all peasant settlements are, of course, passionately regional. The small cultivators of the sandy tracts of Bedfordshire, growing a mixture of vegetables and fruit, are, again, being nursed into a peasantry by the wise leadership of the Duke of Bedford. The holdings are of old standing and very much better farmed than the factory-farms (or firms) of the neighbourhood. The Welsh, small farmers too who own their little properties, still retain something of the old cultural elements of music and festival. But

29

economic pressure has heavily destocked the sheep-runs of the hills. Among the Carmarthenshire smallholders, there is a healthy co-operation.

Both Laxton and the Isle of Axholme represent an authentic descent from the village community, though the " Isleonians " have, like the Evesham villagers, lost their common pastures. But they deserve more than a passing reference, and in 1935, as I described in my *Genius of England*, I visited the " Island." In spite of its shorn privileges in common rights and in spite of the competition from the well-equipped mechanized farms surrounding the Isle, it was supporting a larger population and producing heavier and more varied crops per acre than any big farm in England. There was no native unemployment and the " ladder " between the landless labourer and the small owner-occupier had not the bottom rung missing. The biggest farmer in the Isle was the miller of Haxey who up to 1928 ground whole-meal flour from the local harvest. He farmed 50 acres. Arthur Young's praise of Axholme as cultivated " with all the minutiae of care and anxiety " had not lost its point in 1935.

The traditional farming of the Isle has recently come into sharp conflict with modern commercial and bureaucratic methods. The Trent Catchment Board there established introduces a clerkly and industrial population for wholesale drainage, while the little farmers of Axholme practise warping the land piecemeal and by a traditional co-operation. This is done by a decentralized system of cuts and ducts and by the deliberate flooding of selected areas on a co-operative rotation and according to the local knowledge of conditions of fertility. Warping uses the flood-water and pumping gets rid of it. The one irrigates and the other drains. Pumping takes off the topsoil with the water; warping silts the land in places fifty feet deep. The more the soil-level falls, the more you have to pump, and the more you pump, the lower the fall, which the warped alluvium prevents. The rise of the Trent was due to the partial discontinuance of the old warping system. Hence the Catchment Board to remove a soil " of almost inexhaustible fertility " (Rider Haggard). What a contrast is this urban flouting of local experience to the example of Sir Richard Winfrey (Parliamentary Secretary to the Board of Agriculture from 1916-19)! He saw the connection between the agricultural labourer and smallholdings and established some very successful ones in Fenland, while his far-sighted zeal resulted in the formation of the Lincolnshire and Norfolk Small Holdings Association. Here was a true modernism building up from a stable peasant foundation.

Many readers will regard this retrospect of peasant society and peasant tillage as nothing more. Glance for a moment at Denmark in 1938. It contained 93,800 peasant farms (two-thirds of the total area of land) and 105,700 smallholdings (one-sixth of the area), while 94 per cent. of the holdings were cultivated by the owners. Yet on a soil much poorer by nature than in England this co-operative peasant population of unspecialized mixed farms exported more butter and bacon than any other country in the world, fed its own country abundantly, maintained the fertility of the soil and produced the healthiest and best-educated people in Europe. To contend in the face of such a phenomenon as this that a peasantry is " uneconomic " and devoid of significance for modern conditions is due either to gross ignorance, bad thinking or a deliberate and interested blindness.

20   A Ploughing Team on the Welsh Border

21   Ploughing, new style, in Wiltshire

22 A 17th-Century Farmyard: from a drawing by Francis Barlow

23 Harvest-time in the 17th Century

Chapter II

THE YEOMAN

I THE MEDIAEVAL YEOMAN

The yeoman, wrote Arthur Bryant in *The English Character*, is our common ancestor, and his definition of a yeoman is of a countryman with control over the land he tilled. That, as was seen in the last chapter, equally applies to the peasant or customary tenant of the open field system, much more numerous than the yeoman freeholder. Broadly speaking, then, it may be said that the peasant has been the bedrock of the national character and that the yeoman was the aristocrat of the peasant community. It is easy to be too arbitrary in these divisions, for the landless labourer is the direct descendant of the peasant, while the yeoman shades off both into the tenant farmer and the smaller landed gentry.

It is curious, indeed, how lax and sparse are definitions of what a yeoman is. Technically speaking, the word means simply a local countryman, but there is a secondary derivation of it from the Old English *yeme-mann* or care-man, an attendant, and this is its sense in the military yeomanry, Yeoman of the Guard and Yeoman Usher of the Black Rod. This appears to be the meaning attached to Chaucer's " Yeman," one of the Pilgrims in the Prologue, but not of the tale-tellers. He is represented as a Forester of a " brown visage " and of " yemanly " carriage, " in cote and hood of grene," bearing a " myghtie bowe " and " sheef of peacock arwes," sword and buckler, horn and baldrick and wearing the silver image of St Christopher on his breast. He is the bold and dashing wearer of the Lincoln green, not as an outlaw but a retainer with the Squire of the Knight. This is very curious because these twin yeomen are as opposite in function as Dr Jekyll and Mr Hyde are in morals. The probable explanation is that some of the younger sons of the land-holding yeoman became men-at-arms or archers of the barons. Here was one link between the yeomanry proper and the gentry but a closer one was intermarriage. It was always fairly common and an impecunious member of the squirearchy would often sink into the yeoman class. In other words, he would become a cultivator as well as a landowner or a landowner's son.

The 14th-century granite farmhouse of a yeoman family who lived in it for many generations is set on a hill above Tavistock, untouched up to the beginning of this century. The disposition of porch, doorway, courtyard, terrace, panelled great hall, solar, south window and outbuildings was evidently modelled upon the manor of the lord. Since it is fairly certain that the country gentlemen did marry their daughters to the sons of yeomen who were not the sons of their own retainers, it is evident that the real yeomen were what Stubbs (Const. Hist, Vol. III) calls " a body which in antiquity of possession and purity of extraction was probably superior to the classes that looked down upon it as ignoble." This gives an admirable idea of what kind of a man the yeoman was. Medley (Eng. Const. Hist.) describes him as " the small freeholder of the feudal manor " and Harrison (*Description of England*), Holinshed (*Chronicles*) and Sir T. Smyth (*De*

Republica Anglorum) represent his free land as annually worth 40s. in earlier times and £6 in later.

Since he was not entitled to bear arms, the type-yeoman was a man of peace and independence in contrast with Chaucer's " Yeman," who was a man of war and dependence. Chaucer's Franklin was undoubtedly a country gentleman, though of the lesser breed, while Sir Thomas Overbury's Franklin in the *Characters* was just as evidently a true yeoman. This yeoman survived the *débacle* of the peasantry in the 19th century, though in greatly diminished numbers, and became the family farmer or the " owner occupier," whose plebs is the smallholder, though the latter is so often settled on the land from outside by County Councils and other bodies like the Land Settlement Association that he might be called a probationary or self-made or left-handed yeoman. He is all too frequently a temporary one, especially under the fatal system of hire-purchase.

The distinction between yeoman and peasant is fairly clear. It goes rather further than his " ownership " of more land than the peasant, a hide or 120 acres (very roughly speaking) to the villein's virgate (30 acres) or cottar's bovate (15 acres). As a freeholder, he was the lord's man in respect of rent not labour service and so began where the peasant, by commutation of hand-labour on the demesne for a money-rent, left off in the early 14th century. His personal independence had not to be regained from loss but to be maintained in its original being. Not that he did not suffer with his fellow peasants at the Norman conquest, not so much in status as by deprivation of his land. The single farm appears to have been in existence at the time of the free vills and under the Danelaw, independent holdings being more frequent inside than outside it, the yeoman flourished in the eastern counties.

But his farm was not in isolation from the village co-operative husbandry but a unit interwoven with it. If the lord of the manor was always an integral part of the village community, still more so was the yeoman, himself a peasant, who preceded him. He was the eight-oxen team man of which the hide of 120 acres was the year's " ploughable unit." That, of course, means that his acres were subject to the two-field or three-field system of the village. He had his holdings among the arable strips and in the hay-meadows, while his stock grazed the commons with those of the other commoners. Though his closes and fenced acres were more numerous than theirs, it was not until the 15th century that the freeholder's six-field mixed farm (three arable, three hay, sheep and cattle) appears as an established form of freehold cultivation, still subject to manorial usage.

By that time, the yeoman had become a man of weight and substance, not only locally like the Russian kulak or rich peasant, but, by virtue of his excercising franchise under the Act of 1430 and his freehold being assessed at a certain sum, as a voter who helped to send the knight of the shire up to Parliament. He occasionally found his way into Parliament himself and Sir John Fortescue (*Governance of England*) speaks of the 15th-century yeoman as a highly prosperous countryman. There can be no doubt that he greatly increased in numbers and status through the leasing of the demesne lands after the Black Death. Clement Paston, the good plain husbandman with his pride in his land whose son became a judge, he may properly be counted of the yeoman breed.

Thus, if the yeoman be set apart from the customary villager, it must not be too far nor out of touch with him, still less out of sympathy. Rather he is the bridge between the peasant and the knightly class and after the break-up of the manor, from which both the wage-labourers and the yeomanry increased their numbers, he virtually became the connecting link between the rich and the poor. He possessed the security of the former without their wealth and inherited the traditions of the latter without their lacks. He was only poor among the rich and rich among the poor. He was in fact the rural middle class, and that binding position accounts for the structural stability he conferred upon rural society.

In the 16th century, the great wave of land-speculation and eviction following upon the Dissolution bore hardly upon him, partly because large-scale corn-growing and extensive sheepwalks run for profit replaced the combination of sheep with corn on a subsistence basis and so discouraged the mixed farming which is the yeoman's gift to English husbandry. Many of the *liberi homines* who became Tudor yeomen were forced by the new economic pressure to sell out and become professional men in the towns, just as the evicted cottagers were thronging into them as beggars.

But the Whig Revolution of 1688, when the squirearchy become Government and Parliament in one (not to mention administers of the laws they had themselves made), worsened the position of the yeomanry far more grievously than did the Tudor revolt of the new rich against the old peasant economy. For the Tudor land grabbers and ranchers were not yet the Government which made sporadic attempts to legislate against enclosure. In 1688, gentry and Government became fused, and the commercial idea was disembarrassing itself of the ethical restraints that the Tudors inherited from the Middle Ages. Consequently, the yeomen were bought out in much larger numbers than before, especially during the Napoleonic Wars when specialized corn-growing was extreme, and after thet when the depression began. Just as the large estate rose on the ruin of small properties, so the trader ousted the yeoman, not merely in fact but in that sense of values which transformed the " nation of shopkeepers " (of urban yeomen, so to speak) into one of industrial magnates.

In 1700, one-eighth of the population were yeomen freeholders; by 1830, 88 per cent. of the farmers were a tenantry and only 12 per cent. owners. Up to the time of the " glorious revolution," there were in England 160,000 yeomen, 400,000 cottagers, 150,000 tenant farmers and 16,500 squires. But setting these figures side by side measures the great change that was to follow less vividly than the realization that the different classes represented by these round numbers are not to be cut off, boxed and labelled into separate compartments. There was a flight of stairs between the base-ment and the roof-garden of the social edifice. By his possession of stock, plot and pasture, the labourer could climb up to the ground-floor of the copyholders. Thence up to the first storey of the yeomen was only a few steps, while the more broad-acred of these had ready access to the second floor of the lesser gentry who themselves had descended from the privileges of the roof-garden. The fatal effect of the 18th and 19th century Enclosures upon the smaller yeomen by their loss of stock from the taking-in of the commons, by the high corn-prices breaking up the mixed farm, by the low ones driving them into bankruptcy and by the idea of getting the most out of the land pushing out that of getting the best out of it, may be said to have boarded up the first storey. Add the gutting of the first floor, the darkening and overcrowding of the basement, and, by the time the 20th century had opened, the falling-in of the roof, and it will appear that the new notions of progress were uncommonly like house-breaking with violence. The social edifice of the rural community became a ruin. It still is, though it has been hastily patched up to meet an emergency.

If the 15th and 17th centuries be taken to represent the hey-days of the yeoman, it will be seen how closely his lot was bound up with that of the peasantry proper. They prospered and suffered together. Naturally, because both were the products of the small and moderate property and of the independence and virility that, resulting from it, made England great. The peasant struggle for freedom was paralleled by the yeoman's natural bent for political and religious idealism. The movement for the English Bible was mainly inspired by the yeoman. It will be remembered that Latimer, in his famous sermon before Edward VI, said " My father was a yeoman." He added that he who had once " kept half a dozen men and kept hospitality for his poor neighbours " had lost his land, a passage revealing that Tudor economics were the enemy of the yeoman as well as of the peasant.

But the word " idealism " is not a good one, implying as it does a doctrinaire and dualist element, separating theory from practise. The yeoman and peasant support on behalf of the agitation for the English Bible was one for a closer integration between " our daily bread " and the spirit that was more than bread, for a closer union between the eternal and the temporal, one kind of need and another, a recognition of the interaction between soul and body. In that sense the Reformation was a true and vital enrichment, as it by no means was in the violent separation of sacred and secular which was the course it actually took. The yeoman's movement for the English Bible enriched the content of life no less than the language, especially when it is considered that the official Latin of the day corresponds with the official jargonese of Whitehall and the B.B.C. standardization of speech in our own times.

So far as the annals disclose (the literature of the yeoman is extraordinarily scanty), the yeoman commonly took arms with the peasant in his successive revolts. The Robin Hood Ballads, in which " the good yeoman " figured as the redresser of social injustice, played an inspiring part in the 1381 Rising, while Geoffrey Cobbe of Wimpole, a substantial yeoman, led the Cambridgeshire insurgents. Though he did not actually participate in that last, desperate, forlorn, agonized and futile eruption of Captain Swing and the machine-breakers in 1830, the yeoman certainly sympathized with it. Thus, he is to be sharply distinguished from the tenant farmer who reflected the views of the squires and on his own account was the advocate of cheap and pauper labour.

Cobbett, of course, who climbed up " the ladder " from " starving the crows " as a ploughboy to farming at Botley, was in every particular the typical yeoman. When he wrote:

" Instead of families of small farmers with all their exertions, all their decency of dress and of manners, and all their scrupulousness as to character, we have families of paupers with all their improvidence and recklessness

belonging to an inexorable sentence of poverty for life . . . I hold a return
to small farms to be absolutely necessary to a restoration to anything like
an English community— "

he was articulating the inward mind of the yeoman in its loathing of and
dismay at the changes which were rooting the peasantry out of its soil. Thus,
the yeoman attitude to the peasant was unchanged between 1381 and 1830,
and in a certain breadth of style, a certain stamp of character, the yeoman
never does change, whether in fiction or fact. You can always spot your
yeoman, whether he has a rough tongue like Cobbett or a rough exterior
like Jan Ridd of *Lorna Doone*, whether he is earnest about wrongs like
Cobbett, or earnest about life like Thomas Bewick, whether he talks about
his farm like Henry Best or about cricket like Richard Nyren—" I never
saw a finer specimen of the thorough-bred old English yeoman than
Richard Nyren. He was a good, face-to-face, unflinching, uncompromising,
independent man." In all their many differences they are the same person;
there is a sweetness and soundness about them all, like the chestnut in the
spiky shell.

Arthur Young, on the other hand, a first-rate journalist but a very second-
rate husbandman, spoke for the tenant farmer of his days, though in the end
he repented and, unlike the tenant farmers themselves, perceived too late
the havoc his plea for enclosure had made. That repentence was hand-
somely acknowledged when he spoke for the labourer thus:

" If I am sober, shall have I land for a cow? If I am frugal, shall I have
half an acre for potatoes? You offer me no motives; you have nothing
but a parish officer and the workhouse. Bring me another pot."

The voice of Young but the heart of Cobbett. Henceforward, the yeoman
vanished from the regard of his countrymen, to reappear in a lifting flame
of dying splendour as the master of the Iden family in Jefferies's *Amaryllis
at the Fair*.

II THE 17th-CENTURY YEOMAN

But the yeoman of the 17th century was not quite the same being as he
of the 15th. That is to say, he had become more detached from the co-operative village farm, as the freeholder of the mixed farm, field in rotation with
field, like spring with summer and fallow winter with autumn, livestock
interacting with crops and dung with fertility—the self-contained complex of
interdependent parts which made the yeoman's individual holding. That
rare interpreter of the English country scene, Sir William Beach Thomas,
wrote a book some years ago, called *The Yeoman's England*. It is about
English country, not the yeoman, nothing about him but a great deal about
his handiwork. For, on an all-round view, our countryside as it was before
the suburbs and the arterial roads and the bungalow towns and all the mess
and litter of the towns from factories to swimming baths, omitting too the
great park with the mansion for its dominating eye, this countryside was
virtually the creation of the yeoman in marriage with Nature's England.
He co-operated with the peasant-craftsman in the making of the English
village, so exquisitely faithful to its geological setting and so of as infinite a
variety as Cleopatra's moods.

But " this England," its pattern and human expression of farmstead, bartons, pasture, arable field, hedgerow, coppice, hedge timber, hay- and corn-stack, this is the yeoman's work of art. The peasant's spacious fields have gone; Nature lovingly provided the heaths, the hills, the lakes, the woods and streams, the rock that bears all; the monks set up the great barns and religious houses; the gentry the manors; the Saxons unwound the lanes. But it was the yeoman who husbanded this generous island into that richness of experienced matronhood (though so maidenly in spring, so gipsy-like in autumn) which Drayton, Fielding, White, Collins, Wordsworth, Clare, Jefferies, Hudson, Mary Mitford, Hardy, Barnes, Thomas, Blunden, Adrian Bell, have recommended for heavenly honours.

Thus, the 17th century emerges as the *grand siècle* of the individual yeoman. He has become William Harrison's " oken man," rooted in his native soil.

The 17th century reflects the ascendency of the yeoman in various aspects. Shakespeare himself was of definitely yeoman stock, which largely accounts not only for his country lore and observation (apart from the fashionable pseudo-classical natural history acquired from an urban bookishness) but for the spell laid upon him by the *genius loci*. Shakespeare's rusticity is provincial, not general. If the Stratford countryside held him at both ends of his life, the middle period often lights up with memorial gleans. The abundant imagery of country dances, games and sports—hunting, falconry, coursing, fowling, angling, archery and horsemanship—suggests to us not a picture of Sir Thomas Lucy's pompous equipage but of our robustious yeoman taking the day from his fields either to attend the meet of the lesser gentry or to poach without it or extenuate his muscles with his village kin. Wrote Overbury:

> " He allowes of honest pastime and thinkes not the bones of the dead anything bruised, or the worse for it, though the country lasses dance in the churchyard after evensong. Rocke Monday, and the wake in summer, shrovings, the wakefull ketches on Christmas Eve, the hoky, or seed cake, these he yeerely keepes."

But as our proto-Smiles (did living by machines make " self-help " despicable?), Thomas Tusser, remarks:

> " Ill husbandry spendeth
> Abroad like a mome:
> Good husbandry tendeth
> His charges at home."

and the yeoman was doubtless ten times longer at work than at play.

The " Farming Boke " (1641) of Henry Best, the Yorkshire yeoman, allows us to read behind the lines as to the multiple tasks and manifold responsibilities of his yeomanly labour. By his personal supervision he was his own reeve upon his own little estate, his own cowman, shepherd, plough-man and horse-keeper when the need arose, and all by a personal relation to his men which Sir Thomas Overbury epigrammatically set down as—

> "Though he be master, he says not to his servant ' go to field,' but ' let us go,' and with his owne eye doth both fatten his flock and set forward all manner of husbandry. Hee is taught by Nature to be contented with a little; his own fold yields him both food and rayment; hee is pleased with any nourishment God sends, while curious gluttony ransackes, as it were, Noah's Arke for food, onely to feed the riot of one meale."

36

Henry Best, of the richer type of yeoman, fed better than this. But he was not like the Tudor flockmaster who from the court or the city left his shepherd to pile up his wool-profits wherewith to build up a new mansion from the stones of the derelict Abbey on his lands. When Henry Best spoke of a " goode tuppe " as " large and well quartered, of a snoode and goode stapple," he spoke from his own observation, not at second-hand from his shepherd's report. At shearing-time and anticipating the shearing feasts of Coke of Norfolk, he entertained " forty nine clippers " on the farm, together with the drivers of the wool-carts and " three score of poor folkes gathering up the lockes," who departed with gifts of money and wool.

He preferred " dodded " to horned sheep because the lambs came easier and folded to grass lambs which " proove short runtish sheepe " and were called " dumplings " or grass-bellied sheep by his shepherd. He had his lambs gelded when the moon was " decreasinge." He would not start mowing until July 7 when " pennie-grasse beginnes to whelke " (which sounds like a line out of Edward Lear), while for the scythes of his flight of mowers " the best strickles are those made of proughy unseasoned oak." After his half score of haymakers had spread the hay, it was " raked and cocked " after two days' drying, the shortest and heaviest being kept for feed to the lambs, foals and calves. Before the hay was loaded, the village wrights saw to the axles and " fellies " (felloes) of the wains. He sowed rye on his strong land but not barley because " the stemme will bee stronge and not steare, and the barley itself shoumie and not pubble." His nine sheaves to a stook were banded with a double two-plait twine. His thatching technique was extraordinarily elaborate and fastidious, and he used wheat, rye and barley straw for thatching his ricks, but especially the latter because, well-wetted, " it is sadder and not soe subjeckt to blowe out with everie blast of winde." I have all the equivalents of his thatching tools in my Museum, two needles, an " eize-knife," a "switching-knife," a " slice," a rake and a " jack " or " bow " for carrying the " bottles " (yealms) of straw up to the thatcher on the roof. After the pease-pulling, all feasted on " puddinges, bacon or boyled beefe, flesh or apple pyes, creame in platters, hotte cakes and ale."

Henry Best was obviously a much wealthier yeoman than most but he is as clearly of the breed by his patriarchal relations with his men, his intimacy with their labour, his full-blooded generosity and customary regard for the feast as a decorative tail-piece (but no longer a religious rite) to each chapter of husbandry, his use of the vernacular, his field-learning, his homeliness, the russet colouring of his idiom, the minutiae of his rustic care, his respect for and well-acquaintance with craftsmanship. The yeoman's craft is his farm as an interdependent whole. His sense of devotion to his land made him the trustee of it, and this quality of personal responsibility was the greatest of his gifts to the national character—the reverse of that centralization, committee-rule and bureaucratic control to which we have pinned our faith since his decline.

At any rate, our countryside was " working " as with yeast when the big and little Bests were farming it. The husbandry of the 17th century has been absurdly neglected to the advantage of the 18th, when the four high-farming kings, Tull, Townshend, Bakewell and Coke, are reputed to have revolutionized our agriculture. They did not, as I hope to show by the example of Coke in the fifth chapter. The great age of discovery was the

17th century and what the 18th did was to develop, to improve upon and in some ways to flout these discoveries. The Civil War and the Puritan Victory in it prevented the intensive application of these discoveries, but it is significant that they bubbled up in a period richer in yeomen freeholders than either the 16th or the 18th centuries.

It will be interesting to glance at some few of them not only for their own sake but in the light of a modern assumption to be mentioned hereafter. The Elizabethan " great horse " of war, for instance, became the shire horse of the fallow and the stubble. The Dutch idea of feeding beasts on root-crops was adopted and, indeed, Barnaby Googe had recommended turnip growing as early as 1577. The " black ox," the Gloucestershire and Somerset " blood-reds," shorthorns and various new breeds of sheep were being selected. Henry Best used to shear 80 sheep a day and wash 120. Artificial grasses were bred for the first time. The yeomen were planting gardens to their farms and building cart-sheds, Henry Best's " helmes." The gracious and countrified Yarn Market House at Dunster is a typical example of 17th century regional building.

In the chalk regions with their Tertiary deposits of clays, sands and gravels, brick and timber granaries and bartons were building. The new farm-buildings of the stone regions (liassic and old red sandstone, granite, oolite and other limestones) matched grace with solidity. The hipped roof and the many-windowed façade appeared on the smaller manors, many of which were doubtless occupied by yeomen. Not a few of these had discreet Renaissance porches and fluted pilasters almost flush with the wall, after the Inigo Jones manner but countrified and so blended with the regional and vernacular styles, which remained Gothic in idiom. John Abel (1577–1674) the " King's Carpenter " and " magpie " builder of the " Old House " at Hereford, the Ledbury Market Hall and other half-timbered houses of richness in detail and stoutness in frame, was doing magician's work in timber. The magnificent Jacobean woodwork of church and chapel interiors like those of Rycote in Oxfordshire and Croscombe in Somerset and many other sacred buildings is inferior only to that of the 15th century which excels all others. In the smaller manors and farmsteads of this period, there is as great a mixture of styles as there is in the average parish churches between Norman and Perpendicular, and this indicates a strongly regional squirearchy and yeomanry, differentiated later on in the century from the more uniform and urban style of the big mansion. This showed signs of becoming more aloof from the countryside by clearing the foreground of buildings and vegetation and enclosing a wide bare space with walls.

Corn was being set by means of holed boards and the fallows were four times ploughed before sowing. The " statesmen " of Westmorland (yeomen all) were getting from 4 to 10 quarters an acre from their oats. Manure was ploughed in at once, a great improvement on the bad old habit, very prevalent to-day, of heaping it on the fields. Faggot and stone drains came into use and the proto-mole plough was invented. The " drowner " with his neat irrigation system appeared in the water-meadows. Catch-crops were under-sown to barley or oats. New wheats were bred. Carrots, marrows, parsnips, artichokes, cabbage, fennel, hops, colewort, potatoes, teazle and mustard found their places in the rotations and the old crops of woad, hemp, flax and saffron (one of the causes of Robert Kett's rebellion was the turning

OLD DISHES AND DRINKS

down of the saffron fields to sheepwalks) were restored to husbandry. Tobacco was grown so extensively that in the time of the later Stuarts soldiers were sent from London on the instigation of the Virginia planters to trample down the tobacco fields. Though its time was not yet, big business was beginning to rear its ugly head.

Marling the soil also " put the clock back " and dried blood was used for the vines and fruit. Sow-thistle was sown as temporary leys and both one and five-year clover leys were laid down. " Sallets," nettle beer and " March " beer, syllabubs, possets, preserves, cordials, and home-made wines were brought to a pitch of refinement and delicacy unknown to the coarser plenitude of the Elizabethans. Of the noble old drinks and dishes popular in the 17th century mead, metheglin and spiced frumenty just crossed the threshold of our century. It was the golden age of the housewife's stillroom and the womenfolk both of the yeomen and the squires were practised in the dairy. The herb-garden flourished; new roses were grown and grafting made swift progress. Cattle-cake called " pottage " was made out of linseed, rape and turnip-tops, and this with the cropping of trefoil, lucerne, sainfoin, clovers and other legumes went a long way to increasing the fertility of the land and putting an end to the wasteful slaughtering and salting down of the Michaelmas livestock for winter storage.

The 18th century country gentry certainly ate and drank too much, though, as their victuals were good and fresh and liquor sound, they did not take the harm we do from our dressed and sterilized foods. They did not eat chilled beef, pasteurized milk, tinned sardines and starch bread from germless flour out of exhausted soils. The following is a spot light on the 18th century idea of what Drayton called a " deintie dish " :

Swan Pie " Take a fowl, stuff it with veal and bacon and lay it in the breast of a goose, this again is to be inserted in the swan, which is then to be placed in a dish covered with crust and surmounted by a swan modelled in butter."

At the end of the book that gives this recipe is one for " surfeit water." But the 17th century had a more delicate palate than the 18th and was certainly more fastidious than the 16th.

Hedgerow timber was planted both for shelter and browsing. The reclamation of the Fens was undertaken on a large scale by Vermuyden, Charles I and the Duke of Bedford. Practical country writers like John Evelyn, Speed, Gervase Markham, Worlidge, Blyth and Sir Hugh Platt fostered where they did not create the spirit of novelty and experiment. " Nor can there be found," wrote Speed, " a more ingenious, necessary, delightful and honourable employment than Agriculture."

Perhaps the most fascinating departure of all was the elaboration of the principle of the compost or " compas " heap, mentioned by Tusser but fully developed by Evelyn in *Terra* and Speed in *Adam out of Eden*. For his compost heap Speed used rags from London, skins, shaved horn, trotters, sprats, silt, mud, street-sweepings, hedgings, wine-lees, brew-leavings, the brine of powdering tubs, bay salt, scrapings, trodden straw, " muck-water," seaweed, leaves, blood and offals, garbage, hair, grease and oil, tar, marrow-bones, soot, soap-suds, fern, hop-waste, stubble, rushes, thistles, heath, sedge, haulm, wood-ash, ditchings and earth. These were all heaped into a pit, " bottomed " with clay and the liquid manure from the yards drained

39

off into it. " By this means and with indifferent charge, you may have manure sufficient to serve all your land," and he computed that a ton of this " humus " was worth ten tons of farmyard manure.

Evelyn devoted no fewer than fifty folio pages to his composting. He used haulm, fern, bones, " pourriture " of old wood, leaves, " slub," mud, lime, sea-wrack, " calcinated turf " " bibulous " loam, all manner of dung, including night soil as in China, earth, fat, blood, hair, feathers, urine, horn-shavings, lees, oil, leather, skins, fish, garbage, nettles, rotted fruit, " snail-weed," stalks, cider-lees, weeds, gourds, stubble, sawdust, tannery refuse, rags, " sea-woad," brine, wool, linen clouts, dish-washings, slime, scourings of ponds, dust, road-sweepings, salts, snow, soot, leaf-mould, duck-weed, wood-ash, rick-bottoms, malt-dust, litter and chalk. This enormous debris was dumped into pits, 30-40 feet long, 4 feet deep and 10 feet wide under cover and on beds of clay. Not indiscriminately but sandwich-fashion just like the modern compost-heaps, and he describes how time " dulcified " the mass into a friable mould.

For the composters of to-day, this would have been more than enough, and perhaps even the occult and eclectic school of Rudolf Steiner might feel that Evelyn stood at the porch of the sanctuary. He was not a bad hand at the arcana himself. If soil be too hard, he said, " mollify " it; if too loose, give it " ligature "; if too light, " ballast " it; if too meagre, " impinguate " it; if too rich " emactuate " it; if too moist, apply " exsciccatives "; if too cold, " fermenting composts." Neither Speed nor Evelyn called the decomposed mixture " humus," nor did they talk about " the mycorrhizal association " between root-fibre and soil. Yet Sir Albert Howard's " Indore Process," the most advanced scientific theory of to-day in opposition to the orthodox school of chemical manures, was in being three centuries ago in all the essentials and in all but the exposition of the biological principles governing the compost heap. Anything more confounding to the imbecile lengths which the doctrine of progress has carried the official mind in our days could hardly be presented. I have therefore described Speed's and Evelyn's experiments as an example of " the pattern our forefathers zet " and at a length never previously given them. Indeed, I have never seen them regarded with any seriousness at all. Surely this was an England husbanding its natural resources.

The 17th century, too, was the age of noble gardens surrounded by mellow old walls and great hedges of sweet shelter like Evelyn's own holly one at Sayes Court, 9 feet high, 5 wide and 400 feet long. The pretentious taste of the next age, pandered to by Kent, Bridgman and Wise, grubbed up the old hedges and levelled the old walls for the ha-ha ditch, for the planting of dead trees, the building of " Gothick " ruins, for the vista, the long dull straight walk and the landscape garden. It is a century familiar for its great poets, theologians, diarists, essayists, biographers, playwrights, chroniclers and scholars. Its claim to be the period of great husbandmen has been obscured by the modern obsession with agriculture as a form of brigandage.

III   YEOMAN CHARACTER

This lively and adventurous spirit hoisted its flag over an England predominantly yeoman and peasant. The yeoman was a free man in more than one sense of the term; he also had a free and open mind in which new ideas

24   A Kentish Yeoman's House, near Sandwich

25   An East Anglian Yeoman's House, High Easter, Essex

27 Butter-making: from an engraving of *ca.* 1720

26 "Industrious Girls": from a print of *ca.* 1820

might germinate and flourish. Conservatism and readiness for novelty, independence and aid to his distressed brethren, the practical man with a dash of poetry in him, these made a good foundation for the national character. Had it not been for the Civil War and the dragon's teeth that it sowed . . . but the history of England is sadly full of " had it not been for. . . ." Of all Englishmen, the "oken men " should have been the repositories of that sense of continuity which even more than its memory is the soul of a nation. And in the south-west of England, they did actually make a spirited attempt to preserve the English fabric. The " Clubmen " of Dorset who rose against *both* the Cavalier and Puritan armies trampling their fields and looting their barns and livestock, were undoubtedly yeomen-led. They were dispersed on Hambledon Hill by Fairfax's Regulars, but let us in the midst of the war of a world insane with modernism remember with pride and melancholy this little sensible war of the English yeomen for the peace of the fields.

How well fitted so cohesive and sterling a force was to have been the warp of the weft! In the Oxford Dictionary, the now slightly antiquated term " yeoman service " is defined as " help in need." Evidently we were once proud of our yeomen. Used as an adjective, the word connotes for us a dependability in character, in good workmanship, in honest dealing, in contempt for the shoddy and the makeshift, in self-reliance, in a sobriety free from the mass-psychology of urban life, in strength and traditional wisdom which carries us far beyond the idea of succour in friendship. Yeoman service above all things to the land, the sacred charge which is the essence of a lofty and too often lonely patriotism. H. Harman, in his local sketches of the Bucks countryside, quotes the words of a modern yeoman :

" A cleean land, plenty a dress, plenty a laiabour to get th' increase. That's the way to destroy all malice and hairtred and covetousness."

At the end of a long day, I once came to an upland hamlet of the Cotswolds, naked to all the winds and perched on the flank of the great range that sweeps like a movement in a fugue to the gap at Winchcombe. In the little churchyard of the plain and sturdy church stood a worn tombstone, encrusted with lichens that gave the grey stone the russet patina of age. On it was written in frank, craftsmanly lettering—" John Smith, Yeoman of Sevenhampton." It seemed to me that another England lay buried there, an England we have forgotten and of which the roll of the clouds, the gesture of the bare range, the dusk treading softly into the churchyard, were the mourners.

The yeoman is in a sense identified with his land and, because it was the land of a mixed farm, he too was mixed, something more than that wise, durable, locally pious, confident, truth-loving, home-made freeman who seems to enshrine all the muscular virtues of the English. These elements and good humour into the bargain are implicit in the term " yeoman." But his richness of experience also admitted the beauty of Nature, of his music and patterns of play, of the village crafts he fostered and so of quality in all things. His sense of beauty was his sense of quality, the grain of the man. But still something more. The intense experimentalism of the 17th century in which the yeoman was a John Bull less beefy and bucolic than the later, coarser representation of him, opens out a national figure as eager after new ideas both in husbandry and in social thought as any Renaissance dreamer. But he was the husbandman and married them to his innate conservatism, and so escaped that mad self-deification and disdain of all restraints (later to be called inhibitions) which made the Renaissance man the forerunner of the 19th century individualist in business and the 20th century power-fanatic in the control of his fellows. The yeoman was never a revolutionary, and it was the squire not he who was prominent among the Puritan Ironsides. His provincialism checked him from counting himself among the followers of the abstract and doctrinaire Hobbes and Locke. His land-loyalty saw the new ideas in proportion and the balance of a whole man. This was he who might have carried England through the fevers of the future. Let it be seen what happened to him.

IV YEOMAN'S FATE

In the 18th century, the growth of business methods in farming began to disintegrate the yeoman class. Those of the Best type were shading off into smaller gentry, those of a medium acreage sinking among the copyholders, those of under a hundred acres being bought out by the landlords. Not that the smallest yeomen did not remain men of independent metal. Even when they were holders only of four acres and a cottage by the Elizabethan law still in force:

> " their land furnishes them with wheat and barley for their bread, and in many places with beans and peas, to feed a hog or two for meat, with the straw they thatch their cottages and winter their cow, which gives a break-fast and supper of milk, nine or ten months in the year, for their families " (Marshall).

Even the smallest yeomen had gardens and kept donkeys, pigs, geese, kine and hens on the village commons which were evidently in good condition, else why the eagerness to enclose them? Cobbett in *The Progress of A Ploughboy* said that the cottagers of Horton Heath, numbering 200 persons, not only supported themselves by it and gave their children happy holidays on it, but produced more from it " than any neighbouring farm of 200 acres." Many too of the little yeomen were part-time workers at the village crafts and Chippendale himself was of yeoman stock, as Grinling Gibbons and Eric Gill were craftsmen.

Of the character of the middle yeoman of the century, Thomas Bewick, the son of a Northumbrian yeoman, is the bright particular star. His self-portrait, written in 1822 when he was 69, reveals what it was. Great engraver as he was, his zest for living and earnest liberal mind advanced decided opinions upon " Religion, Morality and Politics, Arts and Sciences " with a homely warmth and sagacity, a fearless probity. He loved husbandry and horticulture, while observing the stars from his garden contributed to forming his independent philosophy of life, sane, broad, reverent and full of that love of Nature that inspired his wood-engravings.

The larger yeomen employed dairymaids, stockmen, carters, shepherd and ploughman, some of whom lodged in the farmhouse and were paid both in wage and in kind, others in free cottages with grazing rights and a few live-stock of their own. A portrait of this type of yeoman occurs in George Crabbe, the younger, his Life of his father, the parson-poet. Mr Tovell " had a native dignity of mind and manners " and lived in a comfortable house with moat, rookery, ancient dovecot and fishponds. But it was not too fastidiously a gentleman's residence because " one side overlooked a farmyard, full of all sorts of domestic animals, and the scene of constant bustle and noise." In the house, spacious hall, oak staircase and the rest. Mrs Tovell knitted with her maids in the kitchen, while the family dined, the heads seated at an old table in the same kitchen and the farm-workers in the scullery, the " female servants at a side table," while a travelling rat-catcher, tinker or farrier was usually present to tell tales to all. Thus, the gradations right up to the gentry were still close and unbroken and, since the great majority of countrymen still possessed control over their own lives, the structure of English rural society remained up to the middle of the century sound and organically vigorous. A proletariat, unemployment and farmers in bondage to the fluctuations of the market, see-sawing between booms and slumps, these phenomena, inseparable from the new idea of progress and the new theory of society being put about by the economists and philosophers, had not yet grown up. Liberty, in short, was maintained by small or moderate properties, and the mark of the age to come was the loss of both. Charles's wish that every countryman should sit under his own vine and fig-tree had not yet become an idle dream.

A beautiful example of the change in social conditions between the 17th and 18th centuries which weakened the position of the yeoman is written upon the trustily regional villages of Upper and Lower Froyle on the Pilgrim's Way in the Hampshire Highlands. These villages or rather this village-and-hamlet in the neighbourhood of Gilbert White's Selborne, George Bourne's Farnham and W. H. Hudson's Alice Holt Forest has been so fortunate as to have been architecturally deciphered by the patience of Mr W. Knight, the local schoolmaster, and by the wide learning of Mr Christopher Hussey.

Briefly, the history is as follows. Froyle was originally a Saxon village strung along the ancient highway. During the Middle Ages and in the 16th and 17th centuries, it was inhabited by an exceptional number of yeomen, many of whose names passed to their farmsteads'—Bonham's Farm, Blunden's Farm, Silvester's Farm, Hodges' Farm and others. All were roomy and medium-sized houses of timber-framing with brick or clunch infillings, and a number of them sub-manors of the mediaeval period either added to or refaced. One reason for this clustering of the " oken men " at Froyle was doubtless the sheepwalks of the chalk Downs, the water-meadows of the River Wey, and the high fertility of the greensand belt that both the Icknield and the Pilgrim's Ways skirt along the Berkshire, Chiltern and Hampshire Downs. Between 1760 and 1780, these yeoman farms were rebuilt or enlarged with brick and stone, while oast houses were erected at their backs. But most of them were lodged no longer with yeomen but with squires. The reconditioned buildings meant corn on the chalk and hops on the greensand, which in the Middle Ages had grown cider-apples and in the 17th century mixed crops, including hops, certainly grown as early as the 13th century. Some of the squires were new men, others, Eggar and Burningham who threw no fewer than four yeomen farms into one, were the descendants of 17th-century yeomen, while others of the old yeoman stock, Messenger, Tarrant, Newman and Westbrook, are tenant farmers at Froyle to this day.

Thus, a triple process appears to have taken place. By 1760, much of the parish land had been enclosed (Selborne next door was not enclosed until 1866), probably for intensive hop- and corn-growing. Some of the yeoman families had become gentry, others had vanished and yet others had shrunk in estate. The Enclosures had evidently not been drastic and on a large scale because the old farm-houses were still not mansions. But the net result was quite definitely a decline in the number of yeomen between 1680 and 1760, together with a sharp turn towards a more specialized agriculture. If the change was less abrupt than in very many other parishes, that decline must have been more precipitate in them than at Froyle. It was a good thing that a number of squires should become yeomen; it was by no means a good thing that a number of the yeomen should become squires. The one tendency underpinned the rural stability, the other overweighted it.

In the more remote parts of the country, the 18th-century yeoman still retained his land and his character, epitomized in the term which became the derision of the 19th century intellectuals and is a quality which is *terra incognita* in our own era—self-help. But a great Irishman of our century, perhaps the greatest of all modern Irishmen, George Russell, he who so passionately pleaded for a natural alliance between co-operation and independence, who believed that the soul of a nation resided in the small free communities of country life and spoke of " the Eden of the bureaucrat " as " the hell of the governed," he it was who restored " self-help," the yeoman's legacy to man, to its pristine virtue :

> " I have always preached self-help above all other kinds of help, knowing that if we strove passionately after this righteousness, all other kinds of help would be at our service."

By a chance felicity, I became possessed of a piece of charming evidence as to the yeoman's self-help in 18th-century Cornwall. This is a duodecimo manuscript book written on local hand-made paper by a yeoman of Morwenstow (Hawker's parish, see p. 45) in 1749, " William Brimacombe his hand and his pen amen." In beautiful clear handwriting, the booklet gives a series of home-made recipes for the sicknesses of livestock, compounded by himself out of his own herb-garden, medicine chest and what in places reads uncommonly like a witch's cauldron. Here is one, a drench for a horse with the glanders :

> " Take a quart of white wine finiger and five eggs and one ounce of dayapenty and five cloos of garlick put this in to a quart cup and stop it close and put it in to a horse's dunghill that is new and hot and let it bide two hours and then give it to the horse and ride him after drenching but be sure to kepe him in that day and night."

The Brimacombe family disappeared in the following century and was succeeded by another yeoman family through Brimacombe's daughter, that of James Woodley who, profiting by the good example of his predecessor, also left manuscript writings, together with a farm account book and a collection of charms most curious and enlightening. Here is one of them, written in 1845 when Hawker was Vicar of Morwenstow :

HIGH FARMING

" *Charm for a Thorn* As Christ went over Willows Bridge he Pricked himself with a thorn he said to himself thou shalt neither wrinkel nor ache so shall thy Leg neither rot wrinkel nor ache so shall thy Leg Be well James Woodley in the Name of the Father and of the Son and of the holy ghost. James Woodley John Woodley."

The formulae at the beginning and end are repeated in all the charms, so that Christ made many journeys over Willows Bridge, and had many misadventures thereby. The blend between Christian faith and pagan sympathetic magic (which would surely have delighted Hawker) is a very striking example of that tenacity in folk-memory (a communal inheritance) which peasant and yeoman shared, and in our old yeomen was combined with self-help, with its concomitants of independence, love of liberty and a Christian recognition of the immortal value of the individual.

James Woodley wrote his charms only a hundred years ago, but how steep the change for the yeoman in that century! Many contemporary writers lament his falling upon evil days, and the heaviest blow he received was through the destruction of the country's domestic industries by the Industrial Revolution. The tenant farmer, not the yeoman, is the hero of the 19th century.

It contains epical narratives about his deeds. James Smith's invention of the subsoil plough in 1831; Billingsley's reclamation of Mendip and Knight's of Exmoor; Bell's reaping machine of 1828; Fowler's steam plough; the meteoric rise of Farmer Mechi; Bates's, Booth's, Williams's, Twynam's, Ellman's and Dudding's improvements of sheep and milking strains of cattle; the Homeric combat between the cow with a dual purpose like the Shorthorn and the cow with only one like the Friesian; Weir's Clydesdales and Crisp's Suffolk Punches—these are some of the glories of 19th century " high farming."

The reverse side of the medal is whitewashed—as when it is stated that the German Leibig's chemical manures made " palpable nonsense " of the " humus theory " and that " soil fertility could now be maintained *for some years at least* (italics mine) by means of artificial manures, unaccompanied by dung or other natural manures." Or the social effects of the new farming are ignored—namely the application of machinery, becoming more complicated, costly and specialized every year and throwing out of work the millwright who made the threshing machine, the wheelwright who made the waggon, the smith who made the plough and the harrow. As Cobbett put it: " All the elements seem to be pressed into the amiable service of sweeping the people from the face of the earth." Or the desperate position of the new landless labourers is described as " the incendiarism and lawlessness " of the " undesirable poor." Or the fate of Mechi (he became a bankrupt), who called the horse-plough driven by one of these wretches " barbarous " and hedgerow trees " villainous stumps," is barely mentioned. Yet the story of Mechi is typical of the high farming days and of the new John Bullism he represented.

Typical too of a change in the farmer's philosophy of life. The ornamental parlour made its appearance in the farmhouse and the wives of the farmers acquired a social status in ratio to their immunity from work. The old days when the ladies worked as hard in their still-rooms as the farmers' wives in their open kitchens were no more. The decline of house-craft dates from

45

THE ENGLISH COUNTRYMAN

the era of high farming. If tenant farming on the grand scale justified the Darwinian canon (derived from Malthus's " war of all men against all men ") of the survival of the fittest by pushing the weakest to the wall, why are there so many stories in that mighty age of distress, decay, bankruptcy and dereliction among the high farmers themselves? Why again did high farming synchronize with the " melancholy long withdrawing " ebb of the tide of landworkers from country to town or colony? Between 1871 and 1931, more than half the labourers on it left the land, while as early as 1892 one hundred and sixty million pounds worth of foodstuffs were bought from abroad.

If the new methods and machines made the old yeoman farming rightly obsolete, why the series of great depressions from '79 onwards and why the cattle-plagues of '65, '70, '77, '79, '89, '94, and 1901-2? The rot has never been stopped. We still spend £50,000,000 a year combating the diseases of livestock. Corn fought pasture (those old allies) and wheat-prices first rocketed up and then dropped like a stone. Between 1876 and 1881, 105,000 sheep disappeared from the Chilterns alone and of the 130 farmers of the yeoman type thereon, only five or six were left by 1914. Between 1874 and 1914, 76,000 acres went out of cultivation in Oxfordshire alone, while the sheep population shrank from 17 to 13½ millions. And why was the English countryside of 1920-39 a jumble of prairie farms, scrub wilderness, suburbs to big towns, dormitories for urban workers, pleasure resorts, beauty spots, derelict industrial areas and opportunities for the speculative builders, that is to say, the furthest removed from stability and fruitfulness? To-day, not one per cent. of our pastures are of first-class quality and less than two per cent. are second-class.

There lies upon 19th century high farming a haggard light of feverish opportunism, of insecurity of tenure, of gambling, of sudden luxury and of catastrophic decline. It was intensified by the " freedom of cropping " granted to tenant farmers by the Liberal Government of the early 20th century in its war against the landlords. As the landlord, influenced by the dominance of urban commercialism, became more and more concerned with his legal dues and the tenant more and more capitalistic in his methods, so the fertility of the land declined with stability in farming it. The system was to end in the almost complete break-down not of the old traditional methods but of what had replaced them. The landlord was forced by excessive taxation to abdicate as a trustee of his property, while one farming corporation after another seized upon the vacated farms. The agent ceased to be a resident squire's and became an absentee landowner's manager. These were a few of the consequences resulting from the growing complexities of international trade and finance, themselves derived from a new parasitism in place of the old self-support.

The reasons for the yeoman's almost eclipse among the blazing and burned-out stars of high farming were both economic and psychological. The effect of the Enclosures upon the smaller yeomen was, as the Suffolk yokels say, " wholly " defeat. Successful tradesmen swallowed up the lands of many. The loss of the commons meant loss of stock ("strip the small farms of the benefit of the commons, and they are all at one stroke levelled to the ground," said a contemporary observer). Great numbers either emigrated or became labourers. I have known many of the latter whose forefathers were yeomen under tombs in the churchyards of their own

46

parishes. Taxation, the fall of corn-prices after the Napoleonic wars and the Repeal of the Corn Laws were other and earlier adverse factors, not only for them but for the small gentry and the small towns. Thus, the ex-peasants lost their natural leaders and the link between rich and poor was snapped.

But for the yeoman the general consequences of the new orientation of society from the idea of plenty to that of power and profit were even more psychologically than economically serious. The novel conception of the land as an investment for the extraction of wealth was quite foreign to him; as a " dirty boot " farmer, he regarded it in terms of produce, not money, as a livelihood, not as a means to affluence and social position. To look upon the land as a means to an end (wealth) instead of an end in itself was an affront to his profound sense of responsible ownership. That sense accompanied him through century after century. Sir Thomas Overbury and Scawen Blunt nearly 400 years later have both interpreted the heart of the yeoman in almost identical terms. " Hee is lord paramount with himselfe," wrote Overbury, " though hee hold by never so meane a tenure," and Blunt:

> " Nor has the world a better thing,
> Though one should search it round,
> Than thus to live one's own sole king
> Upon one's own sole ground."

The quietude of Adrian Bell's shepherd-into-yeoman in *The Shepherd's Farm* is in the same notation as Overbury's:

> " Hee cares not when his end comes, hee neede not fear his audit, for his *quietus* is in heaven."

The amplitude and self-possession of George Eliot's yeoman in the Poyser family and the wisdom of old Iden in *Amaryllis at the Fair* are further versions of the same theme:

> " Iden's flag-basket of tools lay by the gate, it was a new gate, and he had been fitting it before he went in to lunch. His basket was of flag because the substance of the flag is soft, and the tools, chisels, and so on, laid pleasant in it; he must have everything right. The new gate was of solid oak, no ' sappy ' stuff, real heart of oak, well-seasoned, without a split, fine, close-grained timber, cut on the farm, and kept till it was thoroughly fit, genuine English oak. If you would only consider Iden's gate, you might see there the man. . . .
> The neighbourhood round about could never understand Iden, never could see why he had gone to such trouble to render the homestead beautiful with trees, why he had replanted the orchard with pleasant eating apples in the place of the old cider apples, hard and sour. . . .
> When he cut a hedge, for instance, Iden used to have the great bushes that bore unusually fine May bloom saved from the billhook, that they might flower in the spring. So too with the crab-apples—for the sake of the white blossom; so, too, with the hazel—for the nuts.
> But what caused the most ' wonderment ' was the planting of the horse-chestnuts in the corner of the meadow. What did he want with horse-chestnuts? No other horse-chestnuts grew about there. You couldn't eat horse-chestnuts when they dropped in autumn.
> In truth Iden built for all time, and not for the little circumstances of the hour. His gate was meant to last for years, rain and shine, to endure any amount of usage, to be a work of art in itself.

47

If only he could have lived three hundred years, the greater world would have begun to find out Iden and to idolize him, and make pilgrimages from over sea to Coombe Oaks, to hear him talk, for Iden could talk of the trees and grass, and all that the Earth bears, as if one had conversed face to face with the great god Pan himself."

This is a translation, three centuries later, of William Harrison's "oken men."

The yeoman stood firm on his land, like an oak tree growing out of it, but a new, swift and muddy tide was now tearing at the roots, the tide of progress.

The 20th century accentuated and hastened tendencies that had been developing all through the previous century. Since the yeoman's agriculture is a traditional craft, never a mere business, his work is inevitably creative and he found himself in a kind of dealer's paradise. Especially so after 1920, when the Repeal of the Corn Production Act delivered up the land to a swarm of jobbers and speculators. Deflation and specialized ranching following upon the falling-down of arable into pasture and supplying distant townships with dairy products still further weighted the scales on behalf of the distributor and against the self-sufficient mixed farmer. It was not the yeoman but the tenant farmer who turned to prairie farming as an expedient against bankruptcy. The yeoman hung on by his finger-nails to sound husbandry, in spite of the policy of bounties favouring specialization and the craze for more and more machinery making his labour problem practically insoluble. What arable farms were left depended more and more upon artificials from factory and laboratory for forcing their yields, while the grass farms relied upon imported concentrates. The higgler, the advertising traveller and the big processing and distributing firms made the position of the mixed farmer almost untenable.

With the second Great War, when the dealer's paradise was seen to be a fool's one, the bureaucracy demanded a self-supporting England from a farming population pauperized by its own previous policy of the means to secure it, namely abundant labour, a proper rotation of crops, a maximum fertility and the maintenance of the yeoman whose manner of husbandry guarantees such conditions. Nevertheless, both he and the tenant farmer, relieved from the dumping of imports sold below the cost price of home-grown crops and of the debt system interwoven with them, nobly responded. Had the ley-system of alternate husbandry and taking the plough all round the farm been duly nursed and extended, the balanced husbandry of the yeoman would have profited thereby. But his methods and principles were severely handicapped by over-cropping replacing underfarming and the shifts the farmers were put to to cover up the loss of fertility. It wounded his deepest instincts for three crops of corn to be taken in succession with almost nothing but artificials to produce them. This, he knew, was dope, not food, for the land. The tendency was aggravated by the indiscriminate slaughtering of livestock by order (including arable sheep, dairy cows and incalf heifers).

Nor was he relieved from the high interest still exacted by the banks and from the enormous disparity still prevailing between retail and producer's prices. Centralized direction and the multiplication of officials crippled his initiative, and the filling in of unnecessary forms prematurely aged many

48

28 A Yeoman's House in Decay at Kempston, Bedfordshire, 1815 : from a drawing by Francis Stevens

29 A Cottage Hearth in Winter, 1803 : from a print after Hamilton

30   The Kitchen of a Lakeland Farm

31   A Farm Kitchen, 1814

a stout freeholder. Lack of housing, equipment and organic manures yet further hampered him. Jacks and Whyte wrote in *The Rape of the Earth*: " The unprecedented expansion during the 19th century had been followed by a world-wide biological deterioration of the land," and the yeoman was confronted with the need of maintaining the humus content of his land regardless of the demands of the new business farming to turn soil-capital into paper-money. Even local marketing was obstructed or vetoed, and by the excess use of large-scale machinery and the growth of the movement for farming by joint-stock methods he had been further penalized. To such modern improvements (two of them revivals) as ensilage, cover crops, seeds mixtures, to the " golden hoof " of the folded flock, his husbandly good sense could offer nothing but welcome. But his whole philosophy of self-sufficiency is necessarily antipathetic to the attempt on a large scale of the town to control and organize the production of food from the country and to the inherent wastefulness of the modern economic scheme. He sees things from his window and so conserves them. The urban mind sees things over vast distances and so wastes them. Without a change in the modern economic system and a return to the land after the war with plenty of labour to cultivate and humus to keep it in heart, it will be impossible for the yeoman to survive.

That the very existence of the small or moderate farmer is threatened to-day is clear to all. The conditions of war-time farming are all against him. Only the big farmers, the favoured few, benefit by a fixation of prices which at the same time leaves the dealer's exorbitant profit barely touched. But the principal cause (apart from debt) for the depression of the small farmer are the emergency methods of farming itself. They are nothing more or less than the expenditure of capital, soil-capital, fertility reserves, and it is obvious that the small farmer has much less of this capital to spend than the big. He is a conservationist, not a spendthrift.

V   YEOMEN OF THE DALES

Yet how tenacious is the yeoman! I know a yeoman in the Chilterns with a ninety-acre holding who among all the tenant farmers is the only one to persist in crowning his ricks with ornamental " dollies " after harvest. I know another in Worcestershire, a breeder of " Persians " (Percherons) who for fifty years worked his heavy land with a wheel-less, mediaeval " long plough " (now in my possession) and grew the best crops in the neighbourhood. I know a third in Gloucestershire who, in spite of the opposition of his sons, not only crowned his ricks but built them on staddles and elaborate timber frames. A fourth in Dorset I know who grew red wheat for the reed-thatch of the barn and cottage roofs, stripping the flag in a hand-press, and others I know of in Somerset who grow small acreages of the best flax in the world, the family and the neighbours turning out on summer evenings to pull it by hand. Some I know who will have their Harvest Homes, though economic hell may yawn. Others have become innkeepers in their retirement, thus carrying their traditional good manners, good temper and good husbandry into those of hospitality at the village club.

The " statesmen " of Lakeland are still hale and whole, self-acting and each other aiding, practising an uncommercialized husbandry, hardy as their sheep that crop the clouded mountains. A harsh home among these fells,

7   49

for the wheat will not ripen under the rains, only the oats that were once their staple bread and are now their cakes and porridge. They are not tied to the milk-lorry since they still make cheese and butter at home, still home-bake and cure and harvest in the ancient way. Neither are they machine-bound—their hills say no to that—and some of them thresh their beans with the flail. They still manage their own affairs.

They are held together as parts of a regional organism by the interacting and intergrating forces of independent ownership and mutual aid. At harvest and shearing-time, each family lends its full hand to the corn and the penning of the sheep as members of a fraternal community. At these high tides of husbandry, the whole family goes out into the fields, eating great teas together under ricks and stone walls and suppers in stone-flagged kitchens lit by the soft glow of oil-filled lamps. They are yeomen-peasants, " their country's pride," though their country is so little proud of them that it has filched thousands of acres from them by the planting of regiments of conifers on the sheepwalks and so depriving the sheep of their fodder, the landscape of its wild beauties and these husbandmen of their living. But there are still enough of them to preserve this neighbourly and regional yeomanry from extinction.

Not so in Scotland, if the peasant-crofter may be styled a small yeoman. But his passing has been nobly epitaphed, so that his grave has a lettering not yet effaced. There are only five comparatively modern authors who have divined the peasant, labourer or yeoman mentality—Charles Marson, Adrian Bell, Fred Kitchen, William Barnes and Leslie Mitchell. The last has done for the Scottish yeoman what Barnes did for the Dorset land-folk, spoken out of their very selves and in their own language. Only in one book—*Sunset Song* (1932)—and that entirely unknown. None the less, this book, a tale of the crofters of eastern Scotland, is a masterpiece in the severest sense of the term, a book whose greatness in humour, tragedy, beauty and passionate imaginative wholeness, is stamped on every page. At the end of the book, the minister of the Kirk of Kinraddie unveils a memorial to the fallen crofters in the first Great War, cut into a monolith of the stone circle. He speaks:

" With them we may say there died a thing older than themselves, these were the Last of the Peasants, the last of the old Scots folk. A new genera-tion comes up that will know them not, except as a memory in a song, they pass with the things that seemed good to them, with loves and desires that grow dim and alien in the days to be. It was the old Scotland that perished then, and we may believe that never again will the old speech and the old songs, the old curses and the old benedictions, rise but with alien effort to our lips. The last of the peasants, those four that you knew, took that with them to the darkness and the quietness of the places where they sleep. And the land changes, their parks and their steadings are a desolation where the sheep are pastured, we are told that great machines come soon to till the land, and the great herds come to feed on it, the crofter is gone, the man with the house and the steading of his own and the land closer to his heart than the flesh of his body. Nothing, it has been said, is true but change, nothing abides, and there in Kinraddie where we watch the building of those little prides and those little fortunes on the ruins of the little farms we must give heed that these also do not abide, that a new spirit shall come to the land with the greater herd and the great machines. For greed of place and

32   A Mountain Farm in the Lake District, above Ambleside

34   A Cottage Threshold

33   A Smallholding at Bibury, Gloucestershire

possession and great estate those four had little heed, the kindness of friends and the warmth of toil and the peace of rest—they asked no more from God or man, and no less would they endure. So, lest we shame them, let us believe that the new oppressions and foolish greeds are no more than mists that pass. They died for a world that is past, these men, but they did not die for this that we seem to inherit."

Whether or no the yeoman survives elsewhere after the second Great War probably depends upon the amount of tribulation the nation has endured. If it should be very great, he will be nursed into prosperity once more; if it is not so great, he will go. Yet powerful and authoritative voices have made themselves heard more and more insistently on behalf of his reinstatement. Christopher Turnor of *Yeoman Calling*, Lord Lymington, Lord Northbourne, Adrian Bell, Vesey-Fitzgerald, Arthur Bryant, Lord Ernle, Rider Haggard, Henry Warren, Dr G. T. Wrench, Sir George Stapledon, various Catholic and other writers of our century have all urged the restoration of the " owner-occupier," the modern equivalent of the ancient yeoman who has farmed England since before the Norman conquest. From various angles of approach, all these writers look upon him as one who goes with the grain of life.

Apart from a minority of tenant farmers and the yeomen and smallholders that survive (subject to bitter financial pressure and then informed by the advocates of the system that has done its best to ruin them that their holdings are " uneconomic "), it may be considered that there are four types of modern cultivation that perpetuate or maintain under modified or developed forms the traditional husbandry so valiantly safeguarded by the yeoman. One is Laxton where 1,338 acres were cultivated by freeholders in 1635, a parish which has preserved the fertility of its fields for eight centuries. Another is the flower and kitchen garden of a great many country residents from the towns, a fair proportion of whom keep up the health and productivity of their gardens by double digging, rotations and composting. A third is the " Indore Process " of Sir Albert Howard, practised by several market-gardeners with high success. This is the fine flower of traditional husbandry made self-conscious by science. The fourth is those estates managed by a few landowners as self-contained entities. These are branches from the yeoman stock.

Let me conclude with the words of a yeoman, Tom Mann of Virley Hall overpeering Salcott Creek in Essex, and quoted by Mr Wentworth Day:

" There's too much of other people's good money buried in this heavy three-horse land. I'm here to get it out by sweat, not by loan."

There is your yeoman, past and, praise be, still present.

Chapter III

THE CRAFTSMAN

I ARTFULNESS AND CRAFTINESS

The blacksmith hammering on his anvil has of late years been regarded as a " picturesque " figure, like a caballero twanging his guitar beneath his lady's window. The Arts and Crafts movement devoted itself to fostering craftsmanship on the condition that it served no useful purpose and so would not interfere with trade. Whether this attitude still exists among small groups and societies I do not know, but, since it represents the universal modern view of the craftsmanly function, it is important to deal with it. This attitude expresses so complete a misunderstanding of what craftsman-ship is and has always been from the time before man became *Homo sapiens* up to the Industrial Revolution that it enables us to perceive that Revolution and its consequences to-day as an interference with and disruption of the normal patterns of behaviour in mankind. The modern separatist view of the craftsman totally ignores no fewer than five different integrations between man and his labour which are revealed by an historical survey of English craftsman-ship. If they are different, they are not really separable, so that the craftsman is pre-eminently an example of the whole man as a functional being and the direct opposite of that ornamental figure modern opinion takes him to be.

The most obvious of these correlations is that between use and beauty. The most superficial knowledge not only of our own but of human history in general discloses this truism so plainly that the success of the Arts and Crafts thinkers in avoiding it was a triumph in abstraction from reality. Craftsmanship made its appearance in human society as soon as man began to make tools and implements for the common use of his fellows. By the time of the Aurignacian culture (perhaps 20,000 B.C.), these artefacts, as their name reveals, had reached almost as high a degree of finish and workmanship as did the objects of utility in predynastic Egypt. What is more, all the prehistoric cultures of post-palaeolithic man, whether in Thessaly or along the Danube, at Susa, at Anau in Turkestan, among the first Sumerian city-states or in the Indus Valley, achieved their peaks of craftsmanship in the earliest stages of their development, so that, if craftsmanship has nothing to do with mere ornament, it equally will not fit in with the contemporary theory of progress. The beauty of these early artefacts was a by-product of their fitness to the purpose for which they were made, and this is crafts-manship. Once that utility is lost, craftsmanship disappears, though, of course, its biological service must be extended to cover man's spiritual no less than his material needs. Even the gargoyles on a mediaeval church were never ornament for its own sake. The corbel table or the string course was as essential to its structure as the piers and the vaulting.

Ornamentalism as a superfluity was, in fact, an invention with its machines (which were supposed to do the dirty work) of the 19th century. Even in the Italian Renaissance, when the craftsman began to show signs of becoming a specialized and segregated artist handled by the dealer in art-products,

52

painters and sculptors served as apprentices for mastership in workshops as in our own Guild system, and Michael Angelo was a great sculptor by way of being a worker in stone. He revealed the figure in the block by a supreme understanding of the nature and qualities of his material. There is a world of true meaning in Walter Sickert's " An artist is only Greek for joiner." The word " poet " is ποιητής, the maker, and our inability to understand what this means reflects the final divorce between beauty and utility. Beauty ceased to be a common possession in common circulation; the artist became a plant in a pot; objects mass-produced for use had their beauty left out— and the Arts and Crafts movement was founded. Objects of craftsmanship were collected into museums for the simple reason that they were no longer made. The system that created the museums no longer allowed them to be made for the use of the community. It would have " interfered with trade " for everybody to make or to have them instead of a few people to see them. And to interfere with trade would never do. In such conditions even pure ornament became trivial and meaningless.

There is no doubt about the Industrial Revolution being the dividing line by which use became separated from beauty, and thus we find its advent signalled by a holocaust of the crafts. Here is an abbreviated list of the local industries of fifteen counties extinguished as early as 1830 by the discovery of cheap power and the enthronement of the principle of making for profit instead of making for use. In all of the fifteen, dyeworks, malt-houses, mills and tanneries. In Bedfordshire, reed-matting and basket-making from osier-beds, hemp-spinning and pillow-lace. Straw-plaiting in Bucks, Hunts and Cambs. Fabrics for women's dresses, cloth- and linen-making in Lincs. Wool-spinning and combing and hempen cloth in • Suffolk. Baises and rope in Essex. The father of that *gauche* Elizabethan scholar, Gabriel Harvey, was an Essex ropemaker. Coarse woollens, bed-ticking, pottery and worsted yarn in Hampshire. Hops, silk, paper, calicoes, salt-works, copperas, powder-mills in Kent. In Surrey, printing, parchment, leather, snuff. On the Weald, iron-working and charcoal-making. Wool-lens, damask, linen, kerseys and cottons, gauzes, hat-bands, shoe-strings and watch-parts in Berkshire. Weaving, velvets, gloves, blankets in Oxon. Boots in Northants; whips in Daventry; stockings and sailcloth in Notts. China, rope, chains, glass, dyes, fulling and spinning, flannels in Shropshire. Nails and fish-hooks in Warwickshire. This is not by any means a complete list from the counties concerned, but is compiled merely to show the variety of country industries in being as late as the 19th century and *not* what would be commonly dubbed as crafts. In short, they not only " interfered with trade "; they *were* trade, for even a shoe-string or a fish-hook had qualities of durability, shapeliness, good appearance and finish which made the distinction between craft and trade unreal.

Some idea of the vitality of local crafts and small industries may be gathered from Defoe's account in *The Complete English Tradesmen* of how an English gentlewoman of his day was clothed. " The binding of chequered stuff " came from Bristol or Norwich; her petticoat of " black callamanca " which was " quilted at home " came from Norwich; her flannel and swanskin from Salisbury and Wales; her stockings from Tewkesbury or Leicester; her lambskin gloves from Northumberland; her ribbands from Coventry or London; her riding-hood of " worsted camblet " from Norwich; her lace and edgings from Stony Stratford and Great Marlow. By 1851, only 15 per cent. of rural industries survived the débacle. By 1930, only one per cent. of those. Fifty years ago, the village of Finchingfield in Essex (where Quarles wrote his *Emblems* and Thomas Ruggles, the friend of Arthur Young, lived) had two carpenters, two blacksmiths, a wheelwright, a plumber, a painter, a cooper, a glazier, a clockmaker, together with thatchers, millers and experts with the mill-bill for dressing the stones. At the end of the 18th century, the list is more than double, with websters, weavers, cordwainers, tanners and turners thrown in. The sole survivors to-day are a thatcher and a smith. A plaiting shop existed on the village green and the women earned ten shillings a week for their hats and poke-bonnets. Through my friend, C. Henry Warren, I possess a score of examples of straw-plait done by the last of the Finchingfield straw-plaiters, the last of the rural artists, Hannah Firman, aged ninety-three.

A word must be added as to the butchery of crafts more narrowly considered so. The basket-makers were thrown out of work by cheap foreign imports. The factory system and the power-loom accounted for the workers of the hand-loom, descended from the Iron Age Celts, the head man of the " kindred " teaching its use to all the members of the family. The sheep were driven down from the hillside and shorn in pens; the yarn was spun at the farmhouse; the cloth woven in an " outshut " of the weaver's house and, after fulling and scouring at the local mill, was returned to the farm and sold at the local fair. The decline of cooperage, whose tubs, churns, casks and butter-moulds were made from the local oak and hoops from the willows, was due to the importation of American oak, the displacement of wooden by iron hoops and the use of galvanized for wooden tubs and pails, the growth of the big brewery and the despatch of the surplus milk to the factories. Machine-made Torchon and Maltese lace finished off the village lace-schools and the market for Honiton and Bucks Point lace. In the decline or extermination of such wooding crafts as chair-leg turnery, rake-making, hurdling, broom-squiring and the like, the loss of small holdings and the commons together with the creep of the wilderness and the disuse of local markets played as large a part as dumping and manufacturing by the mass. How catastrophic was the effect of the loss of the commons upon rural craftsmanship may be gathered from a side-glance at Lord Winchelsea's estate in 1795. There enclosure was put into practise without dispossessing the peasants. Eighty cottagers owned 174 cows between them with a common for grazing them and their pigs and sheep as well. Every cottage had its garden; the women home-baked by means of the fuel off the common, herded the cows, spun the flax (grown as it should be in small plots) and nearly all the tenants were engaged in part-time cottage industries. So the melancholy inventory might be continued to the filling of folio pages up to the grand, ornamental flourish and finale of the Arts and Crafts playboys. But even if a complete balance sheet could be drawn up, it would not indicate the one supreme phenomenon that underlay the items, namely, the crash of the whole structure of rural society.

II HUSBANDRY AND THE CRAFTS

But even a partial compilation indicates the triple function played by the crafts. The craftsman was the minister to local needs, while each nucleus

35 A Miller

37 Laying a Hedge in Essex

36 Thatching in Worcestershire

THE ORGANIC CRAFTSMAN

of the crafts was in orbital relation to the market-town. Lastly, the intimacy of the bond between craftsman and husbandman since England was first cultivated by the Neolithic farmer is outlined. This is the second integration of craftsmanship. The bond is a family one between man and earth because husbandry conditions the very existence of most of the rural crafts, even though craftsmanship, which is itself a kind of husbandry, is the older. If the cattle were the farmer's, the gate was the craftsman's which kept them in. If the plough broke the earth for the crops, the smith made the plough. The earth and what grew from it were the raw material both for the farmer and the craftsman. Actually, the union was even closer. From times immemorial, the practise of a craft was the part-time or seasonal occupation of the husbandman, while the craftsman almost invariably had a "close" or holding of his own, the hurdler an acre or less of coppice, the basket-maker an osier-bed, the straw-plaiter a plot of corn, the potter a stake in the clay-pit, the mason or waller a share in the quarry. Or the wife of the land-worker practised gloveing or lace-making in the intervals of nursing the baby or getting her husband's dinner. The daughter of a shepherd I know had her bobbins made by her father home from the fold. Nowhere could the peasant art and domestic industry be unpicked from the peasant's tillage—the whole was a seamless garment. The home, the family and the country—craft embraced all three in one.

Even when agriculture was highly developed, no hard-and-fast line of differentiation could be drawn between craft and cultivation. In the village community, the waste supplied not only fuel but material for the carpenter, the wheelwright and the builder of styes, fences and the like. The wool from the sheep was spun and woven by the shepherd's own household. The nettles growing on the headlands were converted into linen by the family of the village shareholders in them. The mower cut and shaped the ash snathe of his scythe out of the hedge and the "thacker" his "bow" or "jack" to carry the straw from the harvest up his ladder to the roof. The stone that ground the corn was grooved by the craftsman's mill-bill. By the light of peeled rushes bestowed by the river, the mediaeval farmers themselves carved their own spoons, bowls, ladles and platters, and the flailer sung by Bloomfield and Hurdis struck his blows with a craftsmanly skill from thorn and holly staves fashioned and thonged by his own craft. A shepherd I know—retired because there were no longer any sheep for him to herd—was a champion thatcher who took first prizes at the shows. No thatcher I know who, if he did not once keep poultry or a pig, had not at one time or another joined the fields.

In Mrs Donaldson's *Approach to Farming* (1941), a labourer stooking barley sheaves and asked what difference it made taking such care to keep the shocks in line, replied, " It don't matter, it looks nice." Was he a field-hand or a craftsman? " Heathering " or wattling the stakes with bramble sprays in the course of pleaching a hedge and a word used by all hedgers I know, was a pre-Roman Celtic term when craftsmanship was even less specialized than it subsequently became. What is the hedger, craftsman or husbandman? What is agriculture, a craft or a business? Perhaps on the answer given to that question lies the future of our own home civilization.

On Henry Best's farm, it was the foreman who cut the underwood in the spinneys and the farm-servants who made flail handles, harrow spindles,

55

rack staves and shafts of " saugh " or sallow of a winter evening in the farm kitchen. They were even saddlers and hurdlers and straw-plaiters for the sedge collars of the draught oxen. They helped the shepherd with the peeled withies for his " folde barres " (sheep-hurdles) and were wheelwrights in the waggon shed. At harvest, the " outligger " (a woman) used to follow the sickleman and bind the sheaf with a knot which traditionally varied from county to county in fold, twist and shape. In Gloucestershire, I have seen a sheaf-knot tied close up to the hedge which the self-binder could not reach and this same band carved on a 17th century tomb-stone of a Gloucestershire churchyard. Was she, the " outligger," different in kind from the mason? Both belonged to the fraternity of the crafts.

Even the most elaborate cabinet-making and wood-carving depended upon a forestry that knew the nature, constitution, habits, properties of trees as a husbandman knows his soils, and I know a saddler who spent many hours of the workaday week going from farmstead to farmstead fitting new horse-collars, visiting the bark-tanneries of stripped oak wood for his leather, the farms where he could procure unthreshed rye straw for the " wale " of his collars, picking out white leather out of horse-hides for his hedging-gloves and selecting his carded " flock " from the woolmen. What does not that man know about horses, sheep and crops? The very indeterminacy of function in craftsmanship, extending even to the towns once belted by the countryside, enables the historian to see not only the craftsman in local development from and organic dependence upon husbandry, not only husbandry itself as the great college of the crafts but England herself as once a federation of farms.

Is not this historical perception a biological one as well? The craftsman was a man who made things that he sold to the people who needed them in the region where he lived through every process from the raw material to the finished article. How very different from the vast complexity our intricate subdivision of labour demands! The organized middleman takes his chance from our pre-occupation with transport, widening the border country between production and consumption. Specialization and dependence upon advertisement for urging the purchase of mass-produced goods upon people who don't want them take us farther and farther from Nature. Disaster overtakes a civilization when it ceases to be biologically adaptable and detaches itself too far from its agricultural matrix.

The intimate bond between husbandry and the crafts may well be epitomized and symbolized by the vernacular terms for the dressed surface of the upper or " runner " millstone, nowadays displaced by steel rollers. The grooves of the ten harp-shaped patterns on it are called " furrows," the largest is the " master-furrow," while the spaces between the furrows are called " lands." The stone that grinds is still the field that grows the corn.

III CRAFTSMAN ADAM

Yet Adam and Eve were makers before he delved and she span, and craftsmanship antedates husbandry. Its bond with Nature is the oldest of all and this introduces our third integration. Our absorption in the artist *qua* artist prevents us from seeing the universality of the artistic instinct in *Homo*. Man was indeed born a craftsman even before he became a man, while the crafts of birds, squirrels, beavers and some insects and fishes preceded even his. Thus, the Industrial was the greatest of all Revolutions since it deprived man of one of the three primary gifts with which Nature endowed him—sex or the power to reproduce himself, the human form or the powers to move and think with it and the hand or the power to make useful and beautiful things with it. It temporarily suppressed something eternal in the nature of man, and this may well be the true cause of the chaos and disruption peculiar to our age. Or some might even say, perhaps with deeper vision though a lonelier voice, that by destroying his craftsmanship or inhibiting its expression, that Revolution had maimed the soul bestowed upon him by the Craftsman of the Universe. There can at any rate be no doubt that the artistic instinct and aptitude in man (I am not only thinking of the Palaeolithic cave-drawings of Spain and the Dordogne) are confined only artificially to the few, and so that the apprehension and creation of beauty have become atrophied or perverted or put to sleep by causes that are not natural. The anonymity of craftsmanship, the immensity of its range, the far horizon of its history, the complex gradations in its degrees, its independence of educational criteria, are final testimony to it as a primeval possession. Agriculture was its golden chance rather than its parent and England, it may be said, one of its most favoured homes.

The mysterious relation of craftsmanship to Nature has a supreme example in the achievement of regional architecture. Neither its prodigal variety in forms and materials nor its developments through the centuries obscure its primary fidelity to its particular rock. The reason for the diversity of the English villages are the varieties of our native rock, and the English village is a better handbook of geology than any printed text. It is not only a guide to the strata underlying it but an exposition of their qualities, texture, capacities and natural vegetation. An observant man does not even have to look out of the window of a cottage interior to tell what kinds of soils surround it, what kinds of crops it bears and even what are its natural features. He can guess the landscape by looking at the roof. I can test the geographical and vegetational changes taking place between the oolite and the lias down from the north-western Edge of the Cotswolds to the Valley of the Warwickshire Avon just as well by going from village to village as by studying the landscape and tapping about with a geological hammer. The transitional architecture from village to village exquisitely registers and translates into vernacular terms the hidden history of the earth on which the homesteads rest.

In the same way, the rather severe rectangular lines and sharp angles of the Cotswold house render into the human medium the linear composition of the wolds, while the discontinuous and fantastic outlines of the liassic hills are expressed in the broken surfaces, the medley of materials, the happy craziness of design in the brick, timber, plaster, thatch, tiling and sandstone of the cottages in the liassic Vale. And because there are no villages in all the world to equal those of England between the 14th and the 19th centuries, so there was no breed of craftsmen like the English who built them. Variety is the English genius of craftsmanship; variety the English genius of landscape. I can at this moment, sitting in my chair, picture to myself four totally different types of cottage limestone-slatted roofs alone, each true to its geological environment, each within fifty miles or less of one another.

If, again, after the geology lesson of walking up the village street, the craftsmanly minutiae be attended to—the chamfering of a waggon in the

8   57

shed, the carving of a corner-post or of a piscina or a poppy-head bench-end in " the decent church that tops the neighbouring hill," the ogee curves to the " guide " of a shepherd's crook, the wrought-iron work of a weather-vane or a chest either in the church or a farmhouse, the moulding of a drip-stone over a cottage window, the geometrical pattern of the thatch below the ridge-board or (if the roof be stone) the " valleying " of the angles of intersection, the setting of the lights to the wall-space and of the houses to the lie of the land, the siting of the church in relation to the secular buildings, the mingling of colours in a cottage garden, the cornering of a thatched wheat-rick, some blue ware on a dresser, the shape and colour of a mug at the pub, a carved settle opposite it, the ball-flower ornament over the chancel arch, the proportions of a pigsty, the raftering of a barn, the brasses on a horse's martingale, a corbel-table along the nave, the slight batter of a dry-stone wall, the harr of a field-gate, the pewter inlay of a butterfly bobbin on a lace-pillow, the finial at the gable-end of a grange, a carved boss in the groining of the church-porch—if the multiplicity of these details be taken in and a Nelson eye be turned to modern intrusions; if, again, another village ten, twenty, fifty or only a couple of miles off be remembered as totally different in its materials, its forms, its mannerisms, its styles, even of the tools (which also will have different names), then it will appear that, if we were a nation of shopkeepers in 1800 and are a nation of card-indexers and committees to-day, we were a nation of artists in 1500, 1600 and 1700.

And what kind of artists? The answer is Gothic artists because the Gothic tradition of village craftsmanship outlived the change in religion for another three centuries, and the Gothic Middle Ages were more favourable to regional craftsmanship than any other. They were peasant artists because the craftsmen grew up out of the village community. John Abel, for instance, the " king's carpenter " (see p. 38) of the magpie style of the west was of Herefordshire yeoman stock. He, one of the very few of the great race of English craftsmen (Chippendale was another) who is not anonymous, is a perfect example of the perpetuation of the Gothic tradition. He is presumed to have built the timber-roof of the great 13th century Cistercian house of Abbeydore, while his Grange house in Leominster, with its arcading, oriels, carvings and overhanging gables, continues the Gothic inheritance. He built, indeed, half Hereford, as a mediaeval town, not by imitation but as it were by his Gothic blood.

Another of these named craftsmen, rescued from the floods of Lethe, was Richard Hyckes who, by the fostering of William Sheldon (see Chapter V.) worked on the looms of Barcheston, Warwickshire, to produce " tapestry, arras, moccadoes, carolles, plonketts, grograynes, sayes and sarges " in the mid-16th century. He also wove maps of the counties, some of which were subsequently bought by Horace Walpole. Thus, like Abel, he was a kind of revivalist, picking up and re-creating the old tradition where it lay in the mire of forgetfulness. One of the very few mediaeval craftsmen whose name has ridden the centuries was Master Richard de Winchcombe who built the chancel of Adderbury Church (Oxon) for New College, and to him should be added Geoffrey Lytster of Felmingham, the East Anglian Dyer, who generaled the Norfolk Riding of 1381 more ably and humanely than most generals. In the 17th century, we have Samuel Malkin and the Tofts, the masters of English slip-ware, still carried on by Cardew's of Winchcombe.

38   The Village Smithy at Fittleworth, Sussex

39   Stake-making in a Kentish Wood

40   Samuel Rockall at his Lathe

Often too the characters of local vegetation and natural resources offered a home to certain types of rural industry. Norfolk reed-thatching lived off the Broads, basket-making off the Sedgemoor rhines, weaving from the Golden Valley of Stroud with its multiple fast streams, timbering from the forests of the liassic, wealden and boulder clays, glass-making from the dense woodlands that once surrounded Chiddingfold.

These artists, too, were Nature-artists because the beauty of English craftsmanship is as unconscious as the beauty of Nature. Its beauty is in fact achieved in exactly the same way as Nature's, as a by-product of utility. There is a kind of eternity in craftsmanship as there is in Nature, and that is why it cannot be fitted in to the modern conception of mechanical progress which, as Chesterton said, is leaving things behind as upon a road, not improving and developing things as in a garden. The whole point of the English peasant art is that it never leaves things behind. No peasant ever throws anything away. So, one spring is never like another, but it is always spring. But not only does the craftsman work in the same way as Nature without hurry or against the grain of things, and obtain similar results, but he is in a special relation to Nature from which he never deviates. This relation is a symbiotic one, which simply means that he uses without misusing his natural material to the mutual benefit both of Nature and himself. His attitude to Nature is never predatory as that of commerce almost invariably is, and so is by inference, though not consciously, ethical. He necessarily subdues his craft to the qualities of natural materials, the grain of the wood, the texture of the stone, the run of the straw, the consistency of the clay, and considers their characters, simply because his object is to make the most of them. He therefore does not impose his will upon Nature as science directs him to do in the phrase, " the conquest of Nature," but works in partnership with Nature, leaving her different but never worse than he found her.

The eyes of the master-man and of the salesman regard the face of Nature from points of view as diametrically opposite as the believer and the atheist regard the universe. And in a sense the craftsman is essentially the believer because his attitude to Nature, being creative, divines that force of generative workmanship which is akin to his own. Though he rarely objectifies this emotional sense, much less gives it a name, all making for him has a sacramental meaning and his very touch upon the works of Nature expresses a life-service towards a creative universal of which he is intuitively aware. " A wrong attitude towards Nature," wrote T. S. Eliot, " implies, somewhere, a wrong attitude towards God, and the consequence is an inevitable doom." The craftsman's attitude is necessarily the right one because he works hand-in-glove with Nature and, employing her methods, translates Nature into a new creation derived from Nature and yet Man's. Thus, in a profound sense, the craftsman works within the complex of God-Man-Nature. As Rilke wrote in one of his Sonnets of Orpheus, addressing Earth—" Unspeakably am I committed to you from eternity. Always you were right . . ." So is the craftsman, creating, committed to Nature.

IV SAMUEL ROCKALL, WOOD-BODGER

Lest this natural piety, whose fruits are a poise and equanimity of temper enjoyed by nearly every craftsman I know, be viewed as an abstract and metaphysical assumption, let me glance once more at one of whose life and character I have often been the chronicler, Samuel Rockall, the wood-bodger of the Oxfordshire Chilterns. If there is a single word that can sum them up it would be integrity in its dual significance of wholeness in multiplicity of labour or through contact with Nature and of devotion to the worth of the work for its own sake, which of course, is Nature's own way in striving for the perfect type. Every process from felling the tree to turning the chair-leg he executes himself, so that he is personally responsible for the entire chain of transformations from woodland tree to domestic furniture. But in serving man he does not rob Nature because his fellings are made with a view to conserving the best timber and regenerating the woodland as a whole. Nature is the source of his industry and each gains by the enrichment of the other.

For many years his earnings have averaged thirty shillings for six full days' highly skilled work a week and procuring or making his own materials for independently modifying the traditional designs of Windsors and Wheelbacks, whether legs, stretchers, spindles, banister splats or whole chairs, that, if they were no longer made would have made him a rich man. His turning is so good that his work has actually been counterfeited as old and disposed of as " genuine antiques," and he thus is paid a wage very much lower than that of the machine-turners whose work lacks all character and variety, for making furniture as beautiful as that which commands a fancy price. In other words, his work is only valued when it is pretended to be obsolete, while he himself, whose workmanship makes artificial the division between past and present has a meaner status even than that of the agricultural labourer. These absurdities are carried to extremity by the moribundity of bodging itself. Mastership means nothing to us unless it be dead. But it is this very continuity between past and present in the designs of Samuel's chair-making which transfers upon the human plane the great continuity of Nature.

He himself made the wheel-lathe (a little more complex than the pole-lathe of the itinerant woodsmen) for his son out of the beech-trees of his own felling. It is the spit of his own lathe which looks as though Nature had made it with the fingers, nerves and muscles of a human hand. Half of the fittings and furniture of his brick-quoined, flint cottage overlooking the heath whose chalk and Tertiary beds supplied the material, were home-made and this versatility is also a heritage of Nature. Here is an example of an hour spent with him recently which illustrates how this lack of specialism responds to the interdependence of Nature.

The bright November day was so full of pinks that it might have been the early blush of spring. Pink were the four-chambered spindle-berries, few of which had yet parted to reveal that defiant scarlet in the face of winter. The hazel catkins delicately suspended beside them were pink and they swung in the light breeze as though they might swing in their youthful colouring across the greys of winter. The woodland was like an Elizabethan cloak worn on the flank of the opposite hill. It had already struck its flag to the autumn gales and was pinkish-brown between the long shadow lying over the crest and the grass-pale slope over against it. Even the chalk fallows were pink and brown or pink and white with the young corn springing out of them to complete the illusion. Samuel's face too was pink not as at the budding of youth (he is in his sixties) but from sheer hard work. Yet the colour of his cheeks under his bright bird-like eyes that express the quickness and litheness of his movements and the general animation of his temperament, revealed one more of his affinities with the Nature all about his cottage on the heath, one I had not noticed before. Samuel is also in his autumn and yet his vivacity is that of youth and spring: Samuel's craft at his lathe may be traced back at least as far as the bowl turning of the Glastonbury Lake Village of 50 B.C., and yet this rock-bottom conservatism not only agrees well with but actually conditions the novelty of the things he makes. And that *is* craftsmanship—re-creation (which is newness) but always in the true line of tradition. Thus in Samuel that day I saw what I had seen in Nature—spring in autumn.

The novelty this time was a stand he was making for an Aladdin lamp. The disc itself was of elm and it was supported by five cabriolet legs of cherry-wood connected by slender stretchers to a circular centre-piece with a mahogany boss in the middle. Samuel bobbed down like a robin on a bird-table into the extraordinary assortment of woods in his workshop in order that he might show me the successive stages which an elm-butt and a cherry-tree had passed before they became a lamp-stand. Glancing down with him, I noticed that everything in the workshop except the tools, the lathe and the chopping-blocks was a cross-section in an evolutionary series. The shavings, for instance, from the lathe (they come curling out of it like a breaking wave) had undergone five different metamorphoses, as though Horse were pictured on a screen in successive appearances back to Eohippus. From kindlings to a powdered dust as fine as sand—for every one of these transformations Samuel had some appropriate use. His very shovel which collected this dust either for his compost heap or his fire and which also picked up pony-droppings from the common he had bought forty years before from a travelling tinker for fourpence. The archetypal peasant!

So it was with the piles of logs on the floor, some with one side in bark, others round and fully clothed, others stripped, others smoothed and shaped, each neat pile one step nearer to the lathe which was finally to domesticate them. These protean piles were like the chapters in Samuel's own life, since from woodland to house interior he is constantly changing one thing into another. Obviously, he derives a deep satisfaction from this orderly flux of material. He showed me the lemon stain of raw cherry-wood, how it fades into the palest flesh-colour after being fashioned and turned on the lathe, and how he restored it when it had become an article of furniture into the faint light of a winter sunbeam—namely by linseed oil. And who would guess what fine shades there are in the technique of seasoning woods according to their variations in hardness and sappiness until they had heard Samuel's discourse on their behaviour under heat?

For making a most elegant little stool Samuel was paid six shillings. He had to select the woods, split and chop them, take the roughness out of them on the draw-shave horse, turn them on the lathe and finish them with beautiful cup and ball mouldings. To say nothing of the new grindstone for his chisels it had taken him three days to fit up. I expostulated with him, six shillings for this little *chef d'oeuvre*, what did he mean by accepting such a price? He explained that, if he had scamped or hurried the job, or omitted the ball turnings, or chosen a poorer quality of wood, he would have been " ashamed to show it to the village."

61

The village—were Samuel's villagers connoisseurs of the fine arts? Or did he think they were because in spirit he belonged to the old village community in which all men were craftsmen and so critics? For to this age Samuel belongs not at all. He is dateless and so Progress means nothing whatever to him. Even the almighty wage-question hardly bothers him, partly because he has a hundred ways of making both ends meet and partly because he is absorbed in the worth of the work, contemplating the habits and constitution of woods, reading the ways of Nature like a sage poring over an old folio. Samuel is not a business man; I doubt whether he has even heard of the joint-stock method of getting all you can out of Nature by means of accountancy, machines and dope. He is of no account to the modern world, though he represents that English tradition which produced Shakespeare and Lincoln Cathedral.

The last time I saw him was in mid-winter when I paid him a visit to receive from his own hands a " Christmas box " he had made for me. It *was* a box, a barrel-shaped and hooped tobacco box with a knobbed lid that a century hence will be prized, if it escapes our era of destruction, as an example of 20th-century wood-carving which by some miracle was true to the great tradition of English woodwork. The body is cherry-wood, taken from a dead cherry-tree in a neighbouring wood and laid aside for fourteen years in case it might come in handy, an embossed annular piece round the lid is of a dark mellow rosewood which had belonged to his uncle forty years ago, and the knob of laburnum, rich and mottled, taken from a tree cut down by him and his uncle when between them they built Samuel's workshop nearly half a century ago. Thus all the woods had family and personal associations for him and had been stored in odd corners as a capital deposit. Things, not counters nor flimsy credit, things that had a history, things not to hoard but to transform, unconsidered trifles to become things of beauty. Here was the quintessence of the peasant-craftsman's sense of possession.

As I sat by his fireside handling my Christmas box, a wisp of flame from the log on the open hearth lit up the fireback of 1650 behind it. It is graved with a winged phoenix. Re-creation along the line of tradition, the quintessence of craftsmanship. Guard him, woods and heaths and hills of creative Nature, for in your midst is creative man, once ordinary man and now a rarity!

V THE SLAT-QUARRY

All craftsmen manifest this same willing and satisfying dependence upon Nature's rhythms, processes, balances and seasonal punctuations. Poetry, said Goethe, was given to man to make him satisfied with himself and his lot. How much the more is this true of craftsmanship which has the vantage of poetry in that the hand creates no less than the eye appraises, and that, though few men read poetry and fewer make it, all men might be craftsmen and most men were. The source of the craftsman's satisfaction is the poetry of Nature which he sees as poetry because his work, resting upon Nature, is beautiful.

This is true of all crafts, but I will give an example of how Nature at once disciplines and attunes the craftsman's work. This is quarrying slats for the stone roofs of the limestone region. Autumn is the signal for " ridding " or removing the turf from the top stratum of " presents," the hardest stone

42   Samuel Rockall using the Draw-share Knife

41   A Wheelwright

43   A Saddle-Tree Maker

44   A Potter

of all, rough, durable and polychrome, and so called because the quarrymen have nothing to do but to pick them out like slices of bread from the quarry-face. When the " pendle " is reached about four feet down, the pick extracts it to be wrapped, each block, in damp sods of earth to keep the " sap " in and so enable the " hammer of frost " to split the stone. The stones are so laid that Jack Frost, the hardest worked of all the quarrymen, strikes clean and in exactly the right place. In early spring, the slatting-hammer taps like a woodpecker where the frost had struck like lightning. After being squared, dressed round the edges and drilled for the peg-hole by the slat-pick, the flakes are stacked in the shape of a diminishing series of transitional Norman-Early English arches in such a way that the spring winds will dry out the sap for despatch to the slatter when they are no longer " green."

A craft like this can be no more mechanized than the shepherd's. Progress is a term without meaning for it because any change in the due order and method of these processes would not " improve " but dislocate them. Nature is the foreman of the work; her apprentices are the weather and the seasons. The co-partnership between man and Nature is balanced into a rhythm and harmony which, once formed, is indissoluble.

VI FREEDOM AND TRADITION

It is only in our eyes that there is anything of paradox in the fusion between variety, independence and tradition which is the fourth integration of craftsmanship. Of the craftsman's loyalty to tradition it is almost super-fluous to speak, since, so far as I know, there are no exceptions to it. But the woodman does not ply the pole-lathe under the golden tent of the autumn beech-woods because of his veneration for the rude forefathers of his hamlet. He is no village Cato nor one obstinately fearful (though he well might be) of that labour by proxy of the machine which has delivered the worker over to a bondage of drudgery incomparably more irksome than any it was dreamed to release him from. These are not his reasons for clinging to his archaic contraption of wood, iron and cord. It is because the pole-lathe is the cheapest (he makes it himself with the aid of the blacksmith), the readiest (the material comes from the beech-woods where he works) and the most efficient instrument for his particular purpose without robbing him of that exertion of skill and exercise of choice which are as much his pleasure as a cinema or a football match are to the machine-minder.

The pole-lathe, the potter's wheel, the hand-loom, the adze, the plough, the axe, the scythe, the trowel, the chisel, the saw, the moulding plane, the awl, the beetle, were invented once and for all. They can be readjusted, carried to a finer point, better poised and balanced or added to like the four-furrow plough, but they and the ways they were used could only be altered by getting the automatic limbs of a machine to operate them and so by depriving the craftsman of his craft, of its natural environment, of the economic conditions of his livelihood and of his social inheritance. The term for this is tragedy, not progress. Not that the machine to the craftsman is altogether what a late frost is to plum-blossom. The small oil-engine could be of signal service to him. But large-scale, " rationalized " mechani-zation adopted for profit rather than use is to him annihilation. Since pride and interest in and responsibility for his work are part both of his family and individual life, his whole being is disintegrated. If man is a natural craftsman as his primitive habits would suggest, the first cause for the dissolving of human bonds during our century is discovered, the obsolescence of craftsmanship.

Quality in the work and vocation in the worker are the secret for the extraordinary tenacity of rural craftsmanship throughout human history and prehistory. There is no essential difference between Adam Bede the carpenter and Samuel Rockall the bodger. I know a villager in the Chilterns (Goodchild of Naphill)* who to this day makes 18th-century furniture not by study and imitation but by continuity of tradition. At Great Hazeley, Oxon, the Cooper family have been monumental masons since 1530 and the last of them still carves headstones with scrolls and winged cherubs in the 18th century manner. This vocational sense is derived from inheritance between father and son, corresponding to the apprentice-journeyman-master hierarchy of the mediaeval craft-guilds. Even in these days when the link between trade and home has been completely broken, I do not know a single exception to this principle of family heritage. In the small market-town near where I live, the hurdler, the blacksmith, the shepherd and the ex-basket-maker, the only surviving mastermen within its bounds, are all grandsons of hurdler, blacksmith, shepherd and basket-maker, while the last can trace his descent from Breton basket-makers of pre-Huguenot origin. Now his osier-bed is a marsh and he sells fruit and vegetables instead of making baskets to put them in. In the Corfe Castle Shrove-tide traditional game of football, the sons of the Purbeck quarrymen were formally apprenticed, and it was a rule of this small society, members of which all were quarry-owners, that only their sons might become quarry-masters.

The father trained his son to step into his shoes and this training was what Arthur Bryant has truly called " a mental and spiritual discipline." Character, judgment, discrimination in values, a scholarship in every sense of the term except the bookish was implanted from father to son and thence projected into the work. This was an education for mastership and its worth is attested by the continuity through millenia of all country crafts. If it was not a son who was thus initiated, it was a nephew or a neighbour's young hopeful and so the cohesion of the village organism was preserved. Ethics were as indivisible from profession as mind from body in its performance and such was the equipment for the transition between entering the workshop and controlling it. Quality in work induced quality in character.

Thus, tradition, passed down the family line like an heirloom, disciplined the craftsman without becoming remote and crystallized. It became variable within certain limits because the human element, nourished by skill and personal responsibility, was always replenishing it. However ancient the tradition might be, it is wrong to think of it as such because it was perpetually renewed and so always present and alive at the moment. It fostered rather than fettered individual treatment and so was inevitably antipathetic to mass-production. Not the least reason for the loss of variety in the graded rural society after the Enclosures was the decay of craftsmanship. Bus-rides to the cinema, local distractions and entertainments (though not village cricket which is a social form of craftsmanship), townified pleasures, all the devices for relieving the dullness of the modern village, are so many patent medicines to cure the pernicious anaemia of that loss of interest in his daily work which

* The yew armchair he made me is the work of a 20th-century Chippendale.

the craftsman, no matter how stern and toilsome the conditions of his life, invariably enjoyed. " My pleasures and hobbies throughout my life have been my work," the carpenter of Winchcombe once said to me. All modern efforts to fill this aching void in terms of comfort or relaxation are inexorably foredoomed to failure. To fix attention on the countryman's leisure rather than on his labour is the fatal error of an urban philanthropy. Our clever modernists never consider the profound significance, the rich organic secret to the good life that Christ was apprenticed to a carpenter before uttering the Word of that life.

But it is impossible to understand this interplay between tradition and individuality except by actually watching a craftsman at work. I think I have seen nearly every one of the dry-wallers of the Cotswolds in the act of building up the wall. Why does Cotswold Balbus seem so careless in the handling and placing of the stones and yet is so unerring, why does he seem so leisurely and yet is so swift? Because invisible hands are aiding him, hands that built the false portals to the long barrows, hands that built the mortarless tithe barns of the region, father's and grandfather's hands. He works in a kind of trance: he is in communion with the dead who live in him. For him there is no arbitrary division between past and present, and yet the wall is built with his mind before he and his forebears with him lay finger on a single stone. The true craftsman always sees the end of his work before he begins it; his hand is guided by his own brain that selects, by his own eye that measures and by the unseen hands which he remembers as the chaffinch remembers the nest-builders of his ancestry.

VII CONDUCT AND SECURITY

The last integration is between economic security and social ethics. This can be as well shown by negative example as any other way. When the commoners lost their commons, the degradation was moral, social and economic, all three. The co-operative peasant became the competitive wage-earner, while the desperate poverty of the labourers found a vent in arson, drunkenness, pitched battles with gamekeepers, the promiscuity of gang-labour and a general demoralization set up by pauperism. The guild system of the mediaeval towns expressly combined ethics in trading (the " just price ") and social solidarity with economic self-protection, and the place of the craftsman in the village community reveals the same synthesis. The village weavers and spinners who made English cloth the best in the world took that personal pride in their work which secured a fair return for it, benefited their neighbours by its utility and brought them into constant social intercourse with their customers. Ethics were a by-product of the craftsmanly status as beauty was a by-product of the craftsmanly job.

At the end of the 15th century, England was a nation of small cloth-makers and small sheep-farmers, interacting with and indispensable to one another. Even when the first factories were beginning to break down this integration, lace-making, glass-making, straw-plait, gloveing, butter-making, bacon-curing, embroidery, metal-work, jam- and wine-making, wooding, even repoussé work continued to be practised, mostly by women, as cottage industries dovetailing into smallholdings. Even woad was grown in small plots for dyeing up to about 1850. I know one village in Oxon where the ploughman still makes rush-baskets in his spare time, and the spare-time occupation is

9

a means to economic stability full of moral implications. The lowered status of house-craft in our own days has had incalculable moral repercussions by undermining the sense of home and family. In the 19th century, idleness, first of the gentlewoman and then of the farmer's wife, had become gentility. I have seen old kitchens in out-of-the-way farmhouses whose fittings and utensils were hieroglyphs of a multiplicity of crafts now forgotten or, if they are remembered, despised for the toil expended upon them, work nowadays having become so dull that leisure is regarded as the means to happiness. But the complex traditions of the old crafts, bound to no time-sheet, united with a regional self-sufficiency, and acting by an interchange of goods and services rather than money, were the pillars and arches of a social structure whose core of soundness was no less ethical than economic.

These five integrations are sub-divisions of one integration, and the destruction of the crafts has, in consequence, been so disastrous that the recovery of them will very soon be a national necessity. The part our surviving craftsmen can play in the conservation of the English tradition may yet become of paramount importance. The history of the craftsman is the story of the intimate relationship between the personal and the functional, the functional working for the personal (to quote Prof. MacMurray's terms) and the personal working through the functional. This is civilization and to destroy it as modern Europe is doing must and will mean the death of civilization.

I have known many craftsmen of various types and trades and I possess many of their works and implements. Is there a family likeness between them as there certainly is between their tools? Since their personalities are probably more diverse than those of an equal number of mechanics or factory-workers for the simple reason that their work gives them latitude for self-expression, it would seem that a family likeness, say between an Oxfordshire saddler, a Dorset thatcher, a Cotswold slatter, a Yorkshire hurdler and a Sussex wheelwright could not possibly exist. From my experience, which is not small, it does exist, this shared quality of being, and, for want of a better word, I should call it serenity. Superficially speaking, this is not to be expected, because the breed of craftsmen is moribund. Their sons rarely now stay at home to learn their fathers' trades; there is either too great or too little demand upon their services; the village life to which they contributed so much is the ghost of itself and they are survivors into an alien new world which takes no account of them at all, or, if it does, only as museum pieces.

To be men of inward peace and balance in such circumstances calls for a toughness of spiritual fibre capable of sustaining no small degree of stress and tribulation. This equanimity of temper, exceeding rare is an age of schizophrenia, is conferred upon them by the nature of their work and their intimate contact with Nature herself. It is not insensibility but poise and, if it owes something to inheritance, still more to lack of frustration, more yet to consciousness of service and even more to the small green world in which they live, it owes most of all to an attunement with the will of Creation itself.

Chapter IV

THE LABOURER

I PEASANT AND LABOURER

It is impossible to gather an authentic impression of the agricultural labourer as he is except in historical alignment with what he was. In a very real sense, he is not what he is but half-way between his old and his present self. The perplexities about him as a type cannot be resolved unless Piers Plowman be clearly realized as the father of Hodge, and the old English peasantry as the ancestral stock of a landless wage-earning proletariat.

To peer backwards in order to detect the first appearance of the landless labourer upon the stage of English country life is a minor and largely academic issue. England certainly knew nothing of him before the middle of the Middle Ages, and there is not the smallest evidence that the hired labourers who worked on the lord's home-farm after the commutation of forced services for payment in money or in kind were landless. They only differed from the average commoners in leaving the lord's farm to look after their own " lands " instead of leaving their own to look after the lord's cultivation. The Tudor Enclosures and the Dissolution of the Monasteries did, however, create a definitely landless class of countrymen by means of fines, rack-renting, eviction and intimidation. But the majority of these uprooted peasants, exposed for the first time to what Tawney calls " the bitter breath of modern commercialism," set in motion that fatalistic drift from country to town which, with changes in the breadth and velocity of the current, has continued to this day. They entered the class of vagabondage and the literature of the period is full of their shifts and " coney-catching " expedients to pick up a living. But the dispossessed of the far more intense and prolonged wave of enclosure from 1750 onwards to its total triumph in 1845 became not vagabonds but paupers, and wage-labourers working on the land. They became in fact a proletariat as the class of beggars strictly speaking is not.

Thus a wedge was driven between peasant and labourer of such violence that the entire social system of the village community was shattered.

The revolutionary precedent of the Enclosures not only drove a wedge between peasant and labourer, past and present (just as the modern theory of Progress does), but drove it deep into the character and mentality of him who became neither one thing nor the other but the ex-peasant, a strange anomalous figure but little understood. We cannot begin to understand his characteristics without reference to this dualism of his historical destiny.

As a means to this end, it has to be computed what his actual losses were, not so much in property and economic security, in his fun and his holidays, his local government and his church, his social life and his employment (of which there is ample record), as in their psychological effects. In a striking passage, Lord Ernle epitomized some in *English Farming Past and Present* :

> " Enclosure destroyed the inherited traditions of the peasantry, their
> ideals, their customs, their habits, their ancestral solutions of the problems

67

of life—all, in fact, that made up the native home-bred civilization of rural England . . . It is not surprising that. . . . they should have remained stupefied by the shock, gradually realizing the full meaning of the change, and then either stolidly acquiescing in their new existence, or impatient to escape on the first opportunity."

Compare the spirit of the Peasants' Revolt in 1381 with that of the convulsion of Captain Swing and the machine-breaking riots in 1830 (when the labourer had become what Hasbach calls " the plaything of prices and taxation "), and the difference is hardly to be measured. In 1381, the peasants broke out of their villages so as not to lose their *independence*; in 1830, they broke the threshing machines in the villages so as not to lose their *jobs* with the flail in the winter barns :

> " Why, here were vourteen men, some years agoo,
> A-kept a-drashen half the winter drough;
> An' now woone's drashels be'nt a bit of good,
> They got machines to drashy un, plague teake em! "

So William Barnes and *Alton Locke* gives a picture of the " insurgents " :

> " As we pushed through the crowd, I was struck with the wan, haggard looks of all faces; their lack-lustre eyes and drooping lips, stooping shoulders, heavy dragging steps, gave them a crushed, dogged air which was infinitely painful and bespoke a grade of misery more habitual and degrading than that of the excitable and passionate artisan."

So Kingsley in 1850, and Cobbett in 1830 wrote of their hovels :

> " Look at these hovels, made of mud and of straw; bits of glass or of old cast-off windows, without frames or hinges frequently, but merely stuck in the mud-wall. Enter them and look at the bits of chairs or stools; the wretched boards tacked together to serve for a table; the floor of pebble, broken brick or of the bare ground; look at the thing called a bed, and survey the rags on the backs of the wretched inhabitants; and then wonder, if you can, that the gaols and dungeons and treadmills increase, and that a standing army and barracks are become the favourite establishments of England."

Disraeli, of course, has left an unforgettable picture of the little rural town of Marley in *Sybil*, of its filth, decay, squalor and disease, of its gaping tenements and stricken dwellers, Marley, the link between the conditions in the new industrial towns and those in the country. " I am ashamed," wrote Cobbett elsewhere, " to look at these poor souls and to reflect that they are my countrymen." Hardly, " a bold peasantry, their country's pride " any more, though of its very blood, its place and its traditions.

That " rebellion " was crushed with ease, not with guile like the first, and then began the hangings and transportations for poaching and stealing whereby not to starve, the passion of relief when the sentence was death, not the convict settlement, and, following the victory of order and progress, the torrent of emigration either to the new factories or the new colonies. Out of 614,800 acres enclosed by the General Enclosure Act of 1845, only 2,223 acres were earmarked for allotments—and these and the ones that preceded them were a Danaan gift since the cost of fencing compelled the holders to sell up to speculators. Doreen Wallace in *Green Acres* (1941) gives a good picture of how Enclosure worked—no wood from the enclosed common to fence in the compensating plots, no stock to manure them, increase of the tenant farmers' acreage giving them the chance to force down wages and refuse to employ the more independent workers. It was the type of the Tolpuddle Martyrs in 1834 that left the village, few of them ever to return; it was the broken and submissive who remained. As John Clare, the so-called " peasant poet," who had tended sheep and geese on the common and learned the old village songs from the last village cowherd, wrote:

> " Then came Enclosure—ruin was its guide,
> But freedom's cottage soon was thrust aside,
> And workhouse prisons raised upon the site.
> E'en Nature's dwellings, far away from men,
> The common heath, became the spoiler's prey;
> The rabbit had not where to make his den
> And labour's only cow was drove away."

Freedom's cottage demolished for the workhouse—this is the succinct history of the Enclosures. Can its psychological reactions be exaggerated?

II   THE LABOURERS' LOSS

They were intensified, of course, by the new premium upon pauperdom by virtue of which the tenant farmers were able (though at the price of rocketing rates) to obtain the cheapest of all labour, that of the destitute, no longer as persons but as units of the gangs. The dread and hatred of the Poorhouse have been in the land-workers' bones ever since the Tudor Enclosures, while a pauper burial is for them the last degradation. What the contemporary voice called " the labouring poor " with, as Cobbett said, " an irrevocable sentence of poverty for life," men and women both, were, some of it, harnessed to the parish carts and fed on sorrel and roots without outraging the sentiments of the heart behind the voice. The new specialized farming, approaching to the conditions of the Roman *latifundia*, was bound to create conditions among the workers not dissimilar from the Roman system of slave-tillage. The remedy sought—Speenhamland—inaugurated the dole-system, which marked the failure of our industrial system in the next century. The extraordinary brutality with which the new labouring class was treated may be illustrated from a few items gathered from *one* district in the Cotswolds. In 1816, forty people were hanged in one day; in 1800, six women were publicly flogged for hedge-pulling till the blood ran down their naked backs; in 1832, a shepherd was transported for life for the customary practise of cooking a lamb that had died; in 1821, three men were hanged at Witney for stealing a sack of flour and some bacon; in 1809, a labourer was sentenced to fourteen years' transportation for stealing a plank by the owner of it. These crimes are not yet expiated, but they will be and perhaps they are now being so.

Be it to Arthur Young's everlasting credit that he repented of his intemperate crusade for enclosure when he saw something of the degradation and desperation that it wrought, though he did not live long enough to see the crime emerging as a blunder. It was through his Tour among the French peasants, not the English, that he was to write a sentence which undid many of his volumes—" the magic of property turns sand into gold." The sagacious Malthus said that, if the poor had property, they would recklessly propagate. What actually happened was that the unpropertied multiplied because the more children, the more labour for the " dark Satanic mills " and the more bastards, the larger the allowance from the parish. Lord Ernle gives an example from a village in Bucks where sixty-four out of the ninety-eight natives were in receipt of poor relief and only sixteen acres of the land were cultivated in a county where the exploitation of the soil on business lines was supplanting its nurture by yeoman and peasant methods. Speculators in abstract thought like Malthus and Adam Smith were not only mistaken about the blessedness of casual labour at a starvation wage on the farms, hardly distinguishable from slave-labour on the plantations, but so, since they confused intensity of labour with intensity of capital, were they mistaken in their estimates of the productivity to be expected from the new era of propertyless competition in place of propertied co-operation. When Joseph Arch from 1872 onwards induced 80,000 of this 19th century helot class to join his Union of Agricultural Labourers, he so far disagreed with the economists of *laissez-faire* as to put the re-creation of peasant ownership in the forefront of his programme.

The condition of the land in our own day, suffering both from infertility and lack of labour, is the direct consequence of the Enclosures, whose predatory spirit at once robbed the soil-capital and demoralized the workers upon it, so true is it that the sour grapes of the fathers have set the childrens' teeth on edge. The building founded in iniquity was to find its top-storey rocking in the wind of adversity. The capitalist farming of the 19th century exalted individualism at the expense of the individual liberty the peasant proprietors had enjoyed. The unanimous verdict of fearless and discerning men as to what the free-hearted followers of John Ball had become may be fitly concluded by the last of them, Richard Jefferies in *Greene Ferne Farm*:

> " Their backs were bowed beneath great bundles of gleanings or faggots of dead sticks, carefully sought for fuel, and they carried weary infants, restless and fretful. Their forms had lost all semblance to the graceful curves of women; their faces were hard, wrinkled and angular, drawn with pain and labour. Save by their garments, none could distinguish them from men. Yet they were not penned in narrow walls, but all things green and lovely were spread around them. The fresh breezes filled their nostrils in the spring and the delicate odour of the flowering bean-field and the clover scent; the very ground was gilded with sunshine beneath their feet. But the magic of it touched them not, for their hearts were pinched with poverty."

" He that is down need fear no fall "—the ex-peasant sank so low beneath 1815 and 1850 that his wrongs can but make a tedious inventory. They must be cut down here to those which were bound to affect his general character. Perhaps the chief of these was the exchange owing to the glut of labour from co-operation with to competition against his fellow-villagers, and they included women and children. George Bourne has well described the effect of the change upon the labourers of the Farnham neighbourhood in *Change in the Village*—the elaboration among them of an unwritten code as to how far that competition in the selling of their only commodity, their labour, should go and where it should stop. This is just what was to be expected, a division between two contrary emotions, the memorial one of mutual aid and the immediate one of rivalry.

Another was the disintegrating consequences of enclosure upon the younger generation, tabulated by Hasbach as malnutrition, the compromising of the love of the land by deprivation of it, unemployment and wasted leisure, loss of thrift (that reminds us of Richard Jefferies's " unthrifty labourer "), lack of schooling, impediments to marriage, inducements to improvidence, depreciation of independence and so of a modest pride and self-respect (reminding us of Arthur Young's famous, " For whom are we to be sober? For whom are we to save? ") and the growth of small dishonesties. These in turn reacted upon the whole principle and art of home-making. The taking-in of the commons also profoundly depressed the varied activities of house-craft from baking the bread in those ovens projecting from the kitchen wall to be seen in so many of the old cottages to making butter from the milk of the cow that was sold when there was no longer pasture to feed it. How angry Cobbett was at the new fashion of drinking strong tea in place of the home-brew! The spring-guns and mantraps in the woods testified to the inevitable growth of poaching as a profession for the desperate, and, as Bernard Darwin has shown (*Early Victorian England*), there was a trade in illicit game like that of bootlegging in America.

The drainage of labour from the land—300,000 labourers were lost to it from 1921 onwards—contributed more than any other factor to the dullness of village life, so that the latter-day labourer trains his sons to become blackcoats who hammer typewriters, add up sums or sell goods over the counter in place of acquiring that soil-wisdom and knowledge of fundamental Nature which the peasants handed down to their families. Lord Lymington has a story of the son of a land-worker whose one ambition was to become an Inspector of Public Nuisances. He achieved it; he rose in the world.

The zero status of the labourer in respect of other workers who exercise not a tenth part of his skill and versatility, a status which he has never recovered, was greatly aggravated by the break-down of the ladder between land-worker and farmer. How many of the smallholders of to-day received their training in husbandry as labourers? As his personal responsibility was shorn by the loss of his land and his initiative stripped by the virtual impossibility of the old-style ploughman " of ancient wise sardonic bones " ever to plough his own land, so the obsolescence of the village fairs and festivals—only the Harvest Home precariously and sporadically surviving—deprived his scanty leisure of the last semblance of life. Long before this atrophy of the village liveliness had reached its climax, Goldsmith detected it and wrote its epitaph:

> " Sweet smiling village, loveliest of the lawn,
> Thy sports are fled, and all thy charms withdrawn;
> Amidst thy bowers, the tyrant's hand is seen,
> And desolation saddens all thy green:
> One only master grasps the whole domain
> And half a tillage stints thy smiling plain;
> No more thy glassy brook reflects the day,
> But choked with sedges, winds its weedy way.
>
> .   .   .   .   .
>
> Sunk are thy bowers in shapeless ruin all
> And the long grass o'ertops the mouldering wall,
> And trembling, shrinking from the spoiler's hand,
> Far, far away, thy children leave the land."

The Hiring Fairs, where shepherd with a wisp of wool, carter with a whip-lash in his cap and others, each with his badge of office, waited to be hired, was hardly a compensation for the loss of the great fairs of old.

So of 1770. Nor inapposite for 1920-39. The farm-labourer of to-day is not, of course, subject to the direct inhumanity and organized persecution that were his lot during the period of the Enclosures, when he had something to lose. Even though Joseph Arch's Union was a failure, it won him a measure of tolerance which he has maintained. But it can hardly be said that either his social or utility value has risen in the estimation of the community since 1770, when a machine-minder who sits in front of a conveyor-belt fitting fragmentary parts to a slot-machine for a railway station can earn more money and work shorter hours than the man on whose knowledgeable devotion to our native earth depend the lives of us all. Under the economic system which came into full dominion after the Industrial Revolution and was given a kind of *carte blanche* of approval by the Darwinian theory, itself anticipated by Hobbes, Locke, Mandeville, Adam Smith and Malthus, it became true not only that he who was down need fear no fall but expect ever to rise up again. If he has won his £3 a week minimum wage, he is as far away as ever he was from winning back his land.

He was the victim not merely of the rage for enclosure most tyrannously exercised, but of a change-over from a rural to an urban attitude, unable to appreciate the values and realities of civilized man's dependence upon the soil. All through the 19th century, the labourers were being replaced by the new agricultural machines and the remainder received a pittance for their experience, their craftsmanship, their fidelity to the land and unrespited physical endurance from dawn to dusk. In our own century, the policy of lending money to the stranger outside the gate in order to beggar the neighbour within it, of importing cheap foreign food as interest upon debt to the ruin of the home market, raised for him the spectre of unemployment in an acuter form than had previously haunted him. All of a sudden, he became the life-line of society and after many days enjoys his three pounds a week. What is to happen to him if agriculture is once more thrown to the wolves of finance?

III THE LABOURER POETS

If the Enclosures combined with the new urbanism debased the currency of the peasant, what kind of a being emerged? Was that coinage turned into paper money? Not so, to the undying glory of a human nature in husbandly bond with the earth. A. G. Street's " gentleman of the party " is a living portrait of a living man who has a touch of undemonstrative grandeur, and so have Adrian Bell's Walter, Wordsworth's Leech Gatherer and Hudson's Caleb Bawcombe. But the truer immortals of the labouring folk are Hardy's Gabriel Oak, Giles Winterbourne and Marty South. All of these heroic figures reveal by an imaginative shorthand the actual history of the labourer, because all three had descended, when or soon after we meet them, from the copyholding class of the peasantry. The old maltster of *Far From the Madding Crowd*, on the other hand, is a peasant, while Joseph Poorgrass and his fellows, together with the Mellstock Choir, are wage-labourers, whose spiced vernacular and almost Shakespearean humour are reminders of their peasant ancestry. How incomparably rich is the English tradition!

The nature of the farm-labourer is still more directly disclosed by the labourer poets, Duck, Bloomfield and the great Clare. These men are persistently classified as "peasant poets," when it is perfectly clear that they are nothing of the kind. First, they were all wage-earners on the land before taking up smallholdings on Parnassus. Next, they were all writing when the Enclosures were in full swing (Stephen Duck rather earlier). Thirdly, and omitting Clare for the moment, they expressed themselves in the literary language of the period, penned into formal couplets, lessoned by the Horatian muse, generalized and, as Ben Jonson sang, "still to be neat, still to be drest." The anonymous peasant poets no more wrote like this than Blake himself, not only because they belonged to a different age but because they were communal singers, as their villages were co-operative farms. Is it conceivable that even John Clare could have written *The Nut-Brown Maid* or *The Ballad of Chevy Chase*? No, *he* did not write it but his old villager sang it:

> "And many a moving tale in antique rhymes
> He has for Christmas and such merry times,
> When ' Chevy Chase,' his masterpiece of song,
> Is said so earnest none can think it long,"

The only post-peasant poet who wrote peasant poetry was William Barnes, and he is to come later into these annals.

Bloomfield's Suffolk Giles in *The Farmer's Boy* was a labourer not a peasant; Duck was a Wiltshire labourer, "engag'd," as Spence said, "in the several lowest employments of a Country Life." Yet underneath the churchwarden costume of their verses lies a gentle detailed conversance with Nature, a faculty for minute observation both of the natural scene and of husbandry, a country-mindedness, a deep humanity and what Edmund Blunden has called "a weather-beaten stoicism." For all the Sunday School manners of their muse, they remain of the earth earthy, of the home homely. Conscious of their wrongs but infinitely enduring and patient, essentially humble-hearted and fatalistic. Duck of *The Thresher's Labour* (1736) writes:

> "Homewards we move, but spent with so much toil,
> We slowly walk, and rest at ev'ry Stile.
> Our good expecting wives, who think we stay,
> Got to the door, soon eye us on the Way.
> Then from the Pot the Dumplin's catch'd in haste
> And homely by its side the Bacon plac'd."

Jefferies has a tragic and ironic picture of the labourer's toil in *The Open Air*. He meets some women fruit-pickers on his walk.

> "They saw no end to their labour, they had waited from childhood, and could see no possible end to labour until limbs failed or life closed. Why should they be like this? Why should I do nothing? They were as good as I was, and they hated me."

But:

> "I envied them that unwearied step, that firm uprightness, and measured yet lazy gait, but most of all the power which they possessed, though they did not exercise it intentionally, of beings always in the sunlight, the air, and abroad upon the earth."

They envied him his idleness, he envied them their power of toil. But the labourer poets thought of the employer who exacted it.

The Egyptian scourge of the tenant farmer whistles through all these plodding poems:

> " He counts the Bushels, counts how much a Day;
> Then swears we've idled half our Time away."

and these lowly records are the shadow upon the high lights of " high farming," competitive against the flood of foreign imports, in the home markets and against their own docile workers.

But the faithful round proceeds as the faithful seasons pass and in the autumn Giles looses the pigs among the oaks that, meeting the mallard startled from her pool:

> " decamp with more than swinish speed,
> And snorting dash through sedge and rush and reed:
> Through tangling thickets headlong on they go,
> Then stop and listen for their fancied foe."

The comfort of Nature is still with the humiliated and the dispossessed, and her shrillest or iciest mood is not the spiritual wound the farmer gives not merely by his sweating wage but the new social cleavage between him and his men.

Through all the defects of the labourer poets, we perceive the husbandly faith still intact from peasant times, the old piety of the labour of the fields. Even in our age it is still with us, though the modern farmers strive to turn farm into firm and the local authority has deprived the labourer of the last item of his peasant property—his pig. Arthur Young in his conversion from Saul to Paul understood the importance of the pig to the cottager and in nothing is the divorce between country and town more clearly exposed than in the urban fantasy that cheap and easy access to the cinema is to the countryman a compensation for the loss of his pigsty. The rational planners who pour out pamphlets about the new England to be fail to realize it and so the variety and interest of a normal country life and so the profound meaning of the little man's private property. The town will plot and plan for the country and under the elaborate superstructure it raises will bury the fundamental needs of the countryman and so of man himself. The flag of Everyman will never wave over the council-chambers of the nation until the self-criticism of urban thought recognizes the place of the cottager's pig in the scheme of things. Is not this perhaps the root of the trouble with Socialism and still more with Communism? It seems to have escaped their notice that private property was abolished by the combine. The core of an authentic country life is that personal responsibility which both State Socialism and the combine deny. For the pig was the labourer's last link with the old peasant community from which he is descended.

In our own days, the inward variety of the average country round has been zealously and traditionally preserved by two English types, the yeoman and the labourer, both of peasant origin. I consider in my mind what I have seen the labourer perform. I have seen him tying the sheaf-knot, stooking sheaves, building and cornering the rick, pleaching a hedge, setting plough, setting hurdles, driving a loaded waggon with shaft and trace horse through a gate, scything a headland, singling turnips, clamping potatoes, directing a sheep-dog, loading the dung-cart, flailing the beans, hummeling the barley ails, broadcasting seed, drawing a furrow, mending a tumbril, pitching hay,

74

45　Seed-time in the Mid-19th Century: from a painting by J. F. Herring, *Sen.*

46   18th-Century Carters: from a painting by George Stubbs

47   Harvesting in Herefordshire a Hundred Years Ago: from a painting by
G. H. Lewis

shouldering corn-sacks, physicking livestock, breaking a foal, delivering a calf, milking a cow, topping sugar-beet, shearing and ochreing pedigree sheep and other things as good. I have known old labourers who performed all the labours of Hercules in a single day, not with strength only but that insinuating mastery which is craftsmanship. From a boyhood spent in " starving the crows " to the old man breaking stones with the fining hammer, the labourers of the past achieved a balance of body with brain that has made their power of work in our automatic days seem legendary, the labour of earthy Titans. Our tinned civilization, protecting itself from manual labour by every ingenuity of mechanical gadget, has come to look upon such labour as beneath the dignity of man, as though arms and legs were a form of bestiality. How should this office-chair culture understand the toils of the old countrymen?

These men, classed and paid as the unskilled, and accommodating themselves to the eternal changefulness of Nature and the earth in the seasons, the weather, the conditions of the soil, the habits of growth, the cycle of life and decay, the alternations and reshufflings of one phase with another, made by necessity an individual response to their environment lacking to the season-less uniformity of town life. At a time when a determined and revolutionary attempt is being made to apply the principles and methods of the factory to organic processes, the assurance we receive from the work of the labourer that country life cannot by the nature of things be standardized is of utmost value. That assurance is confirmed and illustrated in the pages of the labourer poets.

In the volumes of John Clare, on the other hand, whom Edmund Blunden has called " the best poet of Nature that this country and for all I know any other country has produced," the natural unpremeditated impulsive poetry of the peasant, which is social, is fused with the loving log-book of the labourer, which is kinship with earth, and the imaginative meditation of the artist, which is individual. Here something is done far beyond the measure of Robert Bloomfield. John Clare, mystic and naturalist, combining vision with observation, stands as the living sublimation of the countryman as a whole, just as John Langland stands as the living symbol of the village community. It is significant that he, the bound labourer, who loved " sweet freedom and the free," once on his modest earnings as a poet tried to buy a seven-acre holding with a cottage at Bachelor's Hall near his native Helpston where his cottage, when I saw it in 1936, was the most miserable in the village. From this dingy cage the linnet sang.

IV PORTRAIT OF THE LABOURER

We shall note in our labourer, therefore, a duality derived both from his peasant lineage and his modern position as the least esteemed member of the social body. His uncouthness and boorishness are pure myth; he is shy of the stranger as the labourer, genial and social at the inn as the peasant. That composure of his which is incurious of what lies outside his ken is both the peasant's stake in the soil and the labourer's lack of any stake in the country. It goes more often than it should with taciturnity and that not only for the stranger's benefit. The tale told of a courting couple from one of the villages of the White Horse is no *rara avis* :

" John, why doant 'ee say summat? " " Cause I ha'nt got nothen to say." " John, why doant 'ee tell ma that thee loves ma? " " Cause I've telled 'ee that afoor."

75

This is the labourer but not the peasant. They accept without repining their exile—up to the war—from the world of affairs. But it is also a quietude drawn from intercourse with the primal realities which is peasant and labourer nature both. Stray instances have come to my knowledge of how deep-seated is the landless labourer's passion for land. One I know very well planted some apple-pips in his minute garden on the day he left home for the war 1914-18. He is now eating their apples. There is still an elemental commonalty between the labourers (competitive as they have had to be) which is almost a diffused being shared in common and this is an unconscious remembrance of the peasant community. Still, too, they retain the intense localism of the old peasantry, and this sense of belonging to one place was not in the least shaken by their experiences as travellers in the wars of the 20th century. There are swallows who are natives of Long Melford even though they spend half the year with the hippopotamus.

But this peasant conservatism has been broken in their games, darts and shove ha'penny, which have become indoors only. John Clare's *Remembrances* have a double poignancy of loss in this particular context:

" Summer's pleasures they are gone like to visions every one,
And the cloudy days of autumn and of winter cometh on.
I tried to call them back, but unbidden they are gone
Far away from heart and eye and forever far away.
Dear heart, and can it be that such raptures meet decay?
I thought them all eternal when by Langley Bush I lay,
I thought them joys eternal when I used to shout and play
On its bank at chink and bandy clock and law and ducking stone,
Where silence sitteth now on the wild heath as her own
Like a ruin of the past all alone."

In *Our Village*, Miss Mitford mentions a " day labourer " as a bowler in the village cricket match whose " very ecstasy of good humour " she applauds, but how many labourers figured in the deathless game between the Muggletonians and the Dingley Dellers, or, for the matter of that, how many of them played on Broadhalfpenny Down?

Less complete is the break with the past in folk-lore and folk-belief, dying leaves that still whirl in rare gusts through their heads. The wart-curer still flourishes. The grand archaic ritual of " Crying the Neck " as reported in Hone's *Everyday Book*, O'Neill's *Devonshire Idyls* and Fraser's *Golden Bough*, lasted in the west up to about 1850. But the rare " Harvest Hwome " of to-day is hardly more than a supper. A farm-labourer I knew in the Cotswolds used to talk to me about the Wise Woman of Ebrington whom he called the " fey woman." " Do you really believe Hannah Jarvis was a witch? " I asked him. " Maybe her were, maybe her weren't," said Charlie Brotheridge, " but I uddunt a liked to have trusted the old bitch." Many cart- and shire-horses are still called Gilbert after St Gilbert of Sempringham. Jimmy Teapot, the mighty eater of Broad Campden, once said to a friend of mine of the mandrake that " it bled like blood when you drawed it up in the daytime, but it hollers like a child if you draws it on a moonshiny night."

Among the older labourers, I have personally encountered instances of exorcism and sympathetic magic, half-credited. Lord William, a farm-labourer who lived in a hovel in my village has often recounted how he married a mermaid and learned from her tales of wild witchery known to Girth the Swineherd. A few, a very few, of the natives of Long Compton believed up to a few years ago that the stones of the Rollright Circle go down to the stream to drink on Midsummer Eve. But none now tell tales of the pranks of the Devil in disturbing the contours of the countryside. A little, a very little, of the colloquial vernacular survives. I have heard a close game of darts described as " tissicky," a witless fellow as " dummel " and a flashy female called a " bedizened dame," all within fifty miles of London. But the lingo of salty metaphor and sinewy turns of speech is nearly all gone. Mind and speech are no less mass-produced to-day than goods.

The peasant's shrewdness, realism, self-reliance, stability and dignity are still his, though his independence, and his natural good taste have been mortgaged. So his thrift. As Jefferies wrote of Roger the Reaper in *The Open Air*:

> " His cautious old father rendered frugal by forty years of labour, had done fairly well; the young man not at all. The old man, having a cottage, in a measure worked for his own hand. The young man (who had none) . . . scattered his money to the winds."

The social sense of the peasant barely survives except in that unconscious one of a shared being I mentioned above and in such odd and sometimes perverted ghost-appearances as in the story of the woman who cut a hole in the floor to hear and see what her neighbours below were doing. An admirable writer on Essex, R. A. Beckett, has suggested that " village gossip " is a survival of the peasant's communal mode of life. The labourer is still as hard-working as any peasant but, since he works no longer for his own or to achieve his own, there is a certain listlessness in all his labour. In culture, the decline is steep. Flora Thompson in *Lark Rise* has described how the solid old cottage furniture was supplanted by Victorian gimcrackery and most labourer's cottages that I know marvellously achieve snugness in the midst of superfluity.

Hardy has reflected the suppression of the village orchestras by the clergy in the story of the Mellstock Choir and William Barnes wrote the swan-song of musical England.

> " But now a bow do never screäpe
> A humstrum (viol) any where all round,
> An' zome can't tell a humstrum's sheäpe
> An' never heärd his jinglen sound."

Progress finished up with the German Band. Yet a few of the old memories lingered in the breasts of living men as late as the 'nineties of last century and, in one or two very rare instances, even later. Baring Bould in *Old Country Life* has described his personal acquaintance with a few of the old village bards or song-men, descendants of the mediaeval and Renaissance ballad-singers and minstrels. One of these, Richard Hard of Dartmoor, could sing as many as eighty of the traditional peasant songs and one of the Devon song-books records their passing:

> " I reckon the days is departed
> When folks ud a-listened to me;
> I feel like as one broken-hearted
> A-thinking of what used to be.

And I dunno as much is amended
Than was in them merry old times,
When wi' pipes and good ale, folks attended
To me and my purty old rhymes,
To me and my purty old rhymes."

I myself met one of these song-makers in an inn at Blockley, Gloucestershire, but he recited his own verses not sang the peasant ballads and these verses were what David Copperfield's Agnes might have been expected to have sung at her piano. I was just in time to catch a few of the songs the Campden cherry-pickers used to sing before they were supplanted by " Okay, Baby, is it you? " and its fellow urchins. The first verse of one ran :

" My feither died, and I cannot tell how :
He did leave me two hosses for to follow the plough;
With my wim-wam wommle, oh,
Jack sold the saddle, oh,
Blossie boy bubble, oh,
Under the moon."

Only in the cottage gardens with their almost uncanny rightness in choice of flowers and the blending of their colours is the peasant's instinctive sense of beauty unbroken by social and economic change. The common view that the labourer has no love of Nature because he does not say " I love Nature " is, of course, quite unfounded. Living with Nature, he very properly lacks the week-end attitude to Nature, and the word " picturesque " in the 18th century connotation of artificial ruins and landscape gardening, in the 19th or Dorothy Perkins sense or the 20th of the beauty spot, has no meaning for him.

The servility of the Lady Bountiful days has been outlived, though there is a record of labourers' children pulling their forelocks to a stranger as late as 1912. Gone, too, I think, are those wonderful mothers who used to bring up large families on ten or twelve shillings a week, one of whom is commemorated in Fred Kitchen's *Brother to the Ox*. The passionate, almost mystical, feeling for home, certainly a peasant virtue, survives in the face of the urbanization of the countryside, which, of course, weakens the ties of home-life by an attrition almost as severe as the education of the cottagers' children by urban standards and the skimming of the cream of the adult sons and daughters off the land. Consequently, the home-attachment is less strong than it was in the 19th century. Hudson gave many examples in *A Shepherd's Life* of widows and widowers missing the companions of their lives to very death.

Such curious lapses in good husbandry as dislike of double digging or bastard tranching is a labourer's failing, not a peasant's, but the piling of dung-heaps in the fallow for weeks at a time and the burning-off of haulm, squitch-grass and weeds are the farmers' fault rather than theirs. Their distrust of artificial manures, which is universal among them, though being slowly broken down, is altogether a peasant's virtue. To return to the soil what you take out of it is part of the Canon Law of husbandry to peasant and labourer alike. It is the tenant farmer, pressed by the urban view of science, business and government, not the labourer, who is succumbing to the vicious principles of replacing labour by machinery, dung, straw and compost

48   A Half-timber Cottage in Worcestershire, near Castlemoreton

49   A Half-timber Cottage in Shropshire, near Hopton Castle

50   Cotswold Cottages on Ebrington Hill, near Chipping Campden

51   Dorset Cottages at East Lulworth

by artificials. The picture of the old horsekeeper who cared for his team first, the land next, then his master and last of all himself, is now, as Lord Lymington has said, " disappearing in the fumes of petrol." This, no doubt, is a transference of the peasant's thought for the community and the land to the conditions of individualist farming.

V LABOURER'S HUMOUR

The peasant's humour most significantly reveals the unconscious nostalgia embedded within him. I am quite certain of this because, with a friend of mine, C. H. Gardiner, of the Evesham R.D.C., I once collected a great many contemporary specimens (most of them unpublished and never before written down) of the native humour of the western Midlands, properly classified under type-headings and commented upon piece by piece. Out of a score of such headings, at least half and every one of the stories contained in them are nostalgic, memorial or ironical in the remembrance of an ancient wrong. Half the book, that is to say, commemorates out of his own mouth the labourer's sub-conscious awareness of his peasant past—a sufficiently remarkable testimony to the complete futility of the idea of progress as applied to the class without whose aid the nation would perish. Half of these tales, taken down *verbatim*, confess a shadow-world for which the labourer pines, though only rarely does he know it and even the other half, largely taken from the younger generation and sometimes infected with urban slickness, are full of indications of the old peasant ethos.

A dozen or more of these tales are local variations to a universal theme, the reversed epic of the super-simplicities either of the next village or one to which your own has been heraldically opposed, so to speak, " tyme out of mind." Our collection is confined to the rivalry between Chipping Campden and Ebrington (" Yubberton ") but, as Shakespeare's use of rustic humou suggests, this oral jest-book is normal mythological currency in a great many other villages. These inter-village tournaments of ridicule date from the pre-Enclosure period when every village was a little kingdom or self-sufficient commonwealth of its own and the next village was a foreign country. This intense localism had its seamy side, but it was a far, far better thing than cosmopolitanism, with its rancorous sameness and virulently combative standardization. Even when on Dover's Hill in the North Cotswolds, it used to take the form of shin-kicking contests. Ten years ago, I used to take snuff with one of the warriors of the old battles " when Broddy fowt Kyanden." He told me one of his friends used to " thrape " his shins every evening with a coal-hammer in order to keep him in training. These brutalities and the old boxing matches with them reveal, I think, the coarsening effect of the Industrial Revolution upon the old traditions where they were not destroyed. Certainly, that was the fate of Dover's Hill, once Captain Dover's playground, and then the meeting-place of Brummagem racing touts and riff-raff.

These " merry conceited " *corporate* jests of Jack-on-the-Green were handed down to the labourers before he died and are remembered to this day. They show a real power of dramatization contained in the utmost economy of phrase, obviously a traditional inheritance from the times when telling stories and fairy tales developed a high technique as a mode of social intercourse. New stories are, of course, improvised to suit occasions and

79

grafted upon the old stock. Of one such my friend was the victim. In the company of three labourers he had seen Bill Booker at work, the champion breast-ploughman of Yubberton, with an implement as primitive and unwieldy as the Hebridean *caschrom*:

"Now, that's mortal queer," said one of them, "he hant got his bucket o' water with him." "What on earth would he want with that?" ".Well, he allus gets the blade red-hot."

Of course, the life of all these stories is in the spoken word—the intonations, inflections, pauses, the facial expressions, the rhythm and flavour of the old idiom, and to read them is like eating jam instead of the ripe fruit. "Extravagant Humour" is another heading closely allied to the last, the Goliath story, the touch of the marvellous, and the next heading, "Old Time Stories," is a different brand of the same *genre*. Here is one of them that illustrates the revenge of the tortoise over the hare, the country over the town and of an ancient culture in ruins over the barbarism that has overcome it:

"There was a motor mon as took the wrong turnin' up on they hills, and a-moidered he was how to mend his ways. So he comes into a rickyard where old Jim was a-pitching dung into a kyart. 'Hi, you!' starts he a-kyelpin to old Jim, 'What's the way to Cheltenham?' 'Doant know, Master,' says old Jim, peaceable-like. Off guz the motor mon to tun this kyar and as savage as a wild kyat he was and a-callin' old Jim all the fools he could think of. Arter a bit he tuns his kyar and sets off down that dommed old rutty lane. Just then he hears some covey a-hollerin' at his back and, a-twistin' round his yud, he sees another old mon a-standin' nigh old Jim. So wobblin' and whimmin', back he guz to the rickyard and shouts out, 'Well?' Old Jim jerks his thumb at the tother covey and, 'Jarge,' sez he, solemn-like, 'Jarge, zur, doant know neither'."

"Moidered," in the sense of bothered or perplexed, was used by Charles Lamb in a letter to Coleridge of October 17, 1796.

Folk-tales are another section and one I quote here (though I have already published it in another book), partly because it is very short, as the others are not, and partly because it is deeper in antiquity than any other I have personally heard:

"There was four men and a donkey up by Condicote afore these times, when the roads hadnt bin made proper. On Sunday, so as they might have grace, they sets out to gu to church, but not knowing where the church was, they telled the old donkey to find 'un hisself, so off he guz and they traipsed arter him. Sure to be! that donkey stops to nibble a bit o' clover here or some keck over there, but at last they comes to the church. When a main Sundays had gone by, a reglar path was marked, and 'tis due to that okkard old donkey as the roads up on they hills be so desperate twisty."

Keck is Shakespeare's "kecksies" or wild parsley. "So as they might have grace" is peasant religion; the "four men" are doubtless Matthew, Mark, Luke and John and the story is a mediaeval rationalization of the pagan past. A more remarkable example of the tenacity of folk-memory I have never heard. The tale of the okkard old donkey is the tale of the making of England, and so "antiquitates antiquity."

Two last ones reveal in a flash the whole history of the farm-labourer, fined down to the utmost limit of brevity and homeliness:

THE IRONICAL LABOURER

" Old Lord—be a crotchety old codger and so mean as he'd skin a stwun (stone). Tother day he ketchud up with old Willium as works on his estate, a-mombling across the dairy-ground, come day, go day, God send Sunday like. ' Cant ye walk faster than that, my man ? ' snaps he to Willium. ' Sir Lord,' sez Willium, ' I be walking at twelve bob a wik rate.' "

" Come day, go day, God send Sunday " is a country term widely distributed in the South and Midlands. The second :

" Some little 'uns be carny young 'urks. One Thursday dinner—and that be the wrong day of the wik for any vittle except taters or turnups—all the young 'uns had yut their dinner and done their proper duty and said, 'Thank God for a good dinner, Amen,' except young Arthur as was six. 'Ent you a-going to thank God for your good dinner ? ' said his mother. ' Not to-day, our mum,' sez the little 'un.' ' Indeed an you will, I hopes,' sez she. ' I shaunt then,' sez the little bwoy, ' Cos it was only taters and a diddley dwop o' gravy and no pudden and that bent worth thanken nobody for.' "

Thursday's dinner was not a fast (to balance a feast) by church discipline nor indigestion but the necessity of the wages bill. Old farm-labourers have told me that in the 'seventies (when farming was booming), they lived on bread and black treacle or potatoes alone. Notable in these stories is the craftsmanly skill in handling a narrative. The humour of the labourer, indeed, is largely defensive and ironical, so much so that it is nearly always mistaken by the townsman for *naïveté*. I could give many examples of this. Among the older men, it is the harking back to the times before the land was " took in " that is unconscious, not the humour :

" I was born at Yubberton, so a Yubberton Yawny (simpleton) I be; and folks be allus a-kyankering about what fools we be. They say as we mucked the tower to make he grow, as we hurdled the field to pen the cuckoo in, as we kyarred the wheelbarrow round and round for fear the wheel should bruise the ground, and likewise as we put the pig on the wall to see the band go by. Yes, they thinks we be fools—but be we? "

The labourer has lost his land, his culture, his social life, his patterns of play and his religion, but not his character and his sense.

VI   ABOLISH THE LABOURER

There is only one thing to be done with the agricultural labourer and that is to abolish him. His is an anomalous position—locked to the land without having any share in it. There should not be a single labourer in England who does not either cultivate a piece of land of his own or another's as initiation for his own. That, of course, does not mean an allotment hired from the Council. That should be the townsman's respite and refreshment from a very different type of work. The agricultural labourer does not want (quite legitimately) to take up agricultural labour after agricultural labour unless it means looking after his own, feeding his pig, milking his cow or digging his garden. In no other way, which is not the way of high wages, can the drift from the land be stemmed. In spite of his love for the land, the labourer will not stay on it for money alone, but only for the love of his own, which was the property of his forefathers. His workmanship and integrity will, in a saner England, fulfil a dual purpose. He will act as a filter to correct our excess of urbanism and as a check upon that looting of the land which is, through science and commercialism, turning farm into firm.

Chapter V

THE SQUIRE

I THE LORD OF THE MANOR

In the previous survey of the major figures in organic relation with the English countryside, the tragedy has unfolded itself on fairly broad and simple lines. The forces promoting development from within and those brusquely interrupting it from without (called Progress) are more or less clearly defined, while the conflict between external power and inward stability has produced certain results that can be studied without undue perplexity. With the entry of the Squire upon the scene, the spectator is presented with an internal tragedy much more complex and enigmatic than that of his associates in the same English field. The Peasant appears, plays his part and is destroyed, all but a remnant, by an enemy who represents something utterly different from the peasant values; the Squire appears, plays his part and destroys himself through the very act of his greatest triumph. His enemy was from within and his history from past to present has, therefore, an element of paradox lacking to the annals of the lesser members in the rural hierarchy. The peasant drama is like an old Morality with the wrong ending; the squire drama is more like King Lear (with a touch of Macbeth) in which the hero himself plays the fool or the villain and so betrays himself to the all but total loss of his kingdom. It may be that he has not received a wound that is quite mortal; what cannot be doubted is that in his headlong pursuit of wealth and dominion he exposed his own breast to it. It is this paradox of the squirearchy that has been largely missed both by its defenders and its assailants.

To begin with, he changes twice into somebody different—from the lord of the manor to the squire and from the squire to the landlord, terms which, though rarely distinguished, do mean different things, even though the actor changes from one character to the other out of the spectator's eye. The lord of the manor was definitely a feudatory of the king, as his customary tenants were feudatories of him. Secular land was king's land and it would probably have been a great deal better for the peasants if it had remained so. Magna Carta, which saw the struggle between King and Baronage decided in favour of the latter, was by no means a charter of liberty for commoners. So long as the lord held his land and its vills in fief and in trust from the king, his position as a military conqueror in control of the once free vills could not be an absolutist one. So long, too, as the right and means to fix and control the average price-level in all commodities commonly exchanged was the king's prerogative, speculation in land values with its reactions upon rents and prices was frozen at the source. It is one of the curious paradoxes of history that when the second of the Tudors broke his land-trust and specu-lated in the monastic lands, he enriched and empowered the old enemy of the monarchy—the nobility—at the expense of the monarchy and thereby opened the way for Squire Cromwell to cut off the head of the second of the Stuarts who succeeded the Tudors.

That the monarchy did act as a check upon the exactions of the baronage is dramatically revealed by the relation of Richard II to the commoners in the Peasants' Revolt. He was forced to break his pledge by the Parliament representing the lords. Tenure by military service was thus a form of trusteeship (though by no means the best form) which prevented the undue exploitation of the peasantry. To be men of the king, who granted charters, kept the peace and safeguarded customary rights, obviously advantaged the rural community more than to be lord's men only. History indeed has proved it to be so. It was not a king who destroyed the peasantry but a Parliament of squires which had stripped the king of his prerogatives in money and in land.

But if the top of the pyramid held the middle in place by feudal obligation, the broad base of it exercised a gravitational pressure no less strong. By holding strips in the common fields and lots in the hay-meadows, the lord of the manor played an integral part in the peasant economy. Now and again he went even further and identified himself with his peasants even to the sacrifice of his life for them. Roger Bacon of Baconsthorpe, who led the Norfolk Rising of 1381 with Geoffrey Lytster the dyer and attacked the lawyers and profiteers on their behalf, should not be forgotten in a just chronicle of the historic squire. His very home-farm was only an outsize socman's and yeoman's close, so that to break up that economy, as the 18th and 19th century squires did, was contrary to the whole nature of land-tenure. Montague Fordham, indeed, asserts that the Saxon thegns actually were peasants replaced at the Conquest by foreign aristocrats less restrained by customary usages. Thus, the lord may be called simply a development of the head man of the village who certainly had less power than he. Boon-days, when the village turned out for harvest on the demesne, were, as R. A. Beckett reminds us, of old called "love-benes," while the chief harvester of recent days was called "the lord." This looks as though the original lord was nothing more than the village leader. The whole history of the squire is his adherence to or betrayal of this principle. What encroachments the lords did make by the Statutes of Merton (1236) and Westminster (1285) were upon the vaguely defined wastes or sheepwalks and even here they were limited in the number of their sheep that could be turned on them. Having himself become or wedged himself in as the keystone of the arch, the lord could not displace any of the pier-stones, that is to say, remove them by arbitrary enclosure, without tumbling the whole edifice.

II MANOR INTO ESTATE
(The Pastons into Sir Giles Overreach)

This sovereign fact suggests the extension of the well-worn term *adscriptus glebae* as applied to the villein to include the lord himself. I do not mean that he was a good cultivator like many of the later squires. There is precious little evidence that the lords took any but the most perfunctory interest in husbandry, and the example of the Earl of Berkeley who went to all the local markets himself and fished out his corn-samples in leathern bags from the recesses of his walking ironmongery, or of Edward II who was a horse-breeder and expert thatcher, were no doubt exceptions. For the lord hunting and hawking, tournaments, private feuds, civil war, the Crusades, travel and adventure, politics, the founding and endowment of religious

THE ENGLISH COUNTRYMAN

houses, litigation, match-making and marriage settlements, even reading
(did not Sir John Paston sit in his great hall absorbed in Chaucer?) took
precedence of agriculture, the province of the monks.

Yet the Paston Letters do reveal the domestic interior, if comfortless, of
the armoured castle and the details of household administration supplied by
Margaret Paston to her husband, if at times tedious to us (who were never
expected to read them), were plainly not so to him and his like. Sir John
Fastolf, the Pastons of Caistor (stones from the Roman wall in the citadel
of the Iceni helped to build both the church and the castle) and their knightly
fellows hardly exhibit the romantic and chivalrous qualities that the word
" knighthood " not only infers but embodies in Chaucer's Knight and a
thousand mediaeval romances, the lofty even starry ideal of " noblesse
oblige." Possessiveness is perhaps the word that best fits the Paston Letters,
and if it hardens into putting daughters up in the market and having no
truck with their hearts quite as though Trollope were a mediaeval chronicler,
yet this word by no means bears the same meaning as " enterprise "
invidiously assumed four centuries later. It is this sense of property which
distinguishes the lord as revealed by the Paston Letters, a sense that may
shade off into " covetise " or brighten into paternal responsibility but is the
lord's translation of *adscriptus glebae*.

On the other hand, Chaucer's red-faced and white-bearded Franklin, a
man of wealth, a knight of the shire, a sheriff and " lord and sire of sessions,"
is not quite the same type as the Pastons. He is clearly an early draft of the
lesser country squire (his original is presumed to have been Sir John Bussey
of Kesteven) and he is rather derisively presented as " Epicurus onely sone."
His house snowed meat and drink, his open table was always laid and St
Julian, the saint of hospitality, was his patron. Is not this good trencherman
and sack-lover a forecast of Lady Mary Wortley Montague's squire (quoted
by Mr Walbank in *The English Scene*) who believed

" the Greek wines less delicious than March beer, and the beccafiguas of
Italy as not so well tasted as a rump of beef? "

Of one thing we may be sure. The Franklin's house may not have differed
much from John Aubrey's description of the lord of the manor's:

" a great open hall, a kitchen and a buttery, a parlour over which a
chamber for my lord and lady, all the rest lye in common, viz. the men-
servants in the hall (the women in a common room) or oriele, the folk at the
side-tables."

But the Franklin's " folk " in the hall were certainly not retainers but the
villagers.

If Domesday Book be read with an open mind, it must be remarked how
meticulous are the descriptions of manor after manor. The same is true
of all mediaeval documents relating to land. It is as though every grass in
the field were numbered and this peculiar minuteness is lacking from 18th
and 19th century surveys of big estates.* It is true that the mediaeval lords
possessed great estates, but these great estates were multiplications of little
ones in different places, not additions of field to field in one place. The
great lord was master of many manors, not of a Manor. The mediaeval
manor was about as big, to quote a letter of Dr Marett's to me:

* *Their* elaboration is in legal detail and its jargon.

84

THE LITTLE ESTATE

" as would feed a kestrel and, in fact, come within the sweep of his eye. My oldest papers—round about 1400—recite the boundaries and features of a virgate or two of ploughland with perhaps a spinney thrown in or a splash of marsh."

This is the " fine and private place," one's own particular star, and this is the true meaning of the word " bucolic," which the Franklin was and the lesser squires were in the long line of them that succeeded him. We who think in the large and quantitatively naturally attach a derogatory meaning to " bucolic." But it is in the grain that the world is seen or, to use Dr Marett's own expressive imagery, " you can see the whole sky reflected in the raindrop." I do not mean that the Franklin and his descendants regarded the temporal home-patch as a key to the eternal but that their small-scale territorialism was the root of right living. And it is interesting to note how this love of the little place has actually survived into our own day. Three years ago, I had a letter from an English squire in Brittany who described to me with enthusiasm every detail of the crafts and husbandry of his little estate (including basket-making with honeysuckle stems), which was self-contained in all particulars. Lord Innes of Learney wrote telling me about the simplicities and tenantry care of his kinsmen in Normandy on their small estates and in their little manors, and so, he told me, it had been since the days of Duke William. The cosmopolitan outlook which the 18th-century landlords were to acquire was contrary to that wholeness which the home-sense assured, the wholeness " contracted to a span " in which the eternal chooses to reveal itself rather than to those of " great possessions." The difference between the baron and the franklin was that the former was a franklin several times over, between the landlord and the franklin that he was a franklin too big for his boots.

Since the lord was bound to the village community, he inevitably assumed that position of personal leadership within it which *is* the contribution of squiredom to English country life. The bloody-minded baron (as Tawney has truly pointed out) was thus, even when he sweated his tenants, a milder master to them than " the rhapsodist at the court of Gloreana," or a figure like Lord Bathurst of Cirencester Park, Pope's patron, whose Arcadian groves and vistas, whose statuary and parterres, were laid out on the ruin of villages and the eviction of their villagers. The whole of the squire's history lies in his fidelity or treachery to that leadership, and the chivalric ideal must have fructified it, even when it failed in the quest of far horizons to begin at home. Consequently, the commutation of forced services into rent, while restoring his personal freedom to the villein, yet, by making the lord a rent-receiver on the principle of " stock and land lease," and an employer of hired labour only, it tended to loosen his attachment to the personnel of the manor.*

The 15th century was like a St Martin's Summer that presaged spring. The great gale of the Peasants' Revolt was passed; villeinage was at an end; the demand for wool was supplied by a multitude of peasant proprietors; their economy had become much more elastic; enclosure by consent and bargaining with the lord was bringing initiative and experiment into hus-

* " The fundamental character of feudalism is to be found in the principle that it was a system of mutual and fixed obligation," *Mediaeval Political Theory*—R. N. and A. J. Carlyle, Vol 5, p. 99.

bandry and capitalist farming with its loosing of the acquisitive and competitive spirit was not yet. In the south of England, 112 customary tenants
on six manors kept 7,440 sheep. It was these sheep, the mildest mannered
of all quadrupeds, that were to bring the wolf into the English fold, to change
the meaning of land from subsistence into investment and the lord of the
manor into the squire.

How revolutionary was the mutation of the Tudor Enclosures is best
illustrated by Eileen Power's remarkable description in *The Wool Trade in
English Mediaeval History* of the attempt of the financial speculators, given
their opportunity by the Hundred Years' War, to corner the export wool
market, force up prices, upset the Guild principle of " the just price " and,
incidentally, ruin the peasant producers. The attempt was for the time being
successful, and men like William Cade, William de la Pole and Gilbert of
Chesterton (!) became the earliest magnates of money rather than of land,
the first of them building Stokesay Castle as a new financial and so no longer
feudal fortress. But all classes concerned with the wool trade, the king, the
peasants, the guilds, the squireens *and* the big landowners united against
them. The financial conspirators were defeated, went bankrupt or were
imprisoned. The later staplers of the burgher and merchant class who
built Grevel's house at Chipping Campden and Paycocke's at Coggeshall
were traders of modest means and moderate powers. The English climate
was not yet favourable to the growth of the money-power and the part
played by the lords of the manor in suppressing it is of supreme interest.

But the merchants took their revenge in the 16th century by founding a
new landed gentry which disintegrated the personal bond between landlord
and tenant. Now for the first time the great estate is seen as the battering
ram, no longer as the buttress or the protecting shield of the peasant society
and the anarch who breaches the continuity and interrupts the development
of the English tradition is the king. Just as the Hundred and Manorial
Courts supplanted the Open Assembly of the village community, so the
door was now open for the J.P. to preside from without and not within the
rural structure. In both instances, the step was retrogressive from local
and democratic self-government towards autocratic centralization, while
the Dissolution both of the Monasteries and the Guilds of the country towns
marked a shifting of the balance of power from the country to the town.
The new squirearchy was recruited from courtiers, members of the Privy
Council, City of London merchants and land speculators whose rapacity and
contempt for customary rights earned them the name of " caterpillars of the
Commonwealth." There can be no doubt that the true reason for the failure
of government legislation against the Tudor Enclosures of arable common
land into sheepwalks was its administration by the new gentlemen themselves. " What is Government? " wrote St Thomas More of them. " A
certein conspiracy of riche men procureinge theire own commodities under
the name and title of a Common Wealth." Land changed hands almost
as rapidly as bonds on the Stock Exchange, so that gambling in acres was
accompanied by rack-renting and an absentee landlordism. Indeed, it is
interesting to note how intimately gambling was allied with enclosure. The
newly enclosed land in the 18th and 19th centuries was in many instances
a reimbursement by higher rentals for gambling losses at Brooks's and
White's, while the 19th-century tenant farmers gambled in the land itself.

BUILDING BESS

That the new rich who inoculated the countryside with the commercial spirit, to be championed in the next century by the Puritans, were seldom the old manorial lords is attested by example after example. Naboths like Stump of Malmesbury who sacked the great library where William of Malmesbury had worked, like Philip Massinger's Sir Giles Overreach, were parvenus to whom the rural tradition was merely an impediment to self-advancement. Sir Anthony Kingston, who appointed Hangman's Acre near Painswick, the home-town of the celebrated home-carvers of the region, to commemorate his savage suppression of the anti-enclosure riots on his new estate, was nothing but a vulgar butcher. The Fettiplaces of Swynbrook on the Lower Windrush are a nayword to this day for adding manor to manor, park to park, and chase to chase. Sir Thomas Audley of Audley End, grandfather to the Earl of Suffolk, made a name for himself by rapacity,

An Elizabethan Squire

craft and sycophancy. His mean squabble with Cromwell for St Osyth reads like a scrap between a jackal and a hyaena for a disputed prey.

Building Bess of Hardwick, Countess of Shrewsbury, who built Hardwick Hall, Bolsover, Worksop and Oldcote, may serve as a symbol of the more predatory type of Tudor squire. It was said of her:

" She was proud, furious, selfish and unfeeling, a builder, a buyer and a seller of estates, a money-lender, a farmer and a merchant of lead, coals and timber. She kept close accounts and was a terror to her servants."

She married four husbands mainly, it seems, as a means to winning her estates and satisfying her extraordinary passion for building. At the same time, her almost pathological possessiveness links her with the Pastons, and she had a streak of that creative power that was peculiarly Elizabethan. Living till she was ninety and building, building, building like a beaver, she also explains to us something of the dominance and beauty of the more portentous Tudor mansion, while her rough robustious energy and mettle-someness carry her forward to the Georgian two- and three-bottle squires. Once she wrote to her steward:

87

THE ENGLISH COUNTRYMAN

" Let the weaver make beer for me forthwith, for my own drinking and your master's; and see that I have good store of it, for if I lack either good beer or good charcoal or wood, I will blame nobody so much as I do you."

Is not this the voice of Squire Western in *Tom Jones*?
It cannot be said of others of the Tudor land-grabbers that they possessed even the saving grace of strong character. Sir Francis Englefield of Wootton Bassett, who jocketed the villagers out of 100 acres of common by fraud and lawsuits might have been the living model of the Upstart Countrey Knight in John Earle's *Microcosmography* (1628)—" A Justice of the Peace hee is to domineere in his Parish and doe his neighbour wrong with more right." But the infection of gain-getting also caught some of the older families. John Leland wrote that the Duke of Buckingham at Thornbury " took very much fair ground, very fruitful of corne, now fair land for coursing." The Duke of Norfolk enclosed forty-four acres because he did not like the shape of his park, while the enclosure of Attleborough Common raised the Kett Rebellion. The account of how Winchcombe's Benedictine Abbey, the last of whose Abbots was a correspondent of Colet's, was literally razed to the ground to build Sudeley Castle, suggests a banditry looting the countryside rather than a royally sanctioned and legalized change of ownership from clerical to secular hands. And that it really was an explosion of brigandage touched off by the royal incendiary, of moneyed rebels who " dispopulated and overthrew whole townes," even the Whig historians were unable to cover up.

It is, however, the fashionable habit of modern agricultural historians to discover a subtle difference between the Tudor and the Georgian Enclosures, as though imperious greed grew more civilized as he grew older, as though there were some essential difference between the grasping Tudor and Cobbett's landed stock-jobber in *Rural Rides* and Peacock's Ebenezer Mac Crotchet, Esquire, in *Crotchet Castle*:

" He found it essential to his dignity to furnish himself with a coat of arms, which, after the proper ceremonies (payment being the principal), he obtained, videlicet: Crest, a crotchet rampant in A sharp: Arms, three empty bladders turgescent, to show how opinions are formed; three bags of gold, pendant, to show why they are maintained; three naked swords, trenchant, to show how they are administered; and three barber's blocks, gaspant, to show how they are swallowed."

A difference there is. The later and latest imitators of the Tudors are more covetous but more respectable.

III   THE RESIDENT GENTRY

Nevertheless, only one-fifth of the Tudor land was thus despoiled, and out of the desolation rose such proud and ornate piles as Montacute, Compton Winyates and their peers. That they could compensate for the loss of the guilds, the hospitals, the schools, of monasteries, abbeys, chapels, priories and sanctuaries that glorified the face of the land whatever the laxness of their inmates, of social welfare, of continuity, of development from within, of a free peasantry, of order and security in the rural structure and even of the arts of husbandry as practised by the Cistercians, only a partisan could

CHARACTER AND ACRES

claim. Give the partisan rope, and still a bad precedent has interposed itself between the lord's leadership and his responsibility for the little commonwealths he ruled.

In the severing of many of the strands of the social mesh, leaving frayed edges that promised to become unravelled for the future, it is pleasant to dwell for a moment upon the all but seamless continuity of the de Veres of Castle Hedingham in Essex, built by Alberic de Vere, the Conqueror's liegeman, with a monastery beside it, itself granted to a de Vere at the Dissolution and sold by yet another de Vere, the 17th Earl of Oxford, to Roger Harlackenden fifty years later, himself the descendant of the original de Vere's esquire and the forefather of John Addington Symonds. Here is a rootedness, a golden wedlock with the genius of place, that has a virtue of its own. To belong to a parcel of English earth like that is surely to absorb something of its goodness into family bones. And a family thus intimate with its native acres receives a patent of nobility from time itself and cannot but gather the thoughts, the habits, the particular local expression of its tenantry into its safe-keeping as the reaper gathers the wide-scattered corn into stack or barn. A familiarity with place and people like this may shape itself into a representation as telling, and sometimes even more so, than that of election.

This faithfully regional squire certainly does make an impressive appearance during the 17th and 18th centuries, and the varieties of that appearance lay stress upon that individuality which used to be one of the chiefest glories of the English nation. It is one of the most singular aberrations of English history that in its latest hour the nation should have entrusted its destinies to and deeply imperilled its liberties at the hands of anonymous committees, when its traditional contribution to the annals of the world is so emphatically one of individuals. No class in the community has poured out greater abundance in richness of individuality than have the squires. From the vast field of graves, ant-heaps and petrol dumps which is the modern world, it is something more than a refreshment to look back into the diversity and luxuriance, if it be sometimes rank, of the age of the squires. It is also a reminder that the national character has flowered from the roots of the peasant's co-operation, the yeoman's independence, the craftsman's creative work, the devotion of the saints and poets and the squire's sense of personal being drawing its nourishment each from a particular soil.

To the treasure of the county family the gracious tender piety of George Herbert and the baroque eccentricity of Beckford have both contributed. The genial simplicity and dutifulness of Sir Roger de Coverley do not exclude from the common fund the fantastic egoism of Lord Herbert of Cherbury. The stilted Squire Allworthy subscribes to it with his companion, bawdy, tempestuous, mole-eyed, choleric, two-bottle Squire Western. Tony Lumpkin (or Bumpkin) is of the same fraternity as Lucius Cary, Viscount Falkland of Great Tew, in himself the mellowed meditative autumn of the old Renaissance culture shattered by the Puritan Revolution. Squire Somervile (1677–1742), the poet-sportsman who wrote *The Chase*, was in his way two men in one, the reflective appraiser of husbandly plenty and the boisterous hallooer after hounds. The patrician crusader, Scawen Blunt, who cherished his own acres without forgetting the wrongs of distant peoples,

12   89

who saw no disunion between good husbandry and good letters, he also is of the company, though born too late. He is with Sackville, Surrey, Dorset, Fulke Greville, Sir Thomas Wyatt, Sir James Harrington, Sir Thomas Overbury, Sir Kenelm Digby, William Habington, Francis Quarles, the Lytes of Lyte Cary where learning and studious habits seemed to be hereditary, Sir Francis Kynaston of Shropshire, lyrist of charming impassioned oddities and Sir Thomas Urquhart of Cromarty, the translator of Rabelais. Perhaps the most significant of the 17th-century squires in the unfolding of this chronicle is Sir Richard Fanshawe, who wrote the *Ode upon Occasion of His Majesties Proclamation in the Year 1630, Commanding the Gentry to reside upon their Estates in the Countrey*:

> " Yet we, as if some Foe were here,
>   Leave the despised Fields to Clowns,
>   And come to save ourselves as 'twere
>   In walled Towns.

> .   .   .   .   .

> " Nor let the Gentrey grudge to go
>   Into those places whence they grew,
>   But think them blest they may do so,
>   Who would pursue

> " The smoky glory of the Town,
>   That may go till his native Earth,
>   And by the shining Fire sit down
>   Of his own hearth.

> .   .   .   .   .

> " Believe me Ladies you will find
>   In that sweet life, more solid joyes,
>   More true contentment to the mind
>   Than all Town-toys."

Here is a squire who was a conscious and articulate ruralist.

From the particular point of view of our survey, the name of Captain Dover, the " jovialist," is of significance. He it was who revived the Cotswold Games on Dover's Hill, a spur of the north-western Cotswolds. In his honour and that of Endymion Porter, his coadjutor, *Annalia Dubrensia* was written, a book of poems by Drayton, Heywood, Randolph, Davenant, Ben Jonson and the local bard, Francis Izod, a Cotswold name still surviving. This was a remarkable thing to happen: why should these illustrious poets who had no particular associations with the Cotswolds have written a miscellany to the renown of a local squire who organized sports, dances, pastimes and competitions on a hill in Gloucestershire? First, because the Games were very elaborate and splendid; second, because, as we gather from the Account Book of the Weston Subedge village community, they were traditional and dateless in antiquity. But the Tudor Enclosures put them out of action and what Captain Dover did was to resuscitate them.

From my own scrutiny and consultations with my friend, Rolf Gardiner, I am fairly certain that he did more than this. The Cotswold Morris Dancers from Bampton in the Upper Thames Basin to Adderbury in the east and Ilmington in the north-west executed highly symbolic and intricate figures in their performances which were quite different from those of

52   Grevel's House, Chipping Campden

53   Paycocks, Coggeshall, Essex

54   A Mediaeval Manor-house : Great Chalfield, Wiltshire, built by Thomas
Tropenell in 1490

55   The Hall at Great Chalfield
(Both from drawings by J. C. Buckler)

THE RESIDENT GENTRY

the Yorkshire Morris and Sword Dancers. At the same time, they were
extremely old. One village, for instance, took with the troupe on its travels
to neighbouring villages a virgin, *virgo intacta*, and if any man laid a finger
on her, even by accident, he was fined half a crown. Another troupe took
a lamb with them and on the return home it was killed and eaten at a feast
or, in other words, it was sacrificed. Originally, in fact, they were fertility
dances or rather rituals, and Dover's Hill is the site of a Celtic earthwork.
But they were also variants obviously derived from a common source, and it
is highly probable that Captain Dover recreated these dances in a new and
more complex form, each village dancing its own version of the Dover's
Hill original. I also discovered that Rolf Gardiner's own version of the
Plough Monday ceremonial on his estate near Shaftesbury (in which the
surrounding villages take part) is almost precisely the same as Henry Best's
Plough Monday celebrations on his Yorkshire Farm (see p. 15). Here we
have two squires with three centuries between them restoring and replenishing a tradition more ancient than Christianity. To them I add with piety
the name of William Sheldon of Barcheston in Shakespeare's country, who,
marrying the daughter of a wealthy wool merchant and acquiring thereby
the manor and mill, set up the famous Barcheston tapestry looms under the
direction of the master-craftsman, Richard Hyckes (see p. 58). He is an
example of the Tudor new rich who glorified the very best tradition of the
resident native gentry in the face of the predatory self-interest of his fellow
squirearchs in the 16th century. This is leadership recharging the old
village culture with new life, a true functional regionalism.

Horsed or in the study, the record of the resident country gentleman is
not of one who sat upon his acres like a miser over his gold. The dynamism
and forcefulness of the English squirehood, that took such prodigality of
forms and was finally to outrun itself in an ambition divorced from responsibility, are well expressed in the figures of Squire Cromwell and Squire
Hampden. It is one of the paradoxes of history that the men who played
so large a part in energizing a movement which was to separate ethics from
economics and to let loose that commercial self-interest that deprived the
craftsman of the interest in and worth of his work and the peasant of his
fields and recreations, should have been associated in the public mind with
the cause of English liberties. Dictator Cromwell and Hampden (whom his
fellow-squire, Falkland, spoke of as " full of pride, violence and acrimony of
spirit ") were indeed the precursors of that individualism or freedom *from*
ethics in business which in the 19th and latter part of the 18th centuries
was to tempt the individuality of the squire to overreach itself.

The squirearchy's force of character is indeed impressed upon its very
houses, together with that " noblesse oblige " which lends such grace and
dignity to the countryside to which they belong. Though a little withdrawn
from it, they endow it with an aristocratic quality without dominating it.
Great Chalfield Manor in north-west Wiltshire, built by Thomas Tropenell
in 1490, with its grouping of farm, chapel, manor, mill, bartons and outbuildings, exquisitely shuffled together about a little flagged courtyard and
surrounded by a little moat, with its tall square chimneys, wide gables,
delicate oriels, crocketed belfry (to the chapel), great porches to the barns,
carved finials at the ends of the broken façade, let Great Chalfield Manor
in its radiant though reticent beauty stand as a concrete symbol of an ideal

91

squirehood, so perfectly beautiful and moving it is embossed upon the fields and woods. Many others I call to mind, not quite its equal in sheer English-ness and loveliness, but each the secular moon to its portion of English earth as the parish church is the sacred sun to the English village. These regionally faithful modest country houses, the more personable from their very restraint, are a world away from the Palladian mansion whose bleak spacious-ness, urban and foreign style and " air of cold command " no longer yield to the countryside. Something has happened between Great Chalfield, the smaller regional country houses, whether Gothic or Renaissance, and the stately secular fanes of a new hauteur and mastership.

But Great Chalfield and its kin, do they not render into architectural terms that significant tribute of Cobbett to :

> " the resident native gentry, attached to the soil, known to every farmer and labourer from their childhood, frequently mixing with them in those pursuits where all artificial distinctions are lost, practising hospitality without ceremony, from habit and not in calculation."

These are the words of *Cobbett*, the champion of the dispossessed peasantry, and there is a remarkable resemblance to them in the tribute of another great and honourable yeoman who also defended the peasantry, Thomas Bewick :

> " These cottagers were of an honest and independent character, while at the same time they held the neighbouring gentry in the greatest estimation and respect; and these again, in return, did not overlook them, but were interested in knowing that they were happy and well."

And Bewick's and Cobbett's resident gentry were doubtless descendants in way of life of Sir Thomas Overbury's country gentleman :

> " His travell is seldom beyond the next market towne and his inquisition is about the price of corne. . . . Nothing under a *sub poena* can draw him to London."

Even in the higher ranks of the squirearchy, there are notable instances of the same spirit, the Earl of Winchelsea in the 18th and the Earl of Devon in the 19th centuries, he who (the tale is told by Baring Gould), seeing Moggeridge the yeoman walking along, called out to him :

> " Cousin, jump into the carriage with me, and let us have a drive together; we have not met for 180 years."

In her historical novel about the Enclosures, *Green Acres*, Doreen Wallace wrote :

> " There has always been among the English upper classes a small propor-tion of men of conscience, men who are not content to accept the world as a pleasure garden given to them because they are the favoured children of God, but who ask themselves why all God's children are not treated alike."

Frequent intermarriage between gentry and yeomanry (see Chapter II) has been substantiated by court rolls and parish registers. The decline of the county families has thus a double explanation, their own fault and their own virtue, their power *libido* and their fellowship with the sons of the soil. Which is it in the numerous examples of the first who became the last?

92

FROM KING TO COBBLER

The Norman Glanvilles of Whitchurch contracted marriages with tanners and blacksmiths; the Courtenays of Molland became yeomen. The Coryndons of Clovelly survived in a baker, a tailor and a wheelwright who very properly signed himself " gentleman." The great Russell family became represented by small country workers and professional men. In my own neighbourhood, there are Tippings now labourers and thatchers whose ancestors are figured on pompous Renaissance tombs in the parish church and in countless instances the farm-labourer called Durbeyfield was once a knight called D'Urbeville. But what need of this handful of examples when the great-great-grandson of Margaret Plantagenet was in 1637 a cobbler of Newport? *

Sometimes, this process of levelling down or levelling up was due (according to Baring Gould) to servants taking their masters' names (one of Pepys's is a case in point), but this ancient habit can only account for a small proportion of the total. No male descendant of the barons who signed Magna Carta has for these many years sat in the House of Lords.

" I have reason to believe," says an old writer, " that some who justly own the surnames and blood of Bohuns, Mortimers and Plantagenets—though ignorant of their own extraction—are hid in the heap of common people, where they find that under a thatched cottage what some of their ancestors could not enjoy in a leaded castle—contentment with quiet and security."

" Where is Mowbray, where is Mortimer? " What were the dark reasons—the Black Death, the feud and vendetta, the law of attainder, the Wars of the Roses, the Civil War, the '45, the gambling table, the ballot, the aggrandizement of merchants and court sycophants, the corrosive of money? What are all these reasons but one reason?—the breaking of the bond between the landlord and his land. But where mixture of blood occurred, the bond was rather strengthened than broken, and this wholesome and beneficial process was the physical equivalent of that scenic and in a sense spiritual relationship between the small country house and the countryside at its gates. Here lies the organic strength and reality of the squirearchy, in a local leadership which is not domination. As the gentry to the people, so the house to the land. There was something appropriate after all in the christening of so many of our villages—Redmarley d'Abitot, Tolleshunt d'Arcy—by the names of their Norman *seigneurs*. Something appropriate indeed. At the exquisite moated Tolleshunt d'Arcy Hall lives the Eve family who have farmed the land of the parish for 400 years. Mr Weston Eve owns the famous Tudor dado which depicts the daily life of a Tudor squire. This he has refused to sell to America. There is a bond here between people and squire, village and manor which he who breaks violates a kind of law of Nature.

IV   COKE OF NORFOLK

Something certainly happened between Great Chalfield and Blenheim or the mighty mansions that loom out of Trollope's tales. I can best describe

---

* Dr Pooler of Derby informs me that two surviving descendants of " time-honoured Lancaster " were a butcher and a toll-gate keeper, one from John of Gaunt's youngest and the other from his eldest daughter, and both, oddly enough, natives of the same small town, Hales Owen in Worcestershire.

it as the detachment of the country gentleman from the soil, his exchange of responsibility for power. The history of the squire from the Gothic manor to the Georgian mansion is a convincing illustration of Lord Acton's aphorism —" Power always corrupts; absolute power corrupts absolutely."

How could this have been so when the 18th century was the age magnificent of the four monarchs of husbandry, Tull, Townshend, Bakewell and Coke? Nevertheless, it was so and the three stages that mark the transformation of the squire into the landlord were the Statute of Frauds in Charles II's reign which made titles to land invalid without written proof and so dispossessed a quantity of small yeomen whose hereditary lands were held in *customary* fee-farm tenure, the Revolution of 1688 when the landed aristocracy executed their *coup d'état* which was, in Tawney's words " to make the British Empire and ruin a considerable portion of the English nation," and the Statute of 1710 by which only landowners were eligible for a seat in Parliament. Few nowadays realize that the Revolution of 1688, planned and executed by the Whig squirearchy aided by the City of London, deprived the king of his prerogative in the issue of money and vested it in the hands of the Bank of England, whose sole aim was to make private profit out of it. What calamity this great victory of the private money interest has proved to agriculture (and indeed to the peoples of the world) the history of the 20th century has established beyond controversy.

Thus, the bridge between the lord of the manor and the squire were the Tudor Enclosures and the bridge between squire and landlord were the 18th and 19th century Enclosures that followed 1688 and 1710. Both were revolutionary movements of force; the earlier seized upon the monastic lands and threw 80,000 peasant farmers into beggary and the later, more prolonged and ultimately more drastic one destroyed, but for insignificant exceptions, the meaning of the word " peasant " in the English language.

This is plain history and to write the word " progress " upon the tombstone of the peasantry is not, as many modern writers would have us believe, to blur the significance and reality of the *hic jacet* that underlies it. The double enigma that needs to be solved is—how can this century of legalized sabotage be reconciled with the undoubted benefits conferred upon agriculture by Coke and his fellows, and what were the factor or factors which induced the squirearchy to abandon their station of protectorship and responsible leadership to the local community, to turn upon and smash it? What, in other words, is the explanation for the rift between the two ends of the rural economy, the squire and the farm-labourer? The sudden appearance of conflict and ill-will between the apex and the base of the rural pyramid needs an explanation which no historians except Tawney, Bryant and a very few others have as much as attempted to give. Even the great Tawney's is incomplete. I am convinced that one reason was the dwindling of the yeoman, the structural link between the gentry and the peasantry in rural society. This pillar undermined, the edifice tottered and in the end crashed.

The issue becomes clearer if we study the position of Coke, a perfect example of the " resident native gentry," *adscriptus glebae.* Our attitude to the 18th century is out of focus. The 17th, not the 18th century, was the age of discovery, experiment and ferment in ideas of agricultural improvement; it was the absolutist rule of the landlords in the 18th century that enabled them to be ambitiously and extensively practised and no expense

56   A Tudor Squire's House: Montacute, Somerset

57   A Squire's House of the late 17th Century: Bradley, Wiltshire, from a
drawing by J. C. Buckler

58 " The Reapers ": an 18th-century Squire with his Labourers.   From the painting by George Stubbs

59   Thomas Coke, of Holkham, inspecting the Shorn Flock: from a contemporary painting

spared. It has not hitherto been pointed out that the majority of Coke's measures were revivalist, not innovations. For instance, Arthur Young in his *Autobiography* described how Coke reintroduced plough-oxen (imported Devons) to Holkham. He restored marling (as the Celtic and Saxon farmers had done before him) for the light lands he reclaimed (like the Cistercians before him) from the sea. He recovered the almost obsolete industry of home-grown flax and hemp weaving and founded the Thetford Wool Fair as a memento, though not a deliberate one, of the great sheep-fairs of the 14th century. His annual sheep-shearing festival was Henry Best's over again except that it was on a grander and more lavish scale. Both he and Townshend enforced not so much the entirely novel four-course Norfolk rotation of wheat, roots, barley or oats and clover-ley as fitted turnips and potatoes into the old yeoman rotations of the 17th century. Perhaps his most conservative achievement was to re-establish between his leadership and the workers on the Holkham Estate a reciprocity of interests which actually created a contented local community of which he was the well-loved patriarch.

Modern writers, enslaved to the principles of specialized and mechanized agriculture, completely ignore Coke's genius for husbandry as an expression of conservative revivalism and pay no attention whatever to the highly significant tribute Cobbett, the arch-representative of the older England, paid him: " Every one made use of the expressions towards him which affectionate children use towards their parents." The concept of the squire *adscriptus glebae*, bound to the soil, preserving the traditional framework of English rural society but expanding and enriching it so that new ideas might be absorbed into it, Coke was not untrue to this responsibility of local leadership. His example only confirms what I stressed in the first chapter (see p. 24) that the Enclosures might and should have been accomplished without dislocating the rural structure and uprooting the peasantry. But in actual fact they were a destructive force, just as is the modern tendency to turn farms into firms. In executing their predatory designs, the squires brought upon themselves the just nemesis of their impoverishment and partial dispossession in the 20th century.

V THE SQUIREARCHY

The other half of the enigma is—why did the squires turn traitor to the concept which had made the name of squire illustrious both in literature and in actuality? Why did the individuality of the squire spill over into individualism? The answer surely is that, on account of the fateful years 1688 and 1710, they ceased to be local leaders, checked from exploiting their powers by the kingship at the top and the order of rural society at the bottom, and became the Government of England, with nothing whatever to restrain them from taking what they would and how they would. From a regional they acquired a national status; from a rural they took on an urban colouring; from fostering local well-being they moved on to promoting commercial adventure. They tended, that is to say, to become absentee landlords.

But there can be no doubt that the temptation to adopt the new urban and commercial point of view was resisted by some and possibly many of the squires,* especially the smaller ones of moderate means. It is not fair to

* See end of Chapter.

them to swallow the Hammonds' case whole. A good example occurs as late as 1830, that of General Dyott, squire of his well-loved Freeford near Lichfield, who wrote a Diary between 1781 and 1845, the worst years of the Enclosures. He bitterly deplored in it the misery of the labourers and he accused the tenant farmers of " acquiring vast profits . . . and habits and feelings beyond the rank of life to which they belong, instead of being the respectable yeomen " they once were. He, a typical country Tory, denounced the Game Laws with almost the trenchancy of Cobbett or Kingsley. " Commerce," he wrote, " has produced a class of the community almost unknown fifty years back " (see Bernard Darwin in *Early Victorian England*) Miss Matty's squire-lover in *Cranford*, again, insisted on being called " Mr Thomas Holbrook, Yeoman."

There were ominous signs of an understanding between the Puritan merchant and the absentee land-owning courtier as early as Charles II's reign, an this *rapprochment* with urban capitalism was strengthened as the squires became less and less *country-minded*. The gambling at White's; the extravagance and ostentation; the flirting with fashionable vices carried to perverted lengths by such types as Sir Francis Dashwood of West Wycombe and Medmenham; even the high degree of cosmopolitan culture and lettered elegance, these were all symptoms of a new urbanism, good for townsmen like Dr Johnson but not for squires, apparent for the first time after the Restoration. The Hammonds have described from contemporary documents the enclosure of Sedgmoor in which Lord Stavordale, George Selwyn, Fox and Lord Ilchester were all implicated by means of a private bill (there were 4,000 of them in all) to disinherit the small owners for the sake of recouping Selwyn's gambling losses. The extraordinary thing is that, before the full flood of industrialism and the rule of money, the tradition of independence, of free institutions and of the association between property and liberty was maintained even by the enclosing landlords who were engaged in destroying the small properties of the people. Such is one of the many paradoxes oɪ English history.

Even those formal and grandiose mansions which Horace Walpole called " those great rarity-plums in a pudding of country " look as though they were exported from the town and imposed upon the country. Some of them look like government buildings; they *were* government buildings. It was the absentee rather than the resident gentry which appropriated the properties of the peasants, and the example of Lord Winchelsea who in 1795 enclosed his lands without expropriating his peasants is an exceptional one of that responsibility *for* his tenants by the forfeiting of which the landowner took the heart out of his right to own land. The Duke of Grafton, through whom Bloomfield's poems were published, Carnarvon, Suffield and Bedford, too, must be honourably remembered as three of the greater landlords who defended the peasantry against their own immediate interests and their own class, while the tenant farmer must bear an even heavier responsibility for oppression than the lords, by, as it were, grinding his labourers with his own hand down into the dust. At least, the landlords acted by proxy.

Arthur Bryant is right to suggest as a cause for this long tidal wave of oppression in which the landlord turned law, government and wealth against the village that he had grown too rich and powerful, that he had ceased to work on his estate and become arrogant and dictatorial or lazy, dilettante and pleasure-loving. But his sense of local service was the more surely corrupted by his alliance with the new subversive forces of wealth pursued as an aim in itself and with the new philosophy of gain by which economic expediency finally released itself from that moral obligation the Middle Ages had believed should direct all the operations of society. The mediaeval concept of the owner as a trustee disappeared with the idea underlying the Enclosures that a man could do what he liked with his own. When economics came to be considered as a mechanism subject to no moral authority, the landlord, yielding to the Hobbesians, the Malthusians and the Darwinians, put the weakest—his own tenantry—to the wall.

From one point of view, therefore, it is not to be regretted that he or rather his children, paid for his treachery. He paid for it both spiritually and materially. The tapestry of Trollope, for instance, is crowded with squires, and they make a somewhat listless and colourless assembly. The ridiculous arrogance of the De Courcy family; the preposterous pigheadedness of Lord Trowbridge in *The Vicar of Bullhampton*; the pasteboard amiability of Lord Lufton in *Framley Parsonage*; the schoolboyishness of Frank Gresham in *Dr Thorne*; Lord Ongar in *The Claverings*, a reversion to the 18th century type of roué but full of sawdust rather than of bad blood; the sinister and shadowy Duke of Omnium of Gatherum Park; the museum piece Thornes of Ullathorne in *Barchester Towers*—all lack the enormous vitality of the squires of earlier ages. They have ceased to be originals and sit on their properties as in an armchair. They are gorged with lands, boring with their consequence and punctilio and entirely without the quaint homeliness of the prosaic and possessive Pastons. They make little or no resistance to the money-values in which all of Trollope's novels are soaked. They are an aristocracy still in power but run to seed. Power, the worm, has cankered the rose.

The well-bred disdain and hauteur of the earlier Squire d'Arcy in *Pride and Prejudice* on the other hand have an 18th-century flavour, but they are compounded with a provincial attachment to the soil which makes him a mixture between town and country. He half-preserves the tradition of the man of principle, land and home-culture richly accomplished by Squire Knightly in *Emma* but which the Trollope squires mainly lack. Squire Wardle, too, in *Pickwick* returns to the Squire Western type of whom Sir Toby Belch is a preliminary sketch. Wardle is a Rabelaisian figure in a setting of Victorian gentility and prudery.

In the flesh, the last of the old originals was that robustious eccentric, Squire Waterton, whose truth is stranger than any fiction. A prince he of wild adventure in word and deed, not of a park costumed by Capability Brown and a parterre of box and coloured sands. He often left his Yorkshire estate but he took, so to speak, his soil with him, as in archaic days the Polynesian voyagers took it literally across the pathless Pacific. The soil was bound to him rather than he to the soil. Squire Osbaldeston has a greater reputation than Squire Waterton, but what a pursey, horsey nincompoop beside him! Squire Waterton, scholar, antiquarian, naturalist, explorer, humanitarian, athlete, phlebotomist, snake-charmer, crusader, man of letters and scourge of " the Hanoverian rat," who turned Walton Hall into a bird sanctuary, was one of those great fantastics that no other country has ever bred in such profusion as England. Truly has she spawned a giant race when comic heroes and pious madcaps like Squire Waterton, who enjoyed his own absurdities even better than we do, and yet was an earnest man at heart, can be counted by the dozen! What rich life ferments in their veins! Perhaps we machine-slaves who are always babbling about our democracy see these men too much as giants. Small wonder!

Turn to the poetry written between and a little before and after the century (1750–1845) of the Enclosures and a further and most penetrating light is thrown upon the term I have used as an epitome of the squire's relation to the English tradition—*adscriptus glebae*, the treachery to which, I believe, sums up the social history of that century. View the literature of that period so far as it touches upon the countryside and, whatever its diversities, it can all be contained within the fold of this term, sometimes in one way, sometimes in another. Horace Walpole's " Why, I'll swear I see no difference between a country gentleman and a sirloin " is an urban view whole latitudes away from the realities of rural England. The comedies of the time —Henry Cary's *A Wonder or the Honest Yorkshire Man*, Isaac Bickerstaffe's *Thomas and Sally*, the anonymous *The Country Squire*, George Saville Cary's operas and other works, all harp in Walpolian vein upon the oafishness, brutishness, raffishness and gullibility of the squire. Soane Jenyns's satiric eclogue, *The Squire and the Parson* (1748) ridicules the hectoring squire and the toadying parson, while Christopher Smart's *The Country Squire and the Mandrake* is a squib upon his cloddishness and insensibility.

The sentimental and meaningless pastoralism of the 18th century heroic couplet depicts a golden age of sophisticated Swains and Shepherdesses which is completely true to the abstractified mentality of the age and in the economic theories of Mandeville and his kind was the prelude to the 20th century conception of life in terms of mechanization and rationalization. The country scene was classicized and Dresden China figures in it played at country life in the week-ending spirit. The detachment of this Arcadian twaddle is one phase of a real detachment between land and people, squirearchy and tenantry, which can be detected by a careful search into contemporary literature, aided by the masterly labours and brilliant writing of that forgotten book given me more than two decades ago by W. H. Hudson— Julia Patton's *The English Village*. As Soane Jenyns put it:

> " Then each man lived upon his farm
> And thought and did no mortal harm,
> But now, whatever poets write,
> 'Tis sure the case is altered quite."

Traces of realism in this kind of strait-waistcoat versifying and conventional urban opinion are, of course, very rare, but where they can be discovered, are most revealing. Dibdin's *Lord of the Manor* (1781), for instance, exposes the foppery and coxcombry of the new landed gentleman, while Akenside's *Ode to Country Gentlemen* (1758) complains of their deserting their homes and local leadership for riotous living in London, and a jumped-up bourgeoisie acquiring their lands. The novel urban-mindedness of the squire was thus perceived by the urban bard. It is worth quoting here a piece from an anonymous poem—*The Contented Clown* (1757)—not only because it represents the squire's envy of the lowly poor's serenity in his new separation from them but gives a surprisingly graphic and vigorous picture of the small copyholder of the period:

" Young Hodge, a poor but a contented Swain,
Rented a homely Cottage on a Plain;
Homely you'd say, if you the Cottage saw,
The Walls were rear'd of Mud and thatch'd with Straw . . .
Well with the Place the Furniture agreed;
No implements of Luxury, but Need . . .
All that you could unnecessary call,
Were some old tatter'd Ballads on the Wall:
Alike of Wealth was all his Stock and Store,
Two Bee-Hives (one forsaken) at the Door,
And Cabbages and Turnips half a score:
A meagre Tit that on the Common graz'd,
A small runt Cow that from a Calf he rais'd;
One Cock, two Hens, and half a dozen Chicks,
Two little Heaps of Hay, which Hodge call'd Ricks:
Three Pigs within Doors kept, and serv'd with Care;
To these—a Wife—two girls—a Son and Heir;
These were his Stock—nor did he e'er repine,
The Pigs, Wife, Children, often did combine
To greet his Ears, and in loud Concert join.
But midst this Scene of Poverty and Woes,
Hodge, by his Looks, no Discontentment shows . . .
At Work he whistles; when his Work is done,
No more is tir'd than when he first begun;
Homeward he hies, and tunes a merry Song,
His lov'd, though dirty squawling Tribe among . . .
Such Hodge's Life was, which a neigh'bouring Squire
Did often with an envious Mind admire."

As the social effects of the Enclosures unfolded, the colours became more sombre, and still the theme is the same, the havoc of the betrayal of *adscriptus glebae*. How searchingly Wordsworth interpreted that term by his metrical stories of the smallholder's attachment to his land as a something living and of his sense of guilt and of bond-breaking when he sold any of his acres away! But Crabbe was incomparably more direct, lean, acid and un-varnished, if a great deal more prosaic. His stark veracity and a "saeva indig-natio " more to the point than Swift's in *The Village* (1783) and the *Parish Register* (1807) tore all the veils from the labourer's degradation as a con-sequence of the social forces set in motion by the new squirearchy, and his appalling pictures of the Poorhouse were echoed by Ebenezer Elliott, the Corn Law Rhymer, Harriet Martineau and even blessed little Miss Mitford-Muffet on her Hampshire tuffet. Goldsmith's humane and sensitive Muse, significantly scouted by Macaulay, had indeed preceded Crabbe's fiercer one in *The Deserted Village* and heads all the 18-century poetry of this class by his revelation of the wilderness of " sweet Auburn " wrought by the callous and luxurious greed of the urban landlord—" Laws grind the poor and rich men rule the law " is the poetic summing-up of Fielding's Justice Frolick, the oppressor of the poor.

What Elliott called " pauper poetry " steadily gained in strength from Crabbe onwards. The fiery Elliott's own indictment of enclosure in the *Splendid Village* (1831) is more doctrinaire than Crabbe ever was but his descriptions of the impoverishment of the village school, the desolation of the cottage, the absentee pluralist Rector, the inn in charge of constable and bailiff and of the estate ruled *from a distance* are realistic enough:

> " Feast of the happy village, where art thou?
> Pshaw, thou art vulgar—we are splendid now."

" Avenge thy plunder'd poor, oh Lord!" he cried, remembering Milton,

> " But not with sword—no, not with fire
> Chastise the British locustry!
> Lord, let them feel thy heavier ire;
> Whip them, oh Lord, with poverty! "

T. Bachelor's *Village Scenes* (1804) portrays the new-rich squire swelling like a frog:

> " With rapid strides his wide dominion spreads,
> E'en to the eaves of Penury's crumbling sheds,
> And while his friends in boundless prospect rise,
> Scarce views a garden with unenvious eyes."

John Clare, being one of the dispossessed himself, understood very well the meaning of *adscriptus glebae*:

> " When masters made them merry with their men,
> When all the coats alike were russet brown,
> And his rude speech was vulgar as their own."

Pass down the years and we find that even the rose-spectacled Washington Irving made his old squire say—" we have almost lost our simple, true-hearted peasantry." The remedy, he wrote, was for the gentry to pass more time on their estates, mingle with the country people and " set the merry old games going again." But he did not realize that only an organic peasantry plays games, and even Squire Somervile knew that in *Hobbinol or The Rural Games* (1769), though he too looked down on those games from the superior height of power-consciousness. The meaning of the change from the small manor to the great mansion, from a human and personal leadership to a remote and soulless suzerainty was perfectly epitomized by Trollope in *The Small House at Allingham* (1864). Squire Dale speaks:

> " I fancy that our ideas of rural grandeur have altered since many of our older country seats were built. To be near the village . . . seem'd to be the spirit of a gentleman when building his house in the old days. A solitude in the centre of a wide park is now the only site that can be recognized as eligible. No cottage must be seen, unless the cottage *orné* of the gardener. The village, if it cannot be abolished, must get out of sight. The sound of the church bells is not desirable, and the road on which the profane vulgar travel by their own right must be at a distance. When some old Dale of Allingham built his house, he thought differently. There stood the church and there the village, and pleased with such vicinity, *he sat himself down close to his God and to his tenants*." (The italics are mine.)

VI LANDLORD'S ECLIPSE

Fifty years after the last General Enclosure Act of 1845, the landlord found himself hoist with his own petard, as dramatic an instance of poetic justice as history can show and, upon a larger issue, a pointed reminder that in the long run the moral law is not to be flouted with impunity. Death duties from which the corporation, the limited liability company, the college and the county council (nowadays the largest landowner) are exempt, have broken the individual landlord's back as he of old broke the back of the peasantry. The period of agricultural adversity during our century, when the gross income from agricultural land has dwindled from one-fifth of the national income to less than a fiftieth, has certainly not spared the landlord. From 1910 onwards, a vindictive, demagogic and purely urban legislation has crippled him, good, bad or indifferent, responsible or irresponsible, in a variety of directions. As his control of the machinery of government fell away at the end of the 19th century, many of the landlords undoubtedly maintained their estates with much self-sacrifice and disinterestedness. It is quite certain that they saved hundreds of their tenant farmers from bankruptcy, and that the Liberal offensive against them was not a moral crusade but the effect of the shifting of the balance of power from the country to the town and from the idea of private property to that of the combine, the chain-store and the joint-stock company.

Perhaps the most injurious of these urban attacks has been the release in 1923 of the tenant farmer from those tenancy agreements which Coke of Norfolk inaugurated to prevent the tenants from breaking their rotations, selling hay and straw off the farm and exploiting their soils. " Freedom of cropping " has resulted in a great extension of soil-robbery by cashing in on a succession of corn crops and the constant use of sulphate of ammonia to the alarming detriment of fertility. The fact that freedom of cropping or " farming to get out," a characteristic piece of urban dictatorship based on ignorance and guided by the commercial mentality, has stricken both the landlord and the soil in his charge, is an indication of how closely the interests of the one are bound up with the preservation of the other. It is a further indication of how grievous was the error of the landlord in allying himself during the enclosure period and in his capacity as a government with those predatory forces of embryonic industrialism which in our own century made a wilderness of English husbandry. The suicidal *laissez-faire* policy of depopulating our own countryside in the cause of cheap labour to feed the manufacturing industries and of exploiting virgin lands overseas in the cause of cheap food by way of sweated labour and the paralysis of the home market, has not only prevented the landlord from acting as the good husbandman-in-chief but threatened his very existence. The folly, the weakness, the selfishness of " the quality " in yielding to the 19th century demand for quantity and the profit to be made out of it are the more apparent.

Probably the entire urban community, capital and labour, business and bureaucracy, would welcome the extinction of the landlord in the common cry for the nationalization of the land. That in itself should warn the true countryman against allowing his proper appreciation of the social miseries caused by the Enclosures and the ultimate disaster of their effects upon husbandry itself to cloud his judgment upon the indispensability of the squire as a warden both of the English tradition and of English husbandry, in greater peril during our period than ever before in their history. Granted his dubious and parti-coloured record—his futile pheasant-fetichism of a hundred years, his unearned income from industrial and residential ground-rents, his frequent sales of property to timber and land-speculators and his craze for hunting. The sharp, indeed savage attack on the hunting squire in C. E.

THE ENGLISH COUNTRYMAN

Vulliamy's *The Montague-Puffins* (1941), where he is depicted as turnip-headed and hoof-footed, has some justification, though like Oscar Wilde's on " the pursuit of the uneatable by the unspeakable," it represents the point of view of urban intellectualism alone. It is justified, apart from the humanitarian aspect, because the costliness and absenteeism of hunting are incompatible with good husbandry. Granted all these things, yet the squire really is the linch-pin of good husbandry.

There is none but he to take and resist the shock of the urbanization of the country and the commercialization of agriculture, none but he to interpose himself between the traditional rural values and that State-promoted combination of technology with big business which the planners have outlined as the destined controller of food-production in the future. As against his surrender to the idolatry of game-preservation that prevents the regeneration of the woodlands because the pheasants snap up all the young shoots from mast and acorn, that upsets the balance of wild bird life and too often means the control of shooting-rights by business syndicates, must be offset his great work in land-reclamation, drainage, housing and farm-management during the past 150 years. Of the 22,727 cottages built by the landlords according to the returns of 1914, 72 per cent. were provided with gardens, each an eighth of an acre or more. Their designs and general conveniences were, of course, incomparably superior to those of the jerry-built human packing-cases set up by the County Council landlords, the local representatives of the urban bureaucracy. And there is this to be said—that syndicated game-preservation and the surrender of woodlands and building sites to speculators were almost forced upon the landlords by death duties and excess taxation.

The tradition of individual good husbandry has indeed run in the county family since the days of Squire Fitzherbert's *Boke of Husbandrie* in 1523, and assuredly it has survived the specialized mass-producing methods that followed the Enclosures. There is a squiress I know of who had a dispute with the parson and sat in the church-porch on Sundays to prevent the villagers from going to the service. Nobody now goes to that church, though up to the war, the bell was rung Sunday after Sunday. There is by no means a world of difference between this high-handed action and Squire Western's words to his daughter Sophia when she would not have Blifil for her intended :

" If you detest un never so much, you shall have un (oaths). I am resolved upon the match and unless you consent to it, I will not give you a groat, not a single farthing; no, though I saw you expiring with famine in the street, I would not relieve you with a morsel of bread! "

There is a touch of Squire Western, too, but in his jollier and more genial aspect in the story I recently heard of the squire who was reading the lessons. "Here beginneth the second lesson—no (in a loud voice), damme, it's the first." Yet the " feudal village " of this squiress, as it is called, is the neatest, the most cared-for, the best husbanded, the least neglected of any other village within an area of many miles and she better loved by the villagers (all of whom she pensions) than it is possible to love a county council committee.

She possesses the same land-devotion as Scawen Blunt who would not have an acre of his estates at Crabbit Park and Newbuildings sold or exploited or tampered with or changed from what they had been under his ancestors for two hundred years. Some time ago, I received a letter from a landowner

102

in Dorset who with three of his fellow-squires owned 30,000 acres settled by many families which had occupied their cottages and smallholdings for generations. Would I come over and be his guest and see these things for myself? I received another letter at about the same time from a landowner in the North Cotswolds who was forced to sell out all but 2,000 acres of a property his family had held for two centuries. Most of the land was bought up by the tenants whose fathers and grandfathers had rented it from his forefathers. After the sale, the owner was made to feel by the purchasers that the land was still his. Would I come over and see these things myself? These men were the peers of Rider Haggard, who broke his heart and his purse on behalf of English husbandry, and in our own days of men like Lord Lymington, Lord Northbourne, J. L. Campbell, Laird of Canna, Rolf Gardiner and others whose service on behalf of their estates has expanded into a crusade for the regeneration of country England.

I like to place Dr Marett, Rector of Exeter College, beside Scawen Blunt. A seigneur of Jersey and farmer of his own lands, man of infinite learning and an anthropologist who is the fellow of Tylor and Frazer, yet I think of him as the first rather than the last—the veteran Islander. I spent a couple of hours with him while I was writing this book, and he talked to me almost without stopping about his Island, its rocks and seas, its people and its beasts, its folklore and its husbandry, its history and its habitudes, its ancient colonists and its traditional self-government. Known to thinking men of all the world as one of the greatest living scholars, I saw him as a kind of island sea-chieftain, a feudal knight, powerful in frame and utterance, sagacious, patriarchal, deep-versed in all that is to be known about his little place girdled by tides and rocks. He is the interpreter of primitive man to the savants of all countries, and rich are his years in knowledge of the world and its ways. But he is one who has seen the wide perimeter of man and the earth from a speck within it, his native Jersey, of which his ancestors have been squires since Norman days. From his speck, and, when he left it for Oxford, from the spirit it had implanted in him, he cast his mind over the *orbis terrarum*. Was it not perhaps his very island, where change is slow and custom tenacious, which turned his massively granitic mind to contemplating the childhood of man? A man who sees a world in a grain of sand, that is the ideal *seigneur* and so I saw him on that memorable afternoon. He showed me the hidden, almost mystical meaning of *adscriptus glebae*

VII   The Good Steward

In essence, and so long as he is free of the blight of urban absenteeism, the squire stands for the customary England of the yeoman and the mixed farm against the competitive England of the moneylender and the dealer. The worst of landlords is surely a better one than borrowed money. The half-million retailers of agricultural produce receive 682 million pounds per annum to the 500 millions received by the two million primary producers, and of the latter the squire is the natural protector. With the earth and its husbandry, both creative, he is associated by the nature of his office, not with the impersonal and secondary interests which live by and mostly prey upon them. So with mixed farming. If " the farmer's foot fats the land," the squire's eye draws all the diversities of his estate into an organic unity.

Forestry is an eloquent example. It is more or less nationalized in England with the result that the Forestry Commission, neglecting the natural small woodlands on private estates, has over a wide area destroyed the farming of hill-sheep. For our native hardwoods, to which our soils are suited to perfection and by " slow time," it has planted disciplined legions of conifers (particularly the vile Sitka spruce) for a quick-return commercial turnover and to the ruin of our characteristic English country beauty. Now, as Lord Lymington has pointed out, our woodlands are widely distributed but of small extent and are indissolubly related to arable and pasture. They are not, therefore, amenable to what he calls " specialized silviculture." But in the parts they play as shelter-belts, as fertilizers to the fields from their deciduous habit, as conservers of moisture on the watersheds, as guardians against erosion on slopes, as harbourage for bird-life, as lime-producers for the soil, as drainage regulators, as a supplementary food-supply for swine and a variant diet for cattle, as manufacturers of humus, as depôts for certain essential minerals for the soil, as raisers of soil-temperature and last but by no means least as sources of employment for a small host of local woodsmen, hurdlers, bodgers, broom-squires, coopers, carpenters, cabinet-makers, tool-makers, thatchers and the like—they contribute to the balance and interdependence of right husbandry so richly and vitally that their importance cannot be exaggerated. It is significant that one of the propositions of the agronomic planners is to abolish all such belts, groves, copses and hedgerow timber as " nuisances." Who but the landlord whose eye ranges over his estate as a whole, as a little cosmos of interacting parts, can preserve its essential features and maintain in being and in health the human community that makes its living from ploughland, from pasture, from woodland and from market-garden in turn and in mutual relation?

A landlord, therefore, who is conscious of his responsibilities and the good steward rather than the autocrat of his estate, finds himself in inevitable opposition to the non-biological specialization of the laboratory on the one hand and the commercial and industrial values of the town, on the other. In other words, his values are individual, co-operative and regional, and these values, as this survey as a whole has, I hope, demonstrated, are the heart and lungs of the English tradition. For a time, the time of the 19th century, he became anti-social and individualist in step with the new industrialism, whose fruits have been the combine and the power-State, both of which deny the personal and so the Christian view. The regional idea as the nursing ground of the home and family sense is contrary both to individualism and the automatism resulting from it, and the squire is regional both in history and in vocation. His business, therefore, is to recover that trusteeship which is his historical mission, as it is the business of the central authority, be it king or state, to deprive him of his charge together with his lands when he ceases to act as their trustee.

Trusteeship is the binding condition of all forms of ownership and this very forfeiture is advocated to-day by a small group of squires. They have attempted to nurse their estates into a high fertility, to develop local crafts and industries as satellites to husbandry, initiated training camps for land settlement and, in one instance, reintroduced music and festival as organic to the seasonal round. If these beginnings are developed into the definite purpose of restoring a peasantry by education for land-worthiness, the still festering crime of the Enclosure might in time be undone by the very class

61 The Formal Garden Lay-out of an 18th-Century
Country House

60 Rural Activity Around a Squire's House of
the Early 18th Century

62, 63 Squires' Families of the Early 18th Century: from an illustration by
Hayman, and a painting by an unknown artist

that committed it, and a new England be grafted upon the root-stock of the old. That is the practical way, if only one, of building Jerusalem in England's green and pleasant land.

To sum up. To justify his existence, the squire must not only cease to be a leisured class or a wealthy class or a ruling class; it must cease to be a class at all. His office is functional; to become the father of a family responsible for its welfare to the Great Father. The unity of his own group should be a cellular organism preparing for the universal family of mankind.

N.B. (1) I have a postscript to add to this chapter. Some weeks after I had written it, I had a lengthy correspondence with Lord Innes of Learney, perhaps the foremost living authority on feudal tenures and the legal, heraldic and domestic aspects of manorial rights and custom, so far as they relate to Scotland and France. Briefly, his contention was that the manorial order formed an organization of the family descended from the patriarchal system of Celtic chieftainship. The chiefs maintained a true family contact with the whole of the community, while the manorial courts perpetuated the idea of the " family council." The estate was thus the tribo-family unit and the hereditary laird or squire was its personal leader exercising a personal responsibility towards it as the " head of the family." By the council he was both guided and limited and prevented by it from usurping autocratic powers. Thus, it was enacted by the Heritable Jurisdiction Act of 1747: " It is statuted and ordained, by and with the advice and consent of the vassals and tenants of the barony. . . ." This was a reinterpretation of the primary function of the clan council. This democratic and hierarchical order both was broken up in Scotland by the " Clearances," corresponding with our Enclosures and actuated, as ours were, by commercial incentives and inducements of profit. Thus, in 1800, one of the " Improvers " condemned the home farm of the Earl of Caithness at Barrowgill as " uneconomic " because 200 happy people were gathering in the hay, just as in England the idea of the family-community was being supplanted by that of individualist self-enrichment. Many of the lairds and chiefs made vigorous if unavailing resistence to the " Improvers " on behalf of their " families," viz. the local estates.

This digest necessarily omits much of the legal and constitutional support cited by Lord Innes to the effect that the continuity of the manorial system was due, not to a " reactionary " conservatism but because it gave " the happiest and freest and most natural form of life to the countryside." Personally, I am convinced (see Chapter I) that the free vill preceded the manorial community, but the " family " relationship of the lord to the village, as set forth by Lord Innes, in no way conflicts with the freedom and democratic character of the early vill. Thus, the documentary evidence given me by Lord Innes substantiates the argument of this chapter.

N.B. (2) In reference to p. 95, I should mention here the devoted effort of Lord Tollemache, Sir Richard Winfrey, Jesse Collings and Frederic Impey (author of *Three Acres and a Cow*) to undo the Enclosures and restore the peasantry fifty years ago. On Lord Tollemache's large estates, every labourer had three acres and livestock, a reduced rental in proportion to the price of corn, first-rate housing and (very rare in those days) perfect freedom of opinion and belief. Other benefits as well. All honour to this noble band.

Chapter VI

THE PARSON

I THE CISTERCIANS

The history of the parson began with the priest, as the history of the squire began with the Cistercians. They were not only the first of the great line of farmer-squires but the best. Nothing in the world is grander than the story of the Cistercian farmers, nothing more tragic, nothing that so exposes the hollowness of the 19th century theory of progress. In their prime, during the 13th century, the golden age of English monachism, the Cistercians expressed and glorified the ideal of wholeness as no other community has done in our history: wholeness not separable from holiness, and Stephen Harding's *laborare est orare* was faithfully fulfilled upon their smiling acres. They possessed a genius for building-sites, for architecture, for husbandry, for reclamation, for administration, and a genius for simple piety and service towards God and man which were all aspects of one genius, the genius for wholeness of life.

What nobler country buildings in the world than Hayles, Fountains, Tintern, Abbeydore, Jervaulx, Rievaulx and Byland, compensating for severity in absence of ornament by their perfection of structure and the spiritual purity of their pointed arches, the very curves of which express the aspiration of the soul? What achievement more fruitful than their conversion of wastes and barrens into fertility and abundance for man and beast? What were they not—the great flockmasters, the great gardeners, planters of woods, carpenters, road-makers, beer-brewers, bee-keepers, bridge-builders, millers, fishermen, drainers of marshes, miners, iron-workers, quarrymen, horse-rearers, stock-breeders, wool-spinners, cultivators, smiths, builders of the churches with their own hands, and all with frugality, patience, simplicity and devotion? To their peasants and *conversi*, or lay brethren, they were the mildest and best landlords this country has ever known. Their houses were inns, hospitals, guest-rooms, almshouses, agricultural colleges; their abbeys were shrines of peace and poverty for themselves and of peace and plenty for others.

In *Original Letters Illustrative of English History*, Sir H. Ellis has written of them:

> " They never raised any rent or took any incomes of their tenants; nor ever took in any commons . . . all sorts of people were helped and succoured —yea, happy was that person that was tenant to an Abbey, for it was a rare thing to hear that any tenant was removed by any taking his farm over his head. And thus they fulfilled all the works of charity in all the country round."

Surely such an order should be as renowned as Socrates, Shakespeare and Dante? But they are nothing but a rare name in our mouths—it is impossible for us now to understand the association of work with prayer or of husbandry with religion. It will have to be a greater civilization than we are to-day which can appreciate the wholeness of the Cistercians, the richness of their deep organic life of poverty. The tragedy was that they exchanged a material for a spiritual wealth and the cause of that deceitfulness was their own sheep. Their farming methods, diligence, craftsmanship and power of leadership were so successful that their very virtues became the seeds of their corruption.

In Dugdale's *Monasticon*, a record exists of their early wanderings and privations in the Yorkshire wilds. By 1280, the Abbey of Meaux at Holderness possessed 11,000 sheep, and the Abbey flocks became so profitable that specialization in them upset the balance of the Cistercian agriculture. The Abbots became litigious country magnates, and at the last earned the censure of St Thomas More for their responsibility in the soaring prices of the wool boom, so that " poor folkes which were wont to worke it, and make cloth thereof, be nowe hable to bye none at all." Finally, this wealth in wool aroused cupidity in the king whose conscience was on such good terms with his lusts and greeds, and the last act in one of the greatest tragedies of our history was fulfilled : *corruptio optimi pessima*. It seems the hardest thing for the human race to learn by the experience of its past, since the history of the squire took much the same course as the history of the Cistercians, if no squire reached the spiritual heights of the Cistercian brotherhood, and no abbot created such havoc as the Tudor and Georgian landlords.

II VILLAGE PRIEST

What is the essential difference between Chaucer's " povre Persoun of the toun," " that Christes gospel trewely wolde preche " :

> " A bettre preest I trowe that nowher seen ys,
> But Christes lore, and his Apostles twelve
> He taughte, but first he folwed it himselve."

and, say, Parson Adams in *Joseph Andrews*, or many a parson of the parish pump? At first sight it seems that the only difference between them lies in the forms of their respective faiths. But there is a deeper difference, and, in spite of its elusiveness, it is more radical than that between Catholic and Anglican. The distinction is a social one, and, secondarily, an economic one, and in the end its repercussions upon the religious aspect went far and deep.

Though the " povre Persoun " was in orders, his life was identified with the villagers rather than with the diocesan clergy, the friars or the monks, still less with the lord of the manor, and it is probable that more often than not he was a peasant himself, as the inferior chantry priest less commonly was. The parish priest was supported by the congregation—one-third of the tithe going to the upkeep of the parish church, one-third to the poor, and one-third to his living—while the parish church of the Middle Ages was to the cottages and farms what he was to his flock. The Reformation undoubtedly loosened the complex and intimate network of associations between the parish church and the village, just as in the end it completely altered the nature, scope and incidence of the tithe. It detached the parson from his economic dependence upon the commonalty and released him from celibacy. After the Reformation, the parish church gradually ceased to be the refuge, playground, law-court, theatre, assembly room, concert hall, college, picture-gallery, recreational and educational centre of the village, and even its mart and workshop—it was the very creation of the local craftsmen, and there was no separation between sacred and secular. The universals of God-Man-Earth were repeated in the microcosm of church-village-fields. Often too the village inn stood next door to the village church, both ministering, as an old writer has wisely said, " to the natural and universal needs of man " :

" Malt does more than Milton can
To justify God's ways to man "

" Church-ale," at which " all things were civil and without scandal " is a word pregnant of meaning. This organic inter-relationship between village and church was disturbed even as early as the days of Parson Herrick, that true patriot of the village sports and true sympathizer with the pagan memory of the folk. By his station if not always by his acts, the " povre Persoun " was a much more democratic figure in country life than the parson.

John Skelton, the Rector of Diss, our English Villon, whose poems are like old English dances for their liveliness, dexterity, freedom and nimbleness, certainly preserved this popular spirit though he stepped over the threshold of the Renaissance into an age of tyranny. When his fierce, though impish satire caught Wolsey on the raw (for which he had to seek sanctuary at Westminster), he was valiantly maintaining the tradition of the " povre Persoun " against an ecclesiastical authority whose power-politics were now separating it from the people. Scurrilous, tender, whimsical or scathing, the Muse of our Colin Clout is still the voice of the peasants of 1381, sweetly or sourly sung in the person of nearly the last of their shepherds. He was Renaissance, too, in the way he brandished, so to speak, his lusty son over the font and defied the mean-spirited.

III THE 18th-CENTURY PARSON

Take a jump from the end of the Middle Ages into the middle of the 18th century. The discoverer of country England is confronted with a reshuffling of the pieces on the board which is just as symbolic as was the old-fashioned arrangement of parish church-village-fields. In many villages he sees the same church but as an outbuilding, almost an annexe, to the mansion and so no longer the node or focal point of the village. Sometimes, indeed, the church actually stands in the park of the mansion; sometimes there is a private hedgeway from the side-door of the mansion to the west door of the church, while more often than not the mansion dominates and in a sense overawes the church by its considerably greater size.

Inside the church at the top of the nave there is a commodious pew—the squire's—cushioned and fenced off by panelled sides from the seats of the congregation. Evidently, the squire was presumed to leave his earthly mansion for one of those heavenly ones mentioned in the Scriptures. This topographical disposition of church and manor is a visual representation of social, political and economic actuality : the parson is established by the State and the State is the landed gentry. Often the connection was even closer and more personal, either because the squire's younger son was destined for orders or the actual living was held by him to dispose on whom he would. In other words, the parson no longer represents God and Bethlehem but God and Ceasar, and, as the history of the Enclosures reveals, the two masters were decidedly on bad terms. The parson's outlook has become dualistic, and as society in general was moving away from its former conception of itself as a " spiritual organism " towards a new conception of itself as an " economic machine," so the parson's dualism is aggravated. The wind was taken out of the spiritual sails.

There actually was no solution to the dilemma in which he found himself, but he attempted as needs must a *modus vivendi* between its horns. The " squarson " was one idea and " Spurting Bullen," one of the Quorn hunting parsons, and Seabrook, who rode his own horse in the Grand National, are two plums out of this hearty and rather stodgy currant pudding of which the 18th century held the recipe. Not that the 18th century invented the huntin' and shootin' parson. Langland had swung a lantern upon him four centuries before—as *Sloth*, who " could find a hare in a field or a furrow better than construe the first psalm or explain it to the parish." The difference was that the 14th century lashed while the 18th cockaded him. Sydney Smith, one of our cleric scholars but he was a wit as well, said of the squarson :

" I have laid down two rules for the country; first, not to smite the partridge, for if I fed the poor and comforted the sick and instructed the ignorant, yet I should be nothing worth, if I smote the partridge. Two thousand good shots dispersed over the country do more harm to the cause of religion than the arguments of Voltaire and Rousseau."

The squarson was undoubtedly much more abundantly distributed within the society of the 18th century than in the previous one, and it is significant that Taylor the Water-Poet, visiting the centre of the hunting shire in 1640, speaks of its clergy as

" learned, diligent and painful . . . and I did not hear of anyone residing there that is either schismatically opinionated with dogmatical whimsies or Amsterdamnable fopperies,"

and of them being " charitable and careful for the relief of the poor and needy."

The 18th-century parson hunted with the squire's pack, but the 17th-century parson still took some share in the peasant's joys. To this we have no less a witness than Richard Baxter whose *Reliquiae Baxterianae* records how the incumbent preceding his father in the parish :

" read the Common Prayer briefly, and the rest of the day, even till dark night almost, except eating-time, was spent in dancing under a May-pole and a great tree, not far from my father's door, where all the town met together."

Baxter, who was horrified at this way of spending the Lord's day, forecasts Mrs Proudie's Sabbatarianism in *Barchester Towers* two centuries later. But he would equally have condemned the 18th-century squarson.

In the 18th century, too, flourished the " farson " (he might be called) of which *genre* Parson Trulliber, who farmed six days in the week and donned the surplice on Sunday, is the archetype. But he was not like the Cistercians who brought their religion into their farming and their farming into their religion. In Parson Trulliber's times, the division between sacred and secular had become an accomplished fact. We think of Parson Woodforde, also, as only one remove from the farson and whose prolonged bill of fare is more to us than a mile of sermons. A savour as of burnt offerings is exhaled from his pages.

Yet there were many 18th-century parsons who were students, antiquaries, scholars, retired from the world but as individualists not members of a community devoted to the service of God. Of these there have been many illustrious examples, Parson Stukeley, for instance, who had more true insight into and imagination for the meaning of Stonehenge and Avebury than the whole body of modern archaeologists. And Stukeley's friend, the Rev. Francis Peck, the learned recluse of Goadly Horwood in Leicestershire (*ob*: 1743) who took with him to his grave a precious drop of wisdom distilled from his bookish cask. *Illi mors gravis incubat, qui notus nimis omnibus, ignotus moritur sibi* is written on it. Another of these 18th-century pastors who took this way of standing against the indifferentism and hedonism of his age was John Bold, curate of Stoney Stanton (1701–1751), a man so charitable that he starved himself to feed others. A later rector of the same parish inscribed on *his* tomb, " Let me die the death of the righteous, and let my last end be like his."

Parson Skinner, again, was the author of ninety-eight manuscript volumes of diary delicately rescued from oblivion by Virginia Woolf, while Edith Olivier has told the oddities of Alexander Cruden of the *Concordance*. Parson White, of course, is the greatest of this class, he who made Selborne the Mecca of country-minded Englishmen. I have more to say of him when I consider those parsons who reacted against the 18th century ethos. Natural history was indeed a parson's privilege for so many decades that the swanherd of Abbotsbury, because of my interest in it, once mistook *me* for one. But none showed the insight and quality of White. With the learned C. A. Johns in the next century, natural history was ceasing to be a flower of culture and became instead epipetalous, imbricate, didynamous, extipulate, hypogynous, accumbent, racemose, obovate and pedunculate. Nor should the Rev. Gilpin be omitted from the category of parsonic *cacoethes scribendi*, he who invented the word " picturesque " or gave it its fatal literary currency to the delectation of builders of " Gothick " ruins, and so flung the spear that cut in half the useful from the beautiful.

Among the men of letters there are Parson Sterne and in mid-Victorian days Parson Kilvert, both of whom, the classical and the romantic, gave the one a polish and the other an aura to the term " sentiment " very different from the modern degradation of it. Sterne, of course, was true creator but his hedonism was also true to his age, while Kilvert has points that link him with an escape from its legacy. Of the lesser literary brethren of the frock, Thomas Gisborne (1800) joined natural history with poetic numbers in *Walks in a Forest*. But the only rural record I have of the lesser 18th-century parsons who actively resisted enclosure is that of Comber, Rector (1760–1810) of Kirkby Moorside.

The Rev. James Hurdis, Vicar of Bishopstone in Sussex, Professor of Poetry at Oxford in 1793, author of *The Village Curate* (1788) and the *Favourite Village* (1800) and correspondent with Cowper between 1791 and 1794, is a good example of the leisured country divine with a taste for letters who flourished in the 18th century. His poetry was much too highly praised by W. H. Hudson in *Nature in Downland* and, though rural in theme without the earlier bondage to personification, it is almost entirely conventional in treatment. His letters to Cowper, reprinted from the *Sussex County Magazine*, have literary elegance and learning. In one of them he described how he rebuked Tom Paine (whom he compared with Thersites) at dinner with Dr Johnson. But for this narrative his chief interest is his transitional position between the formal 18th-century culture and the equally formal but narrower 19th-century morality, of which I have a striking example to give later. The following passage from the letters to Cowper illustrates a curious blend between the 18th-century style and 19th-century mentality :

" Now since these liberties to a woman of real modesty must be disagreeable, I have advised them again to pin themselves up to the chin, and expose no more of their persons than their own good sense will assure them is laudable and decent. To encourage them the more so to do, I have declared that I believe a great part of the colds, coughs and consumptions which attend the younger part of the female sex, are derived from the absurd custom of clothing the most vital part of the person in the thinnest and coldest teguments, and often leaving it without any covering at all. But if health be deemed a matter of no consequence with the ladies, I have advised them to conceal their persons more effectively, to preserve appearances, and prevent the men from concluding they are destitute of a proper regard for decorum."

Hurdis is also interesting because the *Favourite Village* contains one of the earliest accounts in poetic numbers to village cricket :

" The game laborious of the manly ball
Aim'd at the wicket, and its taper shanks
Levelling certain, but for hindrance quick
And resolute repulse of the strong bow,
That sends it thunder-struck aloft in air,
Or o'er the plain rebounding."

In these lines the Vicar may be said to have bowled a googly.

With Parson Thomas Warton, on the other hand, we are deeply embedded in the culture of the 18th century, and he was one of those who united the two streams of letters and scholarship. Yet even he shows a slight disposition to break away from 18th-century abstractions, since he wrote a pre-Selbornian sketch of his own parish of Kiddington. The old vicarage, the quiet study, the walled garden, the fruit ripening on the grey stone or ruddy brick, are not these the binding of the parson's leisured literature ?

IV THE 17th-CENTURY PARSON

I propose to draw together four very different country parsons of different eras, different calibre and parts and to consider a common ground of resemblance between them which will guide me in estimating the ambiguous position of the rural church. With them I shall briefly consider others between the 17th and 19th centuries who in various ways express the fundamental symbol of Chaucer's " povre Persoun."

These four are Latimer, George Herbert of *The Temple*, Hawker of Morwenstow and William Barnes, the others taking the stage as occasion arises. The parishes of the four are themselves concrete symbols of the English tradition, parishes as different in place as their pastors were in period and character. Latimer's Saintbury is spilled down the steep bluff of the north-western limestone Edge overlooking the oceanic plain of the lias that laps the primordial Malverns. The clustered hamlet of Herbert's Bemerton lies in the wide rich water-meadows of the Wiltshire Avon. Came Rectory is sequestered in a pocket of the sweeping range of the southern Dorset chalk and Morwenstow open to the severe uplands of the Cornish granite. The group of vicars who lived and .worked among these scenes all believed that Nature was a divine ordinance conferring certain rights upon and requiring certain obligations from man, and these the State existed to regulate and protect. Latimer, so valiant in protest against the Tudor Enclosures, and Herbert, the aristocrat who dedicated his life to the welfare and salvation of his villagers, were both heirs of the mediaeval tradition. They were members of a church which still preserved the continuity of the mediaeval idea that no manifestation of the secular life was exempt from the tests and values of the spiritual sanction.

That this was so, and that the link between the " povre Persoun " and the Anglican country clergy in their respective attitudes to the commonalty was not broken up to the end of the first half of the 17th century is completely revealed by a 16th-century Prayer. It was a favourite with Sir Richard Winfrey (see pp. 30, 105), has been quoted in our own days by C. Henry Warren and occurs in the Authorized Prayer Book (1552) of Edward VI's reign, at, that is to say, the height of the Tudor Enclosures. The text is as follows :

" We heartily pray thee to send thy Holy Spirit into the hearts of them that possess the grounds and pastures of the earth, that they, remembering themselves to be thy tenants, may not rack or stretch out the rents of their houses or lands, nor yet take unreasonable fines or moneys, after the manner of worldings, but so let them out that the inhabitants thereof may be able to pay the rents and to live and nourish their families and remember the poor. Give them grace also to consider that they are but strangers and pilgrims in the world, having here no dwelling place but seeking one to come; that they, remembering the short continuance of this life, may be content with that which is sufficient, and not join house to house and land to land to the impoverishment of others, but so behave themselves in letting their tenements, lands and pastures, that after this life they may be received into everlasting habitation."

While this prayer was being read in the churches, the " covetous worldlings " were, as I described in the last chapter, defying it in the country places. The 17th century country church, with George Herbert as its most celebrated figure, cannot be understood except through this continuity with the mediaeval idea passing right through the Dissolution.

Herbert, whom Vaughan called " the blessed man," Traherne and Vaughan himself, the precursor of Wordsworth (the child not only father of the man here but often seeing more than the man) were the three great country poets of the Metaphysical School, a School like no other in the literature of any nation in the world. Thomas Traherne, like Herbert a priest, but greater in his poetic prose than his poetry, was in his turn the precursor of Blake and Christopher Smart's *Song to David*, while Vaughan himself, in his constant use of images of light and darkness as the special properties of Deity, shows a remarkable affinity with the anonymous mystic who wrote *The Cloud of Unknowing* in the 14th century. So these poets look forward and look back.

The attitude to Nature of the Metaphysicals is perfectly expressed by Donne, the prince of them:

" Nature was God's apprentice, to learn in the first seven days, and now is his foreman, and works next under him."

64   The Lay-out of a Great Cistercian Abbey : Fountains, Yorkshire

65　Service in a Village Church, 1790 : from a drawing by F. Wright

HERBERT, VAUGHAN, TRAHERNE AND HERRICK

They saw what Vaughan called " the great chime and symphony of Nature " no less than human society *sub specie aeternitatis*, as the mediaeval church hardly did, and so represent a transcendental extension of the mediaeval idea under the archbishopric of Laud who, like Latimer, opposed enclosure. The mystical-Baroque poetry of this triad (and Vaughan, if not actually in orders, was closer to eternity than either of his two brethren in the spirit) is not commonly recognized as Nature poetry at all, and the continuity of the English tradition is obscured thereby. Yet all three do regard Nature (if only in glimpses) as the porch to the great cathedral of the divine universe. As Vaughan put it :

> " And in these weaker glories spy
> Some shadows of eternity."

Nature to them was the undertones of the heavenly orchestra, the finite projection of the everlasting " I AM," an initiation to the ultimate wisdom. Traherne in his *Centuries of Meditation* explicitly states this view :

> " Into his Eden, so divine and fair,
> So wide and bright, I come His son and heir."

And again :

> " The corn was orient and immortal wheat, which never should be reaped, nor was ever sown. I thought it had stood from everlasting to everlasting."

And again :

> " The world is a mirror of infinite beauty, yet no man sees it. It is a Temple of Majesty, yet no man regards it. It is a region of Light and Peace, did not men disquiet it. It is the Paradise of God. It is more to man since he is fallen than it was before, it is the place of Angels and the Gate of Heaven."

The flaming felicity of Traherne, so different from the enchanting folk-rusticity and joyous worldliness of Parson Herrick, is a new idea both in English poetry and ecclesiastical history. In thought, what a world away indeed was the Rector of Dean Prior from the Rector of Credenhill, both country parsons, both lovers and celebrants of earth, both living in the 17th century ! Herrick's Nature was almost wholly pre-Christian ; Traherne, equally accepting her loveliness and in love with it, saw the green world as the very body of God. Still more so Vaughan, who, calling himself " The Silurist " and " Olor Iscanus," is thus one of the very earliest of our regional ruralists. Except in St Francis and the early saints, this conception of Nature is not to be found in Catholicism. It is a novelty *added on* to the mediaeval tradition, and its due importance in our study of the continuity of the English tradition will be more fully realized when we come to Hawker and Barnes. Therefore, this triple achievement of Herbert, Vaughan and Traherne, if more fragmentary and defective than that of Wordsworth and Coleridge in the *Lyrical Ballads*, takes a momentous place in the history of rural Anglicanism. Abraham Cowley, especially in *Davideis*, carried the same thought into the Restoration, in spite of a very different spiritual climate and a much more urban fashion in literature. After him, the religious attitude to Nature does not *directly* appear (Blake's is indirect) until we reach Coleridge's *Hymn Before Sunrise in the Valley of Chamouny*.

Yet this trio, sharing this mystical experience in common, is entirely

15   113

different in poetic expression. Herbert, whom Vaughan regarded as his master, shows a wonderful dramatic power in his endings, while Vaughan's unearthly inspiration so often goes into sunset before his poem is finished. Herbert loved analogies and similes taken from village lore and the little familiar things of village life. He made a collection of local proverbial sayings and in *Steps to the Temple* laid down self-imposed precepts of a pastor's spiritual courtesies and sympathies towards his flock. Vaughan, though often extremely simple, is at the same time starry and elemental in his choice of natural symbols. Yet these poets all belong to one school, the school of Donne, which, often recondite, tasteless and compromised by what Addison called " false wit," yet has seen further into the ultimate mysteries of life and Nature than any modern.

Herbert's life was written twice over in his own period, by Izaak Walton and by himself in his poems, highly autobiographical and reflecting both sickness of body and much distress and conflict of his saintly spirit. Of *The Temple* he wrote to Nicholas Ferrar:

" that he would find in it a picture of the many spiritual conflicts that have passed betwixt God and my soul, before I could subject mine to the will of Jesus my Master; in whose service I have now found perfect freedom."

His kinsman, Lord Herbert of Cherbury, wrote of him, " About Salisbury where he lived, beneficed for many years, he was little less than sainted." A saintliness won from the high birth, the ambition and the very wit and learning that barred his way to it, so that his life was as dedicated as his Muse. It was a powerful ambition. Walton said:

" He enjoy'd his gentile humour for cloaths and courtlike company, and seldom look'd towards Cambridge, unless the King was there, and then he never fail'd."

Thus his life at Bemerton was a conversion. For " its charity, humility and all Christian virtues " Walton commends it as a supreme example of " primitive piety "—" lowly in his own eyes and lovely in the eyes of others." All his great gifts and station he devoted to the village, as his unique poems were offerings in the heavenly Temple. Layton Ecclesia in Huntingdonshire he restored and filled with exquisite Jacobean furniture; in Bemerton he lived like the " povre Persoun of the toun " ministering to his people:

" Whereas my birth and spirit rather took
The way that takes the town;
Thou didst betray me to a ling'ring book,
And wrap me in a gown."

How significant Walton's expression of Herbert's " primitive piety " is in the history of the English rural church has, I think, not been recognized. We shall see it recurring in Price, Marson, Hawker and Barnes, and what is more relevant at this stage of the narrative, we have it present in the elementalism of Jeremy Taylor, who held the country living of Uppingham before he was sheltered in South Wales from Puritan virulence by his Egerian Lady Carbery. Mr Pearsall Smith in *Reperusals and Recollections* has so perfectly distilled the essence of Jeremy Taylor " of the golden voice and angelic aspect " that there seems nothing left to be profitably said of him. His biographer has written " with the solitary exception of Shakespeare,

66 George Herbert at Bemerton: from the painting by Dyce

67 An 18th-Century Village School: from the painting by Van Aken

68   The Ferneley Family Pew in Melton Church (*ca.* 1828): from a painting
by John Ferneley

there is no writer in all our early literature who has made so fresh and copious and effective a use of metaphor taken directly from the observation of natural objects." Thus, he to whom the ascending lark was a symbol of prayer also belongs among the pietists of Nature. What can, I think, be usefully added on to previous estimates of this tender divine's lustrous and magnificent imagery from Nature is its peculiarly elemental quality and resource, especially in respect of light, the sun, water and " the little houses of birds." If we turn to the writings of primitive Christians like Basil, St Hilary, Gregory Nazianzen and others, we find exactly the same phenomenon, the glorification of primeval Nature, fresh from the mint of God. Thus, the English rural church of the 17th century repeats the achievement of the Primitive Church in reconciling Christianity with Nature from which the mediaeval church had with exceptions departed.

A spell of beauty and richness of inward living was upon the country parsonage of the first half of the 17th century. These annals would be too incomplete if I did not mention the circle, the charmed circle, at Little Gidding, where Deacon Nicholas Ferrar, Herbert's friend, was the presiding spirit. There for two decades he lived, retired from the world's affairs with his brother and brother-in-law, writing semi-biographical histories and tales, partly in the pastoral tradition, partly neo-platonic discourses of contemplation and prayer. Little Gidding became a kind of informal rural university, a school of quietism in which piety, literature, good conversation, metaphysics and country tranquillity made an Academe honoured by the world without and remote from the envenomed theological controversy and disputation that was to culminate in the anarchy of the Civil War. It is in the byways of the 17th century that its deep and mellow culture is to be found, tolerant, catholic, liberal and yet fervent. The Little Gidding circle may be called a duodecimo edition of Viscount Falkland's at Great Tew, where churchmen like John Hales and Chillingworth conversed with men of letters, poets, scholars and reformers of ripe understanding, men of zeal and lovers of liberty. Richard Steward, who preached a famous sermon against usury in 1641 (thus carrying on the mediaeval tradition), and Hammond, another sermonist who preached " The Poor Man's Tithing " the year before, were members of this " session of the Poets," to which the philosophers were as welcome as the " sons of Ben." " An autumn 'twas," this cluster of men of the good life, where sacred and secular met together but never again, never in our history since the Civil War. This sweet aftermath of the mediaeval unity, the Elizabethan curiosity and the Carolean piety was the final glow of the old English culture which the Commonwealth nighted.

Pre-eminently, the Carolean rural divine was a religious zealot, and it seems the more surprising to find among its parish priests a man of science, Jeremiah Horrocks, curate of Hoole (1617–41), whose observations on the elliptic orbit of the moon were acknowledged by Newton and *Opera posthuma* issued by the Royal Society in 1672. This though he died in his early twenties. What Kepler had missed—the transit of Venus across the sun in 1639—he detected from his little screen and telescope. After performing the day's services, he hurried home with his friend, William Crabtree, and saw that the little black circle of the planet had already entered the solar image. *Ecce gratissimorum spectaculum et tot votorum materiem*, he exclaimed to him. Yet he is no misfit in our 17th-century gallery, because Horrocks, Kepler and the

Metaphysicals themselves were all preoccupied with the natural universe as a manifestation of the divine immanence and so recognized no natural division between science and religion. So the Cambridge Platonists and Joseph Glanvil.

V THE VICTORIAN VICARAGE

An enormous gulf separates the still intensity of Herbert and the imaginative richness of Jeremy Taylor from even the best of the 18th-century parsons, living in an age of rationalism rather than reason which looked upon "enthusiasm," the light of the Metaphysicals, as bad taste and the religion of the poor as subversive. The naturalist parsons preserved a veneer of religion in their attitude to Nature as " the works of creation," but it is a kind of politeness rather than a faith. There were, however, a few 18th-century parsons who *partially* and in certain individual ways lifted the mediaeval and 17th-century tradition over to Hawker and Barnes and the " Catholic Revival."

One of these, preoccupied rather with the inner music of life than with its expression in outward deeds, was John Dyer, the Midlands parson and author of *Grongar Hill* (1726) and *The Fleece* (1757). He was both revivalist and precursor, not so much in religion but as a bard of Nature, while his sympathy with husbandry and country pursuits, " the labour of the loom," earned him the censure of Dr Johnson—" how can a man write poetically of serges and druggets? " In literature, he broke with the besetting heroic couplet:

" A little rule, a little sway,
A sunbeam in a winter's day,
Is all the proud and mighty have
Between the cradle and the grave."

More significantly, his fidelity to Nature reacted against that abstract and generalized spirit of thought which dominated the 18th century. He is the meditative quietist:

" Grass and flowers, Quiet treads
On the meads and mountain heads."

—the colourist of the English scene or " prospect " with the eye of the painter, as indeed he was. Thus, he stretches out one hand towards a lost joy in Nature (though without the 17th-century mystical approach) and another forwards to the 19th-century lyrical genius. He was indeed recognized by Wordsworth who overpraised him. With Collins, Thomson, Gray and John Phillips of *Cider*, he renovated the English country tradition and by his slender bridge of pastoral grace closed the great gap between Traherne and Coleridge. In his sensibility to natural beauty and lyrical love of husbandry, he was indeed a rural realist and true rebel against the abstract view of society and of " the law of Nature " as propounded by Hobbes and Locke which anticipated the " economic man " of Malthus and his kind.

With Dyer should be placed in this random chronicle Gilbert White himself, the greatest of all the 18th-century parsons, because in three important particulars he reacted against both the literary classicism and the social thinking of his age. He looks back to the Gothic tradition and, like Dyer, forward to the Nature-poets of the next century. In all other aspects, he was a characteristic product of his own century—but not in these. First, in his devotion to and interpretation of his own place which he made a shrine of the *genius loci*, he truly inherited the spirit of Gothic regionalism, Vaughan's Celticism and Herbert's village sense, and by his fidelity in describing every aspect of Selbornian life added something new to it. Next, his *Naturalist's Journal* is full of forthright Saxon nouns and adjectives which forecast William Barnes, while a number of his descriptions of natural scenes, natural life and natural vegetation are nearer to Dorothy Wordsworth's *Journals* than has ever been recognized. It is not to be expected that the man who wrote of the Selbornian echo as " the prattle of this loquacious nymph " and of spires as " necessary ingredients in an elegant landscape " should have anything Gothic or romantic about him. Nevertheless, it is so, and what, I think, lifted him out of his own period was his extraordinary sense of place.

Thirdly, in my edition of White (1938), I went to some trouble, by the publication of a Tithe Commutation Map of 1842, to show that White was living in a mediaeval village and still in his time rich in Saxon field-names. What is more, Gilbert White and his nephew, James White, in 1793 (the year of his death) defeated the attempt of one Fisher, " a man of a meddling disposition," to enclose the open fields of Selborne parish. He was himself a copyholder with common rights. Therefore, White must be included (to the deep pleasure of his lovers) among those churchmen who from Latimer to William Barnes raised their voices against the deprivation of the villagers' independence and rights of commonage. Gilbert White, who made his village as famous as Stratford and loved it in the same spirit as and with an even greater knowledge than Barnes loved the Valley of the Stour, must be accounted as an authentic descendant of the " povre Persoun," who is the symbolic figurehead of this chapter. Each, the one as priest, the other as naturalist, local historian and man of letters, dedicated himself to the cause and expression of the village.

Another link, this time also transitional in period, between the 18th century and the " povre Persoun " before and after it was George Crabbe. Hurdis's pastorals about Sussex might be anywhere; there is never any doubt that Parson Crabbe was an East Anglian who wrote about East Anglia. His sense of locality suffused his whole being and no poet has caught the genius of place more completely, even devastatingly. The east wind and the salt-marshes of Aldeburgh come right into his pages. Parson Crabbe was a realist, though he fitted his poetic numbers and language into the set patterns of the 18th-century diction, generalized like its thought both about Nature and social life. He was rather too much of a satirist pure and simple (though full of passion about the sufferings of his villagers) for too much stress to be laid upon his bridge-building between Latimer and Barnes. But he was sufficiently close to Skelton in feeling and spirit, though nothing like so good a poet, to be numbered among those who were the spiritual leaders of the village community.

I hardly think myself (though subject to correction) that the Evangelical movement in the country can be so accounted. A vibrant figure among them was John Newton, the slave-trader and hymn-maker who became the Vicar of Olney and so tormented poor Cowper (who called Herbert's poems " Gothick and uncouth "). In their reaction against what an old writer calls " the unwonted timidity and coldness " of the English Church, they threw up a few striking figures of whom Fletcher of the mining village of Madeley (1729–85) was one. He was something of a mystic, and what is more surprising, a humorist. A man who can jest *inside* a volume called *Checks to Antinomianism* is a man of metal. He certainly was that, for he used to rouse the more distant parishioners of his rough village for service at 5.0 a.m. with a handbell.

But the Evangelicals could never recover the 17th century cultural complex of eloquence, poetry, philosophy and translunary vision of God in Nature, something quite different from the crude pantheism with which Vaughan has been foolishly credited. They were not only Low Church but for all their fervour decidedly pedestrian in thought and expression. Both Mr Crawley and Mrs Proudie in the Barchester novels were heirs of the Evangelical Movement, though they were poles apart, both Puritans in mind, while Paul Robarts in *Framley Parsonage* is different from them in kind, being a rather watery descendant of the free-and-easy 18th-century parson with Victorian whitewash. George Herbert was as humble-minded as Bunyan, but he was never a narrow sectary. In pinchbeck morality and desert conditions of mind, there was indeed little to choose between the Low and High Church parson-type of the 19th century. If Trollope has stripped the pretensions from the former, that forgotten novelist, Mary Cholmondeley, not to mention Charlotte Brontë in the first chapter of *Shirley*, have performed the same necessary treatment upon the latter.

When the Evangelicals' impulse with its somewhat Calvinistic furies failed, a pseudo-morality took its place which echoed their Puritanically derived disgust with Nature. How different from the attitude of Vaughan who, in Edmund Blunden's words, " saw God walking in the garden without making others unhappy by applications of didactic insularity." Here is a striking example. In the third quarter of the last century, a simple pleasant book was written about the villagers of Finchingfield by the Vicar's daughter, Eliza Vaughan. She gives a quatrain from the communal song they used to sing to the game of " Kiss-in-the-Ring," undoubtedly a survival of the mediaeval May Day festival. Two lines ran:

" Now you are married we wish you joy,
First a gal and then a boy."

This was suppressed as " indelicate." There was a certain monkish suspicion of Nature in the Middle Ages, but it is inconceivable that a jolly reference to the issue of marriage would have been considered improper in any age, but the Victorian church of class gentility could not hold the sons of the soil, and so the labourers, whose ancestors had been the most religious of men, abandoned it.

Yet the English tradition has been so catholic and tenacious that the spiritual and cultural inertia of the 19th century was broken by a number of gallant Christians. If the church had decidedly ceased to be what Vaughan said of life—" a quickness which my God hath kissed "—it kept on throwing out a number of strange and lovable characters, like a seemingly dead volcano spurting stray flames. Deep down the old fires still burned. In the Victorian vicarage appears Francis Kilvert of Clyro, whose pen is like the brush of an English water-colourist and whose attitude to country misses and wenches was often discreetly pagan. His quality as a man of letters also gave expression to a passion for the countryside, a constant association with his villagers and a delight in village lore and custom which made him one

70   William Barnes

69   Hawker of Morwenstow

71 "The Disturber Detected": Early Victorian service in a country church. From a
painting by George Cruickshank, reproduced by gracious permission of H.M. the King

CHARLES KINGSLEY

of the most graceful and articulate of English countrymen. As one who heard and described with such warmth and sensibility the last of the Welsh harpists, he too is of the tribe of the " povre Persoun." And with Kilvert as thus representative I would place two humbler vicars of the 20th century, the Rev. Hudson, who revived the festival of the Boy Bishop at Berdon, and the Rev. Seddon, who detected the origin of " clipping the church " at Painswick as the Roman Lupercalia, though ultimately older than Rome, and nursed the ancient merriment into life again. These parsons, in reawakening folk-memory of the pagan past, were doing good deeds for Christianity. But in his own century Kilvert had his companions in the spirit, the Rev. C. V. Le Grice, Lamb's friend and a delicate writer of Cornish pieces, Charles Tennyson, William Crowe and William Lisle Bowles, to some extent the poetic master of Coleridge. He too had a regional relation with Herbert, since he was the Rector of Bremhill in Wiltshire, of which Herbert had once been incumbent. Upon the theme of Blake's " dark satanic mills," he denounced the asphyxiation of the cottage crafts by the Industrial Revolution. He is, therefore, one of the spiritual sons of our " povre Persoun." A warm and expressive love of Nature shone from all of these writer-parsons, while Canon Cooper of Filey, the Walking Parson, loved with his legs as well as with his pen.

But it is with Charles Kingsley that we come once more into the mid-stream of the tradition that flowed from the Middle Ages through the 1552 Prayer Book and Latimer to Hawker and Barnes. In *Alton Locke* and *Yeast* he gave a country twist to the Chartist principles and was a true knight on behalf of the agricultural labourer. The rural bent of his Christian Socialism made him regard the new industrial towns as not only a form of slavery for the factory-worker but the beginning of the urbanization of the countryside, and its co-operative values.

" The earth hath bubbles," he wrote, " and such cities as Manchester are of them. A short-sighted and hasty greed created them, and when they have lasted their little time and had their day, they will vanish like bubbles."

If I do not give a conspicuous place here to Kingsley as one wearing the starry mantle of the " povre Persoun," it is because his vehement works on behalf of fraternity and a true democracy losing its life to the money-power, are well known to lovers of literature and the country alike.

Yet another of the fitful Victorian lights was John Price, Vicar from 1859 to nearly the end of the century of Painscastle in Radnorshire and separated from Clyro, where Kilvert had his curacy, by what Bradley calls a " broken but delightful Arcady " of sumptuous hedges banking intricate lanes that wind westward into the mountains. This saintly eccentric, whom Kilvert actually visited and called " The Solitary," lived in three old bathing-machines and, after they had been burned down, in a henhouse, careless as he might well be of all creature comforts but so careful of the spiritual well-being of his parishioners that, in the words of Thoresby Jones in *Welsh Border Country*,

" interpreting literally the parable of the Marriage Feast, he went out to the highways and hedges to procure guests (it was a Dissenting parish) for his spiritual banquet, and soon an offer of sixpence a head per service began regularly to fill his pews with unwashed tramps and their draggle-tailed doxies."

If any of the vagrants were willing to exchange profane for sacred love, each new-wedded pair received five shillings, sometimes doubled or even trebled when, taking advantage of his short-sightedness, they asked for the ceremony to be repeated. In winter, an oil-stove was provided at the end of each occupied pew and on it the black sheep would under the paternal eye of their shepherd cook their kippers and potatoes. The admission fee of sixpence (given, not taken) fell to fourpence, but, by an informal meeting in the churchyard, the rakehelly crew decided to continue as a congregation. But then this prince of charity could only afford threepence per wandering soul and from that day the raggle-taggles went on strike. The church stood empty and the vicar was flockless until he sank to such extremity of destitution that his clothes had to be cut from off his skin, and after a bath he died. It will be a wry smile that greets such a tale of the " povre Persoun of the toun," lost his way in an age when the money-changer had cast out Christ

Sunday Morning (1824)

from the temple. Yes, and from Herbert's Temple. John Price, that holy man, serves as a stepping stone (not in date but spirit) between Latimer and Herbert on one side of the stream and Hawker and Barnes on the other. In the attitude and atmosphere of their respective periods, a sundering flood rolled between them, and yet all four were akin.

Before coming to the two latter among the 19th century band of saints, I must mention a figure who died a little later (1914) than Price, but, like him, an apostle of the " Lady Poverty." Charles Marson of Hambridge, Taunton, is a bright particular star in the crown of our country worthies. He it was who collected the four volumes of Somerset folk-songs, while Cecil Sharp's function was to pick out the airs on his fiddle. He used to sit in an inn on Sedgmoor and get the shepherds to sing their own songs, some as old as the 14th century. In his own village, he revived the acting of mediaeval plays—the *Secunda Pastorum* of the Towneley Cycle—not as an academic and sophisticated frippery like much of modern folk-dancing, the Arts and Crafts Movement and the sham pastoralism of Marie Antionette, but by sheer intuition catching the Gothic spirit of ribaldry and piety mingled. Marson, indeed, had an insight into the peasant mentality extremely rare in an age which the child of the one that destroyed it, and in *Village Silhouettes* he illustrated his own studies of the Somerset folk with his own pen-and-ink drawings. This depth of understanding was buttressed by a combination of profound historical with field scholarship; he was a folklorist, a herbalist and an angler, and this country-mindedness, fired by artistic sensibility, a highly expressive pen and a sacred zeal enables him to describe the effects of the Enclosures upon the dispossessed almost as though, like Kingsley, he had witnessed them in person.

Like Kingsley, too, he was a Christian Socialist before Socialism had ceased to be a human and regenerative force, and in *God's Co-operative Society* he pointed out with as much racy and individual vigour as erudition the social implications of the patristic writings. Marson drew into his own personal philosophy a number of separate but convergent threads of the English rural tradition, that of Goldsmith, of Cobbett, of the 17th-century Churchmen and that of the Celtic and Saxon saints. Since Canon Widdrington of Dunmow, himself a learned and living devotee of the sacred values attaching to that tradition and one of the special lights of the contemporary Catholic Revival, was a pupil of Marson's, the chain is unbroken from the " povre Persoun " to the country vicarage of to-day.

Hawker and Barnes were more than jets of coloured fire eructed from the dead volcano. In an age when political and economic theory had been completely secularized and natural law was regarded as automatic, they both picked up the heritage of the " povre Persoun of the toun " and constituted themselves spiritual leaders of the village community. Latimer, Herbert, Hawker and Barnes (and to these, of course, should be added other figures some of whom I have named) wore the mantle of John Ball, though only one of them would have subscribed to his actual doctrine. But Latimer and Herbert did not live in a period when the church's moral teaching was confined to its own paddock. Hawker in his rough virility, so harmonious with its Cornish setting, Barnes, the poet of country speech, manners, customs and ethics of mutual aid, the champion of the rural tradition, were both revivalists of the mediaeval idea in a church much more unfavourable to it than was early Anglicanism. They restored conviction to a rural church that in the 18th and 19th centuries distrusted it, and the leaven of the old village democracy worked in their souls. Supporters, too, are to be found for them from the kingdom of imaginative creation, no less real than the men who once were flesh—the Vicar of Wakefield, Trollope's Vicar of Bullhampton and Dr Syntax, who, in his " black-cocked hat and wig " played the violin to the villagers dancing round the Maypole, and at whose death

> " The village wept, the hamlets round
> Crowded the consecrated ground;
> And waited there to see the end
> Of Pastor, Teacher, Father, Friend."

VI HAWKER OF MORWENSTOW

The biography of Hawker has been twice written, once incidentally sketched by James Haslam, a fellow-parson, and by S. Baring Gould who also lived in the West Country. Since both these books have long been out of print, let me dwell for a little upon this singular man, whose life was a throw-back, a reversion, an anachronism if ever there was one. But it behoves me to handle delicately that dangerous word " singular," since to regard Hawker as a mere eccentric is to obscure not only his greatness of being but his significance as a churchman in the great tradition. A churchman of what church?—that question has been asked before.

He was born in 1804, the son and grandson of Cornish divines and spent a boyhood very wild and very bookish. He published a book of verse when he was seventeen and a book of ballads, *Records of the Western Shore*, in 1832. His biographers have recorded many tales of his prankishness and practical joking—such as hoaxing the natives of Bude for four days or rather dusks on end in a life-like imitation of a mermaid. This habit is worth mention here not for its own sake nor even as illustrative of a passionate impulsiveness and exuberance that accompanied him through life, but because it so exactly carried into boisterous action the motives of his meditation in verse or from book. When he played ghost or mermaid or legend in his uproarious fashion, he was transporting himself into a pristine Cornish world which haunted all his days. Hawker, whatever his biographers say, was a good poet only in flashes and his poetry never runs on the even keel of William Barnes, who also wrote popular poetry but could never have won the Newdigate, as Hawker did. Scott praised him for a stirring romantic narrative balladry that he wrote himself better than Hawker. But the themes—of the old, old Cornwall—were as true to the man as his extraordinarily vivid and burning feeling for the saints of his native Duchy:

" They rear'd their lodges in the wilderness,
Or built them cells beside the shadowy sea,
And there they dwelt with angels, like a dream!
So they unroll'd the Volume of the Book
And fill'd the fields of the Evangelist
With thoughts as sweet as flowers."

A touch here of the authentic De La Mare magic, but his is secular, Hawker's religious. How different is Hawker's wassailing song to Herrick's— " Drink hael!—in Jesu's name."

He took the living of Morwenstow in 1834 and held it till his death in 1875. Ten years before his incumbency, he married a lady more than twice his age, whose means enabled him to remain at Oxford, absorbing learning like a fish drawing water through its gills. This was not done out of calculation but an access of passion, not for his wife but his studies, and yet he was devoted to her all her life. He took his living also in a kind of transport, but at Morwenstow he neither changed the boy nor reacted against the new man. Rather he settled in like a Cornish chough on its nest among the savage cliffs of black basalt. The land of the saints and the pixies was now his very own. Among those fanged precipices between Tintagel and Bude he built his hut of wrecked ship-timbers, where he would sit for hours contemplating the waves that had given him them and composing his poetry.

There, too, he repaired the well of St Morwenna, the founder-saint of his parish who said to her brother when she was dying, " Raise me in thine arms, brother, that my eyes may rest upon my native Wales." Once a busybody

122

called on him towards the end of his life and asked him what were his views and opinions. He drew him to his window.

" There," he said, " is Hennacliff, there the Atlantic stretching to Labrador, there Morwenstow crag, here the church and graves: those are my views. As to my opinions, I keep them to myself."

I put the words of the saint and the parson together because nearly the whole of Hawker is in their juxtaposition. St Morwenna was a living presence to him and as she felt about God and the wild western land and sea, so he felt. The very spirit of his native place, of " holy Wessex," the land of the saints, was in his bones.

His feeling for the Cornish tradition was so extreme that he wore about his parish a yellow vestment like a Lama's but which he believed was an exact copy of the priestly robe worn by St Padarn and St Teilo. Under this he wore a blue fisherman's jersey and over it a claret-coloured cassock, fishing-boots up to his thighs, a plum-coloured beaver without a brim on his silver hair and, in sharp weather, a pair of crimson gloves. Thus gaily accoutred, he climbed the cliffs or rode forth on his mule, often accompanied by his two stags, as though he had stepped into the 19th century straight out of the pages of Helen Waddell's *Beasts and Saints*. Up the nave of his Norman church (which he restored more lovingly than discriminately), strewn with marjoram, southernwood and thyme, he walked, followed by his ten cats, the man who introduced the Arthurian cycle to Tennyson, a romantic but assuredly not a Byronic figure.

His compassion for animals (*ubi aves, ibi angeli*) was equalled by his stintless generosity and his charity towards all men, even the Methodists of whom he spoke—" John Wesley came into Cornwall and persuaded the people to change their vices." Yet he was always getting jobs for the needy among them, though he had no liking for their Corybantic prayer-meetings and a vehement loathing of the Calvinist doctrine of man's total corruption, holding as he did like the early Christians that he was the blurred image of God. His wild parish was inhabited by a people hardly less wild, wreckers, ex-smugglers, labourers desperate with poverty, uncouth farmers who resented his outspoken championship of the men who were receiving eight shillings a week from them, paid in corn. " They are crushed down, my poor people, ground down with poverty, with a wretched wage, the hateful truck system, till they are degraded in mind and body." If any tale of indigence came to his knowledge, he would rush out of the vicarage with clothing and blankets over his arm and wine and food in his hands. Many a shipwrecked sailor on that pitiless coast he rescued, housed, fed, nursed and clothed, giving, as his grandfather had done, all that he had. He was, as Baring Gould says, idolized by the workpeople who could readily overlook an impetuosity that made them safe from the cold benevolence of a correct behaviour and could share his pagan sympathy with charms and folk-lore, if they could not his visions of a more primitive, less contaminated world. But they could enjoy his drilling of the turnips with the ashes of his own sermons, since they knew all about both. As Baring Gould says, he was a queer mixture of the eagle and the dove, and indeed of whims and convictions, but, so long as they nest close enough together, the dove in Nature gets on well enough with the eagle.

One of the remarkable things about this dreamer and mystic, as bold and fearless in action as he was transparent in honesty, was his introduction of the Harvest Festival (in 1843) into the Cornish Church. That is one of the touches about him that I find most significant: he was a mediaeval revivalist, a seeker after wholeness, trying to draw together the sundered halves of man's estate, the old lost idea of the Manger. Shortly after I had published an account of him, I received a letter from a native of Kilkhampton, the next parish to Morwenstow and enclosing a photograph of the old man in a long mulberry-coloured coat, which, of course, is a great rarity. Her father had been a friend of Hawker's and from him she learned that on " Revel Sunday " (St John's Day), all the congregation went straight from service to the village green where sports and dances were held, wrestling and running matches. " The day," my correspondent writes, " was a recognized one for families meeting and inviting all friends—open houses everywhere. Alas, these hospitable times are gone, but the spirit of Morwenstow remains."

Of these revels Hawker was the leading spirit, so that he was actually performing the same service to the community that Baxter (see p. 109) complained of in his father's parish. It made me happy for a week to have been told of this lovely example of continuity in the mediaeval relation of the church to the community.

But though Hawker was a kind of democrat in the John Ball sense, in the Chesterton sense, as Richard II for a moment had been, he was something more or something further back. All his working life he was a High Churchman, but neither Tractarian nor Ritualist. Before his death, he became a Catholic but in a strange way not a *Roman* Catholic, close as he was to St Francis. Say rather an *English* Catholic, like the good Father Ignatius of Llanthony, almost his contemporary, who read the burial service when his novices took their vows (providing the coffin and bearers) and practically invented his own ritual. But no, that has not quite got it. He was reviled for his change of faith which really was no change at all, and even Baring Gould wagged a deprecatory head. The truth is that neither his biographers nor his contemporary censors paid proper attention to his own words in his own defence.

" I am a priest of the Church, of the Church of God, of that Church which was for hundreds of years in Cornwall before a Pope of Rome was ever thought of."

That explains him-perfectly and is his complete justification. He was a member of the primitive church of St Columba, St Columbanus, St Cuthbert and the Celtic saints of Cornwall whose bloom he retained after fourteen hundred years. Is he not then a significant figure in these annals.

VII WILLIAM BARNES OF CAME

George Sampson, in his *Concise Cambridge History of English Literature*, says of William Barnes that he was " a minor poet concerned chiefly to exploit the dialect of his shire," and that it is doubtful whether his pastoral poetry would have survived without " its unearned increment of dialectial quaintness." So insensitive and superficial a verdict ignores the fact that Barnes's vernacular is so perfectly fused with his meaning and his melody that to separate it from them is to skin his country Muse alive. This urban judgment entirely fails to see that Barnes's lyrics are peasant poetry miraculously reborn. His verse is the old communal folk-song made the vehicle of an individual spirit whose reinterpretation of it was an act of genius. It is a rebirth, not a repetition and so there is novelty—that is to say, the personal and unique contribution of the poet himself. Regional as were Hawker's ballads and regional as was the man, he in his Cornishness cannot compare with Barnes as the inspired translator of the Dorset countryside as a whole, human and natural, into a couple of song-books.

It is not great poetry, no, but where in the world will you find country poetry to touch it? Herrick? A true ruralist but of Anacreontic descent. Wordsworth or Hardy? They are philosopher-poets, Barnes not in the least. John Clare? Yes, but not in pure song; in reverie, in pathos, in intimacy, in lovingness, but there is a detachment even in John Clare. In Barnes there is none, except in his artfulness as a metrist. Otherwise, he simply *is* Dorset country singing out loud. As a country poet (the greater of the two) Clare muses, dreams and remembers alone; as a country poet Barnes partakes in and expresses the life of the village community. The perfection with which he does it from its very speech to its way of life, from itself to its country environment, this is his genius and no one has excelled him in it. The one spoke for the country that has made the husbandman; the other for the countryman who has remade Nature. All the sweetness and greenness and floweriness of the Dorset pastures is in Barnes, and all that lives upon them, man and beast and bird. Man's tragedy, too, no less than his festivals, and English country has been tragic enough since 1830. On page 100, for instance, of *Poems of Rural Life* are two "Eclogues"—" The Common A-Took In " and "Two Farms in Woone "; on page 175, a dialogue on Joseph Arch's Union. The countrymen of his fellow Dorset poet tower symbolically against a sky of sunset fires but the countrymen of William Barnes are just the folk of Blackmore Vale in summer and winter, in joy and sorrow, in work and play, in past and present, in all their moods and tenses, caught into song like the very voice of its rich homely meadows :

> " Tis merry ov a zummer's day,
> When vo'k be out a-haulen hay,
> Where boughs, a-spread upon the ground,
> Do meäke the staddle big and round;
> An' grass do stand in pooks, or lie
> In long-back'd weales or parsels, dry.
> Then I do find it stir my heart
> To hear the frothen hosses snort
> A-haulen on, wi' sleek heäir'd sides,
> The red-wheeled waggon's deep-blue zides.
> Aye, let me have woone cup o' drink
> An' hear the linky harness clink.
> An' then my blood do run so warm
> An' put such strangth 'ithin my earm
> That I do long to toss a pick
> A-pitchen and a-meäken rick."

It is a song-book of the Vale not of the hills, nor the horizon, nor the depths of man's mind, nor longing, not passionate nor visionary, and you can quote from it almost anywhere, so level is it like the Vale itself. It is the cottager's Muse pure and simple, dateless, flowing on and on like the " stwoneless Stour," and so completely does Barnes identify himself with the country scene that in a sense he is the most representative English rural poet that ever breathed and sang. The church-the village-the fields, through William Barnes the poet-parson and the most regional of them, all their ancient trinity is renewed, three in one and one in three. The " povre Persoun of the toun " is with us once more, only now he flutes where once he chanted. But the continuity is restored not by the church but the cleric, not even by the man, zealous priest as he was, but by the bard.

Barnes's love of Nature and love of humanity were bound together by the genius of the place, where they themselves could not be parted one from the other. He was the complete provincial and what the parish lacks in area it makes up in depth. The true provincial makes the utmost of the limitations he gladly accepts. Of no man who ever lived is this truer than it is of Barnes. It is hardly realized what a tremendous scholar he was, a man of unfathomable learning. His songs appear on the surface to be unpremeditated warblings; actually their metrical devices are almost too intricate. He uses in them Saxon alliteration, bardic stresses, Italian metres, Persian assonances and hidden and interior rhymes without the faintest loss of spontaneity and freshness. He knew all these languages, not to mention Hindustani and many other tongues, and beside his linguistic and philological erudition, he was a lexicographer, a prosodist, a grammarian, a playwright, a naturalist, an engraver, a geographer, a historian, an archeologist, a botanist (he called it " wort-lore "), a geologist, a musician, a logician (he called it " speech-craft " *), a translator, a social reformer, a schoolmaster (at Mere) and a very great countryman.

He gave to the term " all-rounder " an epic significance, this simplest of country parsons. Many have laughed at his theory that the Dorset vernacular he wrote was the remnant of the speech of King Alfred but without ever having disproved it. In abolishing all Latinisms and interpolations into the unmixed English he spoke and wrote, he did indeed go too far. But nobody gives him credit for his motive, namely to restore to the language its pristine strength and purity. His poetry and his scholarship were gropings down into the depths of organic being. Why should he have been so preoccupied with this mission? Because his relation to the Christian-Saxon culture is just what Hawker's was to the Christian-Celtic culture. In fact, he *was* a Saxon saint as Hawker was a Celtic one. He was the very origin of the folk he celebrated in song.

> " In stillness we ha' words to hear
> An' shapes to zee in darkest night
> An' tongues a-lost can hail us near,
> An' souls a-gone can smile in zight."

Like Hawker, he dressed like a sage, a kind of spiritual Doge, in kneebreeches, long stockings and a poncho-like cloak, and Gosse saw him on his death-bed surrounded by his brown old books in a red biretta and scarlet robe over which fell his long white beard, a figure most venerable but

* In 1573, Alfred Lever in his *Arte of Reason rightly termed Witcraft* wrote " foreset " and " backset " for " subject " and " predicate" and "saywhat" for "definition."

mysterious too. He had communion with the dead and further back than his own Saxon days. His archaeological researches with the Dorset Field Club were derided in his day; they would not be so now. He was among the pioneers who refuted the common view that our prehistoric colonists were a pack of H. G. Wellsian savages. How interlinked all the facets of his scholarship were! He had a theory of the origin of poetry and music as a trilogy of song-tune-dance and he found it in Stonehenge—*Chorea Giganteum*, the song-dance of the giants. And his own folk-poetry is just like that. I think there is meaning in Barnes's very ancestry, the lords of the manor of Gillingham. There was an extraordinary wholeness about the man.

A sage but, as his daughter truly said who wrote his life, also child-like —but in the scriptural sense. One of his parishioners said of him—" we do all o' us love our passon that we do; he be so *plain.*" Another wrote to him from abroad :

> " I have tried for years to see you and hear you read, and I hope I shall yet; But if not I hope I shall see you when earthly distinctions are past; but may you long live to write, and may you long live to read, and may the earth be always blessed with such lights, and may they always be loved and honoured, and when earthly praise shall cease, may the music of a thousand voices bid you welcome and say ' well done.' Trusting you will forgive me for taking the liberty of expressing my feelings. I remain, etc."

His was the old Saxon kind of democracy (he called it folkdom). He was out in all weathers upon the needs of his parish often without food, and one day, when he was eighty, he walked six miles through deep snow and officiated at two services, a wedding, a funeral and a celebration all in one day. His views on finance were as old as Cobbett's and as new as those of the Economic Reform Club. Labour was the " measure of commercial value," and he had the feelings of the old churchmen about usury and of money that had ceased to be a token and become a commodity bearing yet more money. He was so very old-fashioned (they called him " the hobbyhorse man ") as to apply Christian ethics to economics. He regretted the vanishing of the old-time working squire, " the landlord who lived upon his land : "

> " And while through days of longsome span
> His corn was sunn'd from green to red,
> His son grew up from boy to man,
> And now his master in his stead;
> For him the loaded waggons roll
> To staddled ricks that rustle dry,
> And there for him the grey-wing'd doves
> Around the mossy dovecots fly."

There is something richly appropriate in the squire of Came writing to him and telling him about his (Barnes's) father who saw in the advent of machinery the end of the old cottage home-baking and brewing and virtue leaving things that the people no longer made for themselves. All his life this learned man fought for the unlettered labourer.

When Barnes walked to the top of Ham Hill that impends over his " cloty Stour " and looked over the Vale of Blackmore, he saw in his mind's eye its bones, its green clothing, its buildings, its history and its people as a kind of

tutelary spirit of them all. He would point out the farm where his grandfather
had lived, the clump of trees where he had played as a child, all his favourite
haunts. Not the god of its meadows and woods, but the home-saint; not
only the wise man of his little kingdom but the child of its very heart.

VIII THE CHRISTIAN TRADITION

It is clear that men of the godly stamp of Latimer, Herbert, Hawker and
Barnes with their like-minded or like-living fellows, more illustrious or less
so than they, each picking up the Christian tradition in his own special way,
it is clear that men like these whose lives or works or both translated into
contemporary terms the inward meaning of the Manger and the Workshop
in Galilee were not of the same world as that of Jack Russell whom Baring
Gould recorded as calling out of his pulpit:

> " O Tally Ho, O Tally Ho!
> Dearly Beloved—Zounds, sir! "

Nor were they of the same world as the old-time scholar-parson.*
Both the hunting and the antiquarian parson, so typical of the 18th century,
survived into our own period. One of them, remembered from youthful
days, was a big burly man with a booming voice who thought the M.F.H.
was God's deputy on earth. He was like a big bluebottle booming round
and his wife was like a wasp. Another was a passionate Egyptologist who
every Sunday chose a text from the Old Testament that had something to do
with Pharaoh or the Egyptians. He would then deliver an address on
Egyptian archaeology to his bewildered parishioners.

Nor were those who preserved the continuity of the old tradition of the
pluralist breed or the type which put an end to the old village choirs or of
those whose Christianity was that of a text on the wall, a vague benevolence,
a sentimental propriety or a set of minatory injunctions to their poor
parishoners to be respectful to their betters—still less of those who lived in the
squire's pocket and ate out of his hand. The undistinguished host of these
is represented by an immortal trio—Mr Slope in *Barchester Towers*, Mr
Elton in *Emma* and Mr Collins in *Pride and Prejudice*. The Roman Church
attempted to dictate to the State; the English Church of the 18th and 19th
centuries went over to it. That which had tried to be the State's master
succeeded in becoming its servant, and one of the milestones in this record
of ecclesiastical progress was the material benefit derived by the parson hardly
less than the squire from the Enclosures.

Nearly twenty years ago, there appeared in the pages of the *Nation* a
number of anonymous articles on the countryside which elicited such
applause in the Liberal camp that they were republished in a volume called
England's Green and Pleasant Land. Though he had some good things to
say about housing, the writer, as an apostle of rural progress, made much
of his book the substance of an attack upon the parsons, on the ground that
they were " out-of-date," " mediaevalist," " remote from the stimulus of
London," anti-rationalist. " Gramophone sermons," he thought would be

* There is a denigrating sketch of this type, divorced from the humanities, in
Doreen Wallace's admirable historical novel of the Captain Swing period, *Green
Acres*.

73 The Communion: from a painting by Francis Wheatley

72 A Vicar Receiving Tithes, 1799: from an engraving after Singleton

75 The Parson and his Clerk Caricatured in 18th-Century Porcelain

74 An 18th-Century Parson's Return from Tithing

quite a good idea. If the writer is still alive, he surely could have no ground for complaint as to the rapidity with which the country has been urbanized. All frowns in 1925, he must be all smiles to-day.

The part played by the parson during the Enclosures, his divided allegiance, that is to say, between God and Caesar, produced a supine and diluted Christianity which proved to be a broken reed in resistance to the growth of the new urbanism that, since the beginning of the 20th century, has been undermining every aspect of rural integrity. Parson Crabbe, with his usual shrewdness and biting penetration, put his finger on the mischief:

> " Thus he his race began, and to the end
> His constant care was, no man to offend;
>
> .   .   .   .   .
>
> He was his Master's soldier, but not one
> To lead an army of His martyrs on:
> Fear was his ruling passion."

And elsewhere:

> " Now rests our Vicar—They who knew him best
> Proclaim his life t'have been entirely—rest."

This Laodicean parson has been happily limned by Baring Gould in *Red Spider*. His waggon, having become unhitched from its star, was driven along the icy roads of the " Economic Man " by Mr Facing-Both-Ways. The trouble with the country parson has been, not that he has been too much " out-of-date " but too little. He has compromised too dangerously with the progress that has from the Enclosures onwards been putting Christianity out-of-date altogether.

Chapter VII

THE ENGLISH TRADITION

I WAR UPON THE ENGLISH TRADITION

In the foregoing chapters, an outline of some of the main qualities and characteristics which distinguished the English country-born tradition has taken shape. It covers, of course, many fields I have not had room to wander in, such as the fair province of the English water-colourists and wood-engravers who painted and incised the England of that husbandry which itself modelled it out of a bountiful Nature. The illuminated manuscripts of the 14th century, Samuel Palmer and Thomas Bewick the yeoman, Constable, Calvert, Cotman and Crome, and in our own time Wilson Steer, are as much part of the tradition as Lincoln cathedral and a thatching spud. The little towns of the guild-masters belonged to it as intimately as the cob-cottage.

The solitary individuals share it in company with the anonymous co-operators of field and building. Use in this kingdom is at one with beauty and religion with art, just as piety and buffoonery are at home together in a Gothic church. This tradition makes up a single complex as a Gothic cathedral does and, like it, it is definitely Christian but without excluding its Pagan background. But its source of power is ultimately the Christian religion, whether directly or indirectly in its ethical manifestations, so that it is predominantly and in the broadest sense a spiritual culture. It was only when that inspiration began to fail it that it began to disintegrate, slowly but inevitably. Its wholeness began to break up into separateness, and that is most clearly seen in the history of the parson after the church had ceased to claim or to exercise any influence over the life of man in society and particularly in economics. But the parson's abdication is only a short-hand of what happened to the whole tradition itself, since the binding force of all its activities was the genius of folk, family, and faith, rooted in place but branching out into multiplicity of expression.

If, without going into politics and economics, you look at the five representative rural figures which translate into human terms the siting of every authentic village into church-houses-fields, themselves a microcosm of God-Man-Earth, you gather that what has happened to each one of them has happened to all. If the old term, *adscriptus glebae*, be used in its simpler, non-technical sense, we see that all five figures have in course of time ceased to become *adscriptus glebae*. The peasant has been jocketed out of his land; the intimate association between land and craft has been broken; the yeoman has ceased to have security in his land; the squire and the parson lost, the one his personal, the other his spiritual responsibility for the village. All five figures became uprooted. There were exceptions, and they were those who carried on the continuity of the tradition. Progress has detached every one of these type-figures from the village. Judging by its results, the term *adscriptus glebae* means something more than a social order which has been disrupted. The three primaries—God-Man-Earth— have been disintegrated and the village pattern faithfully reflected it. Thus,

130

76   The Great Timber Mill at Houghton, Huntingdonshire

77 Market-Day at Thame, Oxfordshire

78 A Village Shop at Heytesbury, Wiltshire

the term has practical and spiritual implications both; its meanings are aesthetic as well as functional. Good husbandry may be historically called the root of good literature, true piety and the art and craft of living. The peasant, the yeoman, the craftsman, the squire and the parson are what you might call basic England. In the sphere both of values and of practical life, the structure of the village is as indestructible as the family. And if we look at modern developments, they can all be boiled down to one thing —the separation of its people from the soil.

Consequently, the tradition is at its weakest to-day when a concerted attack is being made upon it. All that it has meant in the development of the authentic national character is not only threatened by a revolutionary movement in high places of great power and energy, but its elimination is openly advocated. An alliance between the forces of agricultural technology and big business with the bureaucracy as their willing promoter has appeared whose professed object in its own words is " to overcome tradition " and be rid of " out-of-date customs which delay progress." The abolition of private ownership in land; the destruction of " nuisance " features in our countryside such as hedgerow timber, copses, hedges, lanes and the like; the abandonment of balanced farming for specialization in crop-production; the unlimited use of machinery and artificials; total nationalization accompanied by the profit-making motive as the sole stimulus to initiative in agriculture—these proposals are put forward, not by irresponsible paper-ideologues but by men of weight and authority in national affairs.

Their advocacy of " larger economic units " represents the last stage, the final act, of the 18th and 19th century Enclosures. This formidable body of opinion is flanked by the tenant farmers on the one hand, numbers of whom profess themselves as guided by the cash principle alone (" I don't go in for ' good farming ' as some people know it. I just go in for profitable farming and the two are not by any means synonymous," is the way one of them puts it) and by the doctrinaire " rational planners " on the other. Their new orders, abstractly conceived from the top downwards, bear no relation to the needs of the countryman, have little or no knowledge of husbandry and are purely urban in mode of thought. Thus, the English tradition which is as deeply a " part of an Englishman's constitution," as Crawford said of Shakespeare in *Mansfield Park,* is in danger of its death.

If you look at a common or yard-fowl with the eyes of the English tradition, you will see three things—the husbandman's Wyandotte or Rhode Island Red, the Nature-lover's " timekeeper on green farms " and the visionary's

> " Father of lights! what sunnie seed
> What glance of day hast thou confined
> Into this bird? "

All three aspects are true to the English tradition and something of each usually occurs in one or the other. This is our ruralism.

The main cause for all this activity against it is not so much the present interdependence between national safety and the production of home-grown food as the dawning realization that at the close of the present war it will not be possible, at any rate for an unforeseen number of years, to repeat the abandonment of our native agriculture at the close of the last. Our foreign investments having been " liquidated " our position will be no longer that of a creditor but of a debtor nation. The urban population will no longer be able to depend upon imported cheap foods as interest-payments upon non-existent foreign loans nor will foreign nations, with their fully-equipped industrial plant, be willing to receive from us exported cheap manufactured goods which they will in future make for themselves. The conclusion drawn is not a complete revision of an economic system which forced debtor countries into cut-throat competition with one another for producing food and raw materials out of exploited soils as debt-charges paid off below the cost of production. That is not the end in view; it is the commercialization of our own countryside as a substitute for the loss of profitable fields of exploitation in distant lands, regardless of the examples in the spendthrift wastage of capital resources in soil-fertility, phosphates, timber and the like entailed by it.

The contempt expressed for any and every form of tradition shows quite clearly that it is not only the husbandman who is the object of attack but the whole English tradition, material and cultural. The revolutionary not only regards the yeoman and the craftsman and the smallholder and the landlord as " obsolete " but English country and the English countryman as Marvell saw them and as, though fallen upon evil days, we see them:

> " O thou, this dear and happy Isle,
> The garden of the world erewhile,
> Thou Paradise of the four seas
> That Heaven planted us to please."

II THE JUST PRICE

Is our native husbandry, on the busy stage of which the actors I have represented played parts of such lustre, really obsolete? One of our champions of reconstruction of a different stamp from the mechanists and economic agronomes, Montague Fordham, has argued persistently on behalf of a " standard price " fixed by the State for agricultural home-products as the only non-palliative measure to secure the farmer from his ruinous exposure to cut-price competition and alternating booms and slumps, as has been the history of agriculture since the 19th century. This is nothing more nor less than the " just price " of the mediaeval guild and country workshop alike.

Many anti-revolutionary land-reformers of the calibre of Sir George Stapledon, Lord Lymington, Lord Northbourne, the late Christopher Turnor, Adrian Bell and others have stressed decentralization as the first of all needs, and the nursing of regional centres and nuclei from a foundation of local practise, soil-conditions and human intercourse. Their reasons have been manifold. Locally raised fresh foods are a remedy for sterilized and faked ones and for the notorious malnutrition from which, according to Sir John Orr, twenty millions of our people suffer. The excess profits of dealer and distributor, sometimes five times those of the primary producer, batten through costs of transport and processing upon centralization, while prices are manipulated by them against both the grower and the consumer. Mr Clifton Reynolds, a business man turned farmer, makes the following comment in his book, *Glory Hill Farm* (Lane, 1941):

> " I am told that the big retail milk combines exert a powerful influence on this Board (the Milk Marketing Board), but that they do not make much money out of selling milk. Yet I see that one of them made profits of more than £600,000 a year for several years and wonder how it was done, if not from

milk. And while on this subject, it is interesting to note that the milling combines regularly paid out dividends of 20 per cent. and 25 per cent., and a certain company interested in root-crops a cool 400 per cent. on its original investment . . . these figures represent net profits for distribution to people who do nothing at all in the way of working for them."

When the Ministry of Food by confidential instructions condones the removal of part of the wheat-germ from and the use of damaged flour in its " National Loaf " against the repeated and express recommendations of the Medical Research Council, and it is widely known that tampering with the nation's food-supply has been to the profit of the big milling interests, then producers and consumers alike are victims both in health and in pocket of a gigantic conspiracy of money operating through the distributing trades and at a time when the home-production of nutritious foods is bound up with the national existence.

Regionalism obviously checks such parasitism, while the basis of a true democracy is in local self-government. It also counters a non-organic suburban spread from top-heavy cities. It prevents that waste endemic to an over-industrialized nation and would encourage the revival of a host of local industries, of which country milling is perhaps the most vital. It is a means to fostering co-operation as well as the only practical method for reconditioning the land (Stapledon). Perhaps the best reason these writers give is that regional centres are the only practical mode of recharging the moribund village with life. These are very different proposals from those of the " rational planners " to dump irrelevant industries upon villages and small towns and thus urbanize them. But Trystan Edwards's *Hundred New Towns*, complete with factories and different centres of civic activity and depending on the surrounding countryside for fresh produce, could do nothing but good towards the reawakening of an authentic rural life. Good for the towns and good for the country, for the interdependent balance between them *is* a true modernization of the English tradition, a fulfilment, not a destruction. It is needless to go further than the bare assertion that its husbandry has always been regional and never centralized except through the focal points of market towns.

III THE MIXED FARM

Three other issues, deeply involving both the past and the future, are so closely intertwined as to make a composite unity. They are the balanced or mixed farm, the health and fertility of the soil and intensive production. That all are characteristics of our traditional husbandry calls for no exposition. The first and second interact for the obvious reason that the mixed farm of arable, pasture, livestock and woodland is the only one which can restore to the soil what it extracts from it, and recognizes the basic wholeness of Nature by its own correlation of parts. Nature is the first of farmers; the mixed farm is the nearest to Nature.

It is a very curious fact that, though the specialized and mechanized farm, the modern version of the Roman *latifundia*, actually produces less yield of crops per acre than the mixed farm (large or small) and the smallholding, yet output and again output (the Research Institute, the government office and the business firm only think in terms of output), is put forward as *the reason* for supplanting the mixed farm and smallholding by " large-scale economic units." The figures prove it beyond controversy. In Sir Daniel Hall's *Reconstruction and the Land*, the spearhead of the " land as investment " attack upon our time-honoured husbandry, a table is given of the production per acre of wheat, barley, oats, potatoes and sugar beet between 1927 and 1936 in eleven countries. In every instance and by wide percentages, the list is headed by Denmark, Holland and Belgium, the type-examples of peasant and yeoman farming, and bottomed by Canada, Australia, the United States and the Argentine, the type-examples of large-scale mechanized farming for profit.

Peasant and yeoman farming is, of course, always intensive (when not crippled by finance and saddled with debt) partly by the stimulus of owner-ship and partly by that element of personal care and intimate knowledge which a farm run by machines and for profit alone necessarily lacks. It lacks something else as well. A fifty-acre holding properly cultivated and fed with humus has an internal surface equal to one of 150 or even 200 acres, so that throwing a number of smallholdings into one large one is actually wastage of soil. Thus, the relentless revolutionaries of " progress " are in flouting the tradition of the past mortgaging the welfare of the future, and from this conclusion there is no logical escape. Those very countries at the bottom of the list are now a byword throughout the world for the soil-exhaustion and soil-erosion of millions of their once fertile acres. In material terms alone and at a moment of supreme crisis in the relation of population to food-supply, the traditional husbandry of the country types I have been considering emerges as the one safe anchorage against a potential world-starvation. To say nothing at all of Sir Albert Howard's contention that a sick soil (viz. over-driven or denuded of organic humus) is ultimately respon-sible for disease in plant and animal and a human population subnormal in health.

Since the assailants of the English tradition, nowadays so vocal and power-ful, only refer to the question of values as one merely of " sentiment " and " nostalgia " and so presumably as out-of-date as private property in land, why should I refer to them in this chapter? Because the history of our peasant, our squire, our land, is pregnant with them, inseparable from them. The beauty of our landscapes and villages and little towns chimes with the inward beauty of those who have lived in and upon them, ranging the whole gamut from Shakespeare to the ploughman's song. A competitive world riven into chaos and going up in flames would seem to stand in need of that co-operation the peasant expressed not for emergency but in normal usage. A humanity perilously near the servile state and the automatism of the ant-heap has something to learn from the independence of the yeoman. A society in bondage to machines whether of the body or mind might look with something like longing upon the creative individuality of the craftsman and from the rapacity whether of countries or corporations turn with relief to his absorption in the worth of his work.

Is the individual leadership of the squire to be despised in a world of State absolutism and mental abstraction? Are the Christian values of Herbert, Barnes and the " povre Persoun " outmoded by the chaos of their denial? And is the quality of being exhibited by all these actors upon our stage not an alternative to the sense of mass which levels all things and persons to a row of numerals? Or, if we pass from the men to their work,

79 Norwich Market-place: from a drawing by J. S. Cotman

80 Cuckfield Market, 1790: from an engraving by Rowlandson and Alken

81   A Country-house Meet at Buckland, Berkshire

82   A Country-house Meet a Hundred Years Ago: from a drawing by
Rowlandson

material and spiritual craftsmen all, is not craftsmanship the true antidote to a humanity almost insane from something more than economic frustration? All the amenities of the most Utopian of Leisure States, all the ideologies from Communism to the Corporative State could never compensate the human being for the loss of individual craftsmanship in work. These things are the illusion of the urban mind.

I take it, then, that the English tradition of which our native husbandry is the base, being as it is true to the nature of the Englishman, is the concern of the future rather than a pleasant tale of the past. The fatal error of the modern theory of progress is that it interposes a destructive wedge between the past and the future, and at the same time regards itself as almost immune from criticism. A recent authoritative book has this sentence: " No sacrifice is too great to check the black plague (Nazi-ism) that would set us back to the 13th century." One can but wonder at the complacency of the modern illusion that considers as lower than its own barbarism the age that perfected the guild system and created the Early English style. The qualities I have been reviewing in previous chapters are always in date and only out-of-date at the expense of the human living-power and the national well-being. They are the conditions of a permanent satisfaction in the act of living; time may modify them to meet changes of circumstance but to destroy them is suicide. We cannot initate them by " putting the clock back " because we have lost the knowledge of and the key to them. What we can do and what the times we live in will compel us to do, if we wish to continue as the English nation, is to recreate the English tradition in a form compatible with certain modern developments which are real and salutary, not fictitious and thoroughly harmful as many of them are. We do not want more bureau-cracy, more regimentation, more commercialism, more bank-debt, more machinery, more competition, more complexity, more urbanism, more organization, more parasitism, more occasions for future wars, more and more imitation of the totalitarian or the communistic State, since all this is quite simply the way of death. The business of modernism is to fulfil the English tradition, not to destroy it.

It we desire to have more life and have it more abundantly, we have to control, not to give full reign to these tendencies and to reassert our native humanity, our particular Englishness in spite of them. The example of the English tradition is before us who have become its prodigal son. Whether the inward rottenness of modern civilization as a whole has gone too far or whether the strain of suppressing the State-cum-military despotism of the openly predatory nations will exhaust us too much, cannot be foretold. But the effort must be made for our redemption as a nation.

IV   THE FUNCTION OF THE STATE

Having lost the art of self-help and the power of co-operative self-govern-ment, we are hardly fit to look after these things for ourselves, as our fore-fathers did. Therefore, we have to call in the State. As this is in itself a confession of failure, it behoves us to invite the State not into the kitchen and the living room (much less the bedroom), but to guard the front-door against the financial wolves, rather than allow it to turn armed burglar itself, as is the habit of modern States, which Nietzsche called " the coldest of all cold monsters " and George Russell " Apollyon." Germany and Russia enable us to see the fruits of Hobbes's *Leviathan.* A very sharp distinction should thus be drawn between State control and State ownership. The extraordinary bungling of the urban bureaucracy in its misdealings with agriculture during the present war and what would seem deliberate attempts to discourage and even suppress such healthy and productive local activities as country milling should warn all countrymen that saurians have not only cold blood but small brains. Where individual responsibility is lacking, so is humanity and it was when the squires became the State that they acted like savages towards their tenants. The fact that we have to call it in, therefore, is the measure of what economic babes we have become, our lips, as George Russell said, " for ever nuzzling at its nipples." To grow up we need some power to chain up the financial man-eater and, until we do grow up, than the State there is no other power. How should it be exercised?

If China can or could feed three people per acre on a moderate soil, we could easily feed one person for every three-quarters of an acre of superlative soil. The only genuine argument against self-help in feeding ourselves is that we prefer making money to healthy and happy human beings. But some imports there must be and it is the business of the State to regulate and adjust them to exports so that they shall not interfere with the home market. That implies a drastic revision of an economic system whose whole object has been to undersell competitors by " a favourable trade balance " of exports over imports and thus to foment ill-will, exploitation, sweated labour and all the diverse evils of economic warfare which have plunged the world into a chaos of physical carnage. We fight the Teutonic Beast of Revelations on behalf of humanity, but it was our industrialism and our economic system that created that Beast. The security of the English tradition depends upon the State or King creating money on the credit of the work and character of the people instead of leaving it to the banks to do so on behalf of their own profit and a " credit-worthy " affluence.

One of the duties of the State is surely to put an end to land-speculation, especially in building-sites, unless ribbon-development is to put out of production an even greater acreage than exists already. A State control that acquired the power of distinguishing between predatory and legitimate enterprise and made finance the servant instead of the master of nutrition and husbandry could not do other than release them, and the English tradition with them, from an intolerable incubus upon both culture and cultivation. In putting money in its right place as the medium of exchange between village and village, region and region, nation and nation in the passing to and fro of surplus goods and services as adumbrated by the Lease-Lend Act, the State would have quite enough to do without turning England into a chain-gang of collectivist farms. For money is simply a convenience in facilitating barter, the barter of our forefathers and President Roosevelt the realist rediscovered an ancient truth.

The provision of credit; the diversion of sewage from polluting the rivers to fertilizing the fields; fostering reclamation; facilitating land-purchase, especially of bankrupt estates; the regulation of markets; the checking of dishonesty and adulteration in the handling of foods; the maintenance of security for the cultivator; a general supervision of our natural wealth which is our native land, the birthright of free men; these and functions like them

83 The English Summer : Sussex Cornlands overlooking the Weald

84   Mousehold Heath, Norwich, by John Crome

85   Sheep-shearing, by Samuel Palmer

but not beyond them are State business. This is no Utopianism nor New Order; it is the removal of obstructions from the right and duty of farmers to farm and the owner-occupier (be he landlord, yeoman or smallholder) to own. If they fail to fulfil that duty by their land, then forfeiture, as I mentioned before, is the right and duty of the State. On an estate in my neighbourhood stands a small mediaeval chapel with a roof painted like the sky with stars and clouds and the interior filled with a unique set of Jacobean furniture and fittings. The present owner, a rich man, has allowed it to fall into a pitiable decay, so that the rain drips through the roof, without lifting a finger to repair it. In a civilized community, a clear case of forfeiture and, if I were the Government, I would not pay him one penny of compensation. The function of the State is to encourage its nationals to do as far as is humanly possible without it, so that a vigorous and regional self-government is its true purpose, not a bureaucracy using revolutionary powers to paralyse it. As the seat of the nervous system of the body politic, to preserve the continuity of the national tradition, nursing its richness and discouraging its ranker growths, is the only object of the State's existence.

V COUNTRY-MINDEDNESS

No thinking person to-day would dispute that the modern educational system is hardly more than a forcing-house for the acquisition of urban values, while even our agricultural colleges train the sons of the soil to become blackcoats. Proficiency in passing examinations and collecting certificates has been the means of suppressing the cultural individuality of both teacher and pupil. The idea that education is a continuous adventure of body and mind together and so an initiation into what Sir George Stapledon calls the wisdom of wholeness is pure heresy to our sausage-machine methods, at the end of which the made-up article is ejected for sale into the urban market with the newspaper heading and the cinema poster to put the final touch upon the mass-mind. The mechanization of knowledge as a prelude to the mechanization of work is surely the worst symptom of the Machine Age, and there can be no alternative whatever to it except an education in rural values as a means of countering a spiritual poverty and a practical deficiency.

A vast exciting territory opens out at once at the mere mention of them, favourable to all kinds of sproutings except for the pot-plants of specialization and standardization. Nature being the source of life as the country is of the national character, they teach the virtues of a solitude which forms a philosophy of life and of a co-operation in labour which avoids the competitive basis of urban civilization. The theme is inexhaustible, horizon opening beyond horizon, from the home paddock to the fields of the world, since every civilization has sprung from those same rural values and man himself from their womb. The Hadow scheme which destroyed the village school was the last step in the process of urbanizing the mind of the child.

I have not the space here to develop the theme as it cries out to be developed, and better minds than mine have already done so. But there is one fresh contribution that I can make. I have before my mental eye two examples of what true education means and might mean. The first is that of the Danish Folk Schools, as expounded by Sir Richard Livingtstone in *The Future of Education*. At the beginning of the 19th century, the Danish peasantry were an ersatz and a crestfallen people, victimized and without spirit. Through these High Schools it evolved a generalized culture which incidentally made Denmark one of the most agriculturally productive countries in the world. The agronomic experts of to-day demand a purely technical education for potential farmers. The curriculum of the Folk Schools was not only non-technical but non-agricultural. It was an introduction to the possibility of the " good life," and if the young adults after leaving the Schools took to farming, it was because they had been taught to see it as the basis of a civilized society. They understood the full meaning of the word *agriculture.*

Kierkegaard's inspiration upon these Schools was a religious one, while Grundtvig's method was not to teach the pupils " how to farm well," but to produce in them " a passionate desire to do so." They learned " to hear, to see, to think and to use their powers." They gained " an enlarged outlook on life," combined with a strong feeling for fellowship, a love of Nature, a sense of values, and a relish for life and knowledge whose fruits were the peasant prosperity which survived all the depressions of world-markets and only succumbed to the German invasion. How was this miracle accomplished? In two ways. By the study of history and literature as book-learning on the one hand; by craftsmanly practise on the farm on the other. By, that is to say, an education in that wholeness which is wisdom.

If education is not Christian, then it is anti-Christian, and, if it is anti-Christian, it is, in Dr Micklem's words (*The Theology of Politics*) " materialist or Communist or Nationalist or Nazi." Assuredly, there is nothing sectarian in teaching every pupil the Bible and Shakespeare. Without them, all education is the husk without the grain. And I am convinced that any school, no matter what its educational programme, which avoids inculcating the religious mode of thought, commits a sin against that wholeness. In Denmark, it was a leavening of genius.

There is only one established (since 1925) school in England which bears the faintest resemblance to the Danish Folk Schools, and that is Avoncroft College near Bromsgrove, Warwickshire. It teaches agriculture, plant and animal husbandry, economics, some mechanics, woodwork—and English literature and history. The students have informal discussions as well as teaching every morning, and in the afternoons their time is devoted to practical farmwork. There are serious deficiencies at Avoncroft, no vital association with village life, no apprenticeship to neighbouring village craftsmen, no music, no religious philosophy (which, of course, need not be in the least sectarian), and these are all organic needs. I have been told, too, that there is a certain bleakness in its atmosphere, which seems inseparable from all Quaker foundations, magnificent as is their social work. But at least Avoncroft is a tentative step in the right direction.

With these examples in the back of my mind, I turn over once more these pages I have written about the English tradition that was created by the English countryman as far back as the Neolithic villager. I find in these pages a rough account of the husbandry of succeeding ages, quotations from the poets and prose-writers and oral singers of our literature and a rather halting historical retrospect. In other words, my study of the basic types of the English countryman has compelled me, in order to do justice to them, to combine all three elements by the very nature of the theme and so, all unconsciously, to pursue a method analogous with those of Avoncroft and the

Danish Folk Schools. Therefore, since these separate elements form an indivisible trinity, the English tradition should surely form the groundwork of all young Englishmen for an education in right values which may extricate us from the ultimate consequences of the Industrial Revolution. And the gaps in my narrative would fill a library.

VI THE ENGLISH PATTERN

This looking backwards also discloses that all the figures represented have their part to play not only in a regenerated agriculture but an England depending on it and redeemed from the money-power. If the peasantry has been the foundation not only of rural stability but of civilization itself, as history shows it to be, both the labourer and the squire, the ground-floor and top-storey of the rural structure, are the means to its restoration. It certainly cannot be achieved by planning machinery from without. The labourer with his skill, his experience, his all-roundness and knowledge of how to do the right thing at the right time in the right place is the potential by virtue of being the post-peasant.

But there are all too few of him, and those not the men their fathers were, to form the nucleus of a peasantry. It cannot but be built, therefore, through the education of the younger and willing townspeople who fail to find the good life though the cinema and football pool at one end and the conveyor-belt at the other. A firm step in that direction would be dual occupation for the factory-worker, namely the allotment after the factory. And perhaps (as Adrian Bell has suggested), the suburban gardening amateur is indeed a potential peasantry in the making. He is plastic since he is attached to nothing, neither town nor country. He is something of an inarticulate passive resister to urbanism by the very act of sleeping outside the industrial city. If he could wake up one day, the country might dawn on him and he would realize that he had brought the town with him into it. If the suburban householder were to become country-minded in will and action as he already is in a nebulous pining, he could move mountains and the small-power engine would help him to do it. It is simply waiting to be used by the smallholder who needs to be relieved from overwork.

Both the labourer by example in the field, and the squire through the facilities afforded by his estate, each should play a dynamic part in that education. Rolf Gardiner's estate at Springhead with its training camps, its rural industries in the processing of flax and the spinning of wool, its fine forestry and all-but rural university of land-culture in the widest interpretation of the term is a wonderful example of actual achievement. Lord Lymington has experimented in the same direction on his estate at Farleigh Wallop. These holiday and training camps are a means to that fellowship which the Danish Folk Schools cultivated in its pupils and without co-operative marketing in the actual profession of farming, it is impossible for the small man to hold his own. Such communal activities as the jam-making of the Women's Institutes point the same way towards the recovery of the much more than team-spirit of the peasant. And the manorial village farm might well be recreated in a new form by the estate grouped about by family farmers doing seasonal work upon it as a " dual occupation," just as the peasants did week-work and boon-work on the demesne No peasantry can be recreated except on a co-operative basis, and the estate is the natural centre for co-operative activities. The County Council smallholdings have been largely a failure for the very reason that each cluster of them is not thus nucleated.

If the Agricultural Colleges and Research Institutes were anything like Sir George Stapledon's Plant Breeding Station at Aberystwith, what a part they might play in the reawakening of the countryside! Doubtless there are other exceptions—South Moulton, for instance. But those that lack experimental farms of their own have tended to become more and more detached from true husbandry, more and more separatist in method, abstract in thought and subdivided in specialized function. They tend to become more and more dictatorial and too obsessed with machinery, chemicals and other devices of the inorganic to play any creative rôle in the concrete and organic realities of rural life, whether in the soil or on the soil. Some even of those that have farms show a biological unsoundness and lack of vision which unfit them for any kind of leadership as does their association with an economic system that first puts every obstacle in the way of a smallholder being a good husbandman and then rounds on him with, " you are uneconomic. Out you go." The landowners of to-day are much freer from any such contamination and, were their sense of responsibility nurtured by freedom from the paralysis of Death Duties and their irresponsibility subject to forfeiture of their land, there is a chance that they might take the opportunity of exorcising the curse of the Enclosures.

The problem of the yeoman, the craftsman and the family farmer (and one third of English and Welsh farming is still by the owner-occupier) is a very much simpler one, threatened with extinction by the forces arrayed against them as they are. They contribute something of irreplaceable and inestimable value to the soul and body of the nation in any period and in all conditions. Off their own bat they really unriddle the perplexities of the how much of artificials and the how much of machinery. The experienced small farmer knows what is good for his land and what is not; he is the husbandman and so stands for healthy crops, a fertile soil, a proper rotation, fresh food and a sufficiency of livestock. He is not the man to deceive himself that artificials can replace humus or machines the work of hand and eye, and so he will have so much but no more of them. He is our guardian not only against scientific fantasy but that predatory spirit which has to some extent corrupted the tenant farmer. He takes kindly to the modern development of an old idea like alternate husbandry, because it does not go against the grain of good cultivation.

As for the craftsman, he is for ever. No civilization that replaces him can survive nor does it deserve to. He at once shapes its anatomy and is the root of its culture. The only two things he needs in order himself to survive are the very ones that modern society denies him—security and apprenticeship. About the parson there is only one thing to say: his job is Christianity, not on Sunday only but all the days of the week and given to the village not as a cluster of naughty or ailing gossips but as the universe in a grain that grows.

The English tradition is the national root whose leaves have been practise and flowers the spirit of life. Because of late what William Barnes would have called " the old woak " has been defoliated by caterpillars and deflowered by the frosts of neglect, that does not mean it is not still sound in limb. Yet if we succeed in scotching the supreme expression of modern mechanized man, the Teutonic Predatory State and its imitators at the expense of that tradition, we win only to lose.

Though nobody says it and everybody talks in the air about democracy, what we are really fighting for is the English tradition, fighting for it but also against it. A recent writer has posed three alternatives before us at the conclusion of the war—the anarchy of the old *laissez-faire* of competition for profit, a State despotism on the Soviet model or the Christian life. I should prefer to speak of the third alternative as the English tradition which is Christian and secular both, each irrigating the other. By " secular " I do not mean enclosure by legal compulsion which was both secular and revolutionary. I mean by it two things—development from within growing up from organic life as opposed to " progress " breaking away from it, and those expressions of culture and husbandry which, though secular, were yet influenced by the polarity between the temporal and the eternal. The whole point of the Christian tradition is the worth of the individual, opposed in grain to mass-regimentation, whether collectivist as in Russia, racial and corporative as in Germany or by way of the profit-making combine as in England. This polarity is not difficult to understand because it is expressed in the English village and small town (church-secular buildings-fields), in themselves a bulwark against the evils of nationalism. Thus, so long as we fight for Christendom, we fight *with* the English tradition. Should that tradition be snuffed out altogether, the future can only be:

> " A tale told by an idiot,
> Full of sound and fury, signifying nothing."

But does the English tradition survive? Does the English landscape? There are places in it undefiled where Drayton and Campion might walk without knowing they had left their own span of time behind them. Chaucer would still find the daisies growing if his shade grew tired of the asphodel or the heavenly lilies, and Ophelia's emanation could see the willow stretched over the stream as where she fell. Wordsworth could still lift his eyes to the everlasting hills and Blunden hear the same bluetit tootle as John Clare heard it enlivening eternity. There are hearts living now to whom our woods and streams sing as they did to Vaughan and Collins. There are quiet men in England to whom the lift of a hay-fork, an old book and the glistering coat of a shire-horse are like the evening sky, and there are men of zeal too whose Jerusalem is full of primroses. Theirs is the holy war not lost by death.

As it is with England and these Englishmen, so it is with the native character that inherits the English tradition. It inherits it not only by the deeds of courage and self-abandon in the convulsion of man's inhumanity to man, but in the ways of peace and fruitfulness that violence cannot touch.

INDEX

(The numerals in italics denote the figure numbers of illustrations)

INDEX

Chippendale, 42, 58
Chipping Campden, 15
Christian tradition, the, 128f.
Christmas, 14
Church, the, 11–14, 128–29, 130
Church, The Country, by Cruickshank and Wheatley, *71, 73*
Church Ales, 15
Cistercians, the, *64*, 106
Clare, John, 36, 69, 72, 73, 76 quoted, 100 quoted
" Clearances ", 105
Clergy, the, 10
" Clipping the Church ", 119
Clopton Bridge, Old, 18
" Closes ", 4
Cloud of Unknowing, The, 112
" Clubmen " of Dorset, 41
" Coaration ", 3
Cobbe, Geoffrey, 34
Cobbett, 34 quoted, 35, 42, 45, 68, 69, 71, 88, 92, 95
Coke of Norfolk, 37, *59*, 93–95, 101
Coleridge, 2, 80, 113
Collet, 18th century Alehouse, *12*
Collins, 36
Comberbach, Cheshire, 14
Commonalty, 4
Commoners, 25, 65
Common at Goathland, Yorks, *8*
" Commons ", 1, 4, 7, 9, 10, 46
Commons and Common Fields, by Scrutt, 7
Common Wealth, 86
Compost, 39–40
Compton Wynyates, 88
Concise Cambridge History of English Literature, 124
Cook, Brian, 6
Coomber of Kirby Moorside, 110
Cooper of Filey, Canon, 119
Cooper Family, the, 64
Cooper's Hill, 15
Copyholder, the, 1, 23, 26
Corn Laws, the, 47, 48
Cotswold Games, the, 15, 79, 90

Cottage Hearth in Winter, (1803) after Hamilton, *29*
Cottage Interior (*ca.* 1850), by Webster, *14*
Cottage Scene in Essex (*ca.* 1820), *11*
Cottage Threshold, A, *34*
Cottages in Dorset, East Lulworth, *51*
Cottages on Ebrington Hill, Cotswolds, *50*
Cottages, Half-timber, nr. Castlemorton, *48*
Cottages, Half-timber, nr. Hopton Castle, *49*
Cottar, the, 2, 7
Country House Meet at Buckland, Berks., *81*
Country House Meet at Buckland, Berks., in the 19th century, by Rowlandson, *82*
Courtleet, the, 2
Crabbe, George, 42, 99, 117, 129
Crabtree, William, 115
Crafts and husbandry, 54f., 106f.
Craftsman, the, 52f., 130f., 140 ; tools and tradition, 63f. ; conduct and security, 65f.
Cranborne Chase, 8
Cranford, 96
Crofter, the, 50–51
Crome, John, *84*
Cromwell, Oliver, 82, 87, 91
Croscombe, Somerset, 38
Cruden, Alexander, 110
Cruickshank, G., *71*
" Crying the Neck ", 76
Cuckfield Market, by Rowlandson and Alken, *80*
Curbery, Lady, 114
Cymbeline, 21

" Dales " (Lakes), 3
Dalesman, 29, 38, 49–50
Dancing and the peasant, 18–19, 22
Danelaw, 32
Danish Conquest, the, 9
Danish Folk Schools, the, 137f.
Darwin, Bernard, 71, 96
Davies, 25

Day, Wentworth, 51
Defoe, *The Complete English Tradesman,* 53
de Henley, Walter, 14, 22
" Demesne ", the, 5, 10, 25, 32, 83
Democracy : as element in peasant life, 4, 5, 9
Demonology, medieval, 21–22
" De Migrantibus ", Salic Law, 7
Denmark ; Peasant and smallholder, 30 ; enclosures in, 26
De Republica Anglorum, 32
Devon, Earl of, 92
Dissolution, the 23, 25, 33, 67, 82, 86
Domesday Book, 7, 84
Donaldson, Mrs, *Approach to Farming,* 55
Donne, 112 quoted, 114
Dorset Field Club, the, 127
Dover, Captain, 18, 79, 90–91
Dover's Hill, 15, 18, 79, 90–91
Drainage and flooding, 30, 38
Drayton, 28 quoted, 36, 39
Drove Roads, 21
Duck, labourer poet, 72f.
Dugdale's *Monasticism,* 107
Dunstable Down, 15
Dunster Yarn Market, 38
Dyer, John, 116, 120–21
Dyott, General, 96

Earle's *Microcosmography,* 88
Early Victorian England, 71, 96
Eden, 25
Edward II, 83
Edward VI, 34
Edwards, Trystan, *Hundred New Towns,* 133
Education, the value of, 137
Egerton MS., the, 26
Eliot, T. S., 59
Elizabeth, Queen, 22, 27
Elizabethan squire, An, 87
Ellis, Sir H., 106
Emma, 97, 128
Enclosure Act, the, 1845, 1, 2, 9, 10, 24, 68, 100

143

INDEX

INDEX

INDEX

INDEX